The Light Reading of Our Ancestors

The Light Reading of Our Ancestors : Chapters in the Growth of the English Novel

By the Right Honble. LORD ERNLE
(Rowland E. P. Ernle)

 BOOKS FOR LIBRARIES PRESS
FREEPORT, NEW YORK

First Published 1927
Reprinted 1970

STANDARD BOOK NUMBER:
8369-5422-X

LIBRARY OF CONGRESS CATALOG CARD NUMBER:
73-124234

PRINTED IN THE UNITED STATES OF AMERICA

CONTENTS

PREFACE

THE title and sub-title of this volume are taken from two articles which I published anonymously in 1886. Both those articles represented a considerable amount of reading during several years before their publication. I am, therefore, parting with a book which has been my intimate and more or less constant companion for half a century.

I cannot remember the time when stories were not one of my chief amusements. To read for myself the fairy-tales of Madame d'Aulnoy and Perrault was the chief bribe which overcame my childish reluctance to learn French. I was encouraged to read Walter Scott, and, before I was ten, I had read all the Waverley Novels, even *Count Robert of Paris*, and my own favourites many times over. My birthday presents were generally novels, like Bulwer Lytton's *Last of the Barons*, *Harold*, or *The Last Days of Pompeii*. In other directions, my reading was more clandestine. *Charles O'Malley* and *Jack Hinton* were read aloud to me, perched on the pantry dresser, by my father's servant, his voice choked with laughter over the exploits of " Micky Free." Lever's novels always bring back to me the faint smell of the pantry sink. Another event in my life was the discovery, in a little-used bedroom, of *Oliver Twist*, with Cruikshank's illustrations. For weeks afterwards I expected to see the baleful face of Fagin glued to the window of my nursery. The first book that I bought with my own money was *Jane Eyre*, which I had heard discussed by my elders. At Southampton railway bookstall, on my way to my first school, I purchased, out of my scanty pocket-money, a copy of the novel bound in yellow cloth. The morning after my arrival at school the book was taken from me by the master, on the ground that it was improper reading for a small boy. I never saw it again. I felt sure that my *Jane Eyre* was either kept for his own use or presented to a friend. The sense of injury rankled.

As years passed, the taste rather grew than faded. After leaving Oxford I tried to study the prose fiction of the past, period by period. In my leisure from other occupations, I began to haunt the Reading Room of the British Museum, curious to discover who were the writers whose works had entertained successive generations of our ancestors, and why the development of the modern novel was so long deferred. Half a century ago such enquiries were difficult. In general histories of English literature the subject was practically ignored; bibliographies of prose fiction did not exist, and catalogues in public libraries had no subject-indices. Dunlop's *History of Prose Fiction*, without the valuable notes of Wilson (1888), was the only available authority. Dealing, as it does, with the prose fiction of all countries, the space devoted to English writers is necessarily inadequate. Especially is this true of the period which elapsed between the invention of printing and the publication of *Pamela* (1740). Until M. Jusserand broke new ground with *The Novel in the Times of Shakespeare* (1888), it was almost possible to believe that Samuel Richardson was the father of English prose fiction. More recently, another French scholar, M. Abel Chevalley, has laboured in the same field, and his *Thomas Deloney et le Roman Corporatif* (1926) has thrown new light on the literature which entertained the Elizabethan artisan.

It was the poverty of literature on a great subject which brought me a proposal from a publisher to expand my articles of 1886 into a volume. I declined the offer. I had to forgo the delightful luxury of concentrating on literary work of a kind which, even if successful, is unremunerative. But the subject of prose fiction never lost its fascination. In the midst of other occupations it persisted, and I went on reading, accumulating notes, and from time to time writing, on detached portions of the subject, articles which now fill three bulky, closely-printed octavo volumes Mainly out of these materials this book is condensed.

Meanwhile the opportunity slipped away. Numerous writers occupied the empty space with all the thoroughness of modern scholarship. Whatever special novelty my book might have possessed forty years ago it has lost. Facts on which I stumbled with the thrill of discovery are now matters of common knowledge. I dare not attempt to enumerate the living scholars to whom the students of to-day owe an incalculable debt. But one book I may mention. In 1894 the late Sir Walter Raleigh published *The English Novel*. With incomparable grace of style, and with a power of selecting salient features that was exercised and strengthened by years of successful teaching, he answered the question, Who were the writers of prose fiction whose works had entertained successive generations of our ancestors? To the other question—why the modern novel was so long deferred —he gave no direct reply, and probably none can be given. The only thread which I have tried to follow is the gradual growth of the perception that truth to life is the aim of novelists. Not until imagination and observation were yoked together, could prose fiction claim to be an independent branch of representative art. The slow recovery of that touch of reality which thrills us in the Canterbury Pilgrims or in the story of Lancelot and Guinevere is what I have tried to trace.

With leisure to piece together fragmentary materials came an unexpected difficulty. Work that might have been done in a few hours extended over months. More and more dependent on the eyesight of others, I owe the completion of the book to Miss Crow, Miss Law, Mrs. Macbean and, above all, my wife, who have read to me, typed and re-typed dictated passages, corrected and re-corrected drafts. I record also my debt to Mr. R. H. Hill, of the Bodleian Library, Oxford, who has carefully revised the manuscript throughout. In conclusion, I offer my thanks to the editors of the different periodicals in which portions of the following pages have appeared, and, above all, to the editor of the *Edinburgh Review*, who has permitted me to reprint from the issues for January and April 1926 the chapters on Richardson and Fielding.

ERNLE.

The Light Reading of Our Ancestors

CHAPTER I

INTRODUCTORY

In the form of imaginative prose fiction, change is life. It must express from age to age the varying needs of society. Its future cannot be predicted. There is no reason to think that the novel of to-morrow will resemble the novel of to-day more closely than the novel of to-day resembles that of yesterday. The prose fiction of the twentieth century and that of the eighteenth are as dissimilar as are the conventional dress-clothes of Mr. John Galsworthy and the ratteen coat, bloom-coloured breeches, and silk stockings of Oliver Goldsmith. With rare exceptions, the light reading of one generation becomes the heavy reading of the next.

The instinct to which prose fiction appeals is universal. Story-telling is as ancient as time. A tale is often the first key which unlocks the mind of a child. Often, also, it is the last voice to reach the sluggish brain of the aged. In intermediate stages of life, it is in a story that many men and women seek refuge from anxious realities. Even the most robust appetite for useful information sometimes loses its " roast beef stomach," rejects solid fare, and craves the lighter diet of a tale. Thus it is that, at every period of life, from childhood to age, in almost every country, at nearly every stage of history, stories have supplied recognised needs of human nature.

So venerable and universal is the love of a story that the origin of imaginative fiction in prose is blurred by the mists of antiquity. But novels of contemporary life, and historical romances, as we know them to-day, are, comparatively, mushroom growths which have not yet celebrated their two-hundredth birthday. Thus the art of prose fiction is at once immensely old and intensely modern. In one sense the novelists of to-day boast of ancient lineage. The simple tellers of tales of wonder, of old wives' fables, of legend and tradition, which passed from lip to lip with all the freshness of oral transmission, are their remote ancestors. It was on these materials that early writers of romantic fiction tried their 'prentice hands, adapting their forms to the changing needs of society. Generation after generation elaborated the instrument, adding new notes, enlarging its compass and variety. Every stage in the protracted development of the novel is represented ; each ebb and flow of the tide, now of idealism, now of realism, has left some mark ; each advancing wave is enriched by something which its predecessor has left behind.

Of all these experiments in form and method of literary expression our contemporary masters and mistresses of prose fiction are the heirs. They were born in one of the seven cities which claim the honour of the birthplace of Homer. They were nourished and taught their letters by French nurses. They were doctored by Arabian physicians, schooled by wise men from the farthest East, tutored by Greek, Latin, Italian and Spanish masters. They began their career as minstrels in the halls of the great, or as wandering entertainers in open streets and ale-houses, before they settled down to paint, etch or photograph their scenes from real life, or to chronicle their blood-curdling adventures in the Kingdom of Nowhere, or to seek the romances of modern society in the strangeness and mystery of crime.

Ancient as is their origin, modern novels are yet a new creation, so complete is the transformation which they have undergone. Their relation to the past is not so close as that of descent ; they had predecessors rather than ancestors. In their progress no law can be traced ; nor can the theory of evolution be applied to their growth. Englishmen do not attempt to distinguish accurately between novels and romances. In common speech the words are used interchangeably to describe imaginative representations of life, either as it is, or was, or is desired to be. The border-line between the two branches of prose fiction is so often crossed and recrossed that it affords no definite frontier. But the modern novel is broadly distinguished from older forms of fiction in aim, in construction, in material. It aims at truth to real life in the representation both of facts and of human nature ; it combines with a picture of events and circumstances the moral and mental phenomena which give them their human interest ; its narrative is compacted into a plot, by the unravelling of which the characters of the actors are illustrated.

In all these respects, the prose fiction which enthralled the Middle Ages, or our Tudor and Stuart ancestors, was essentially different. Early writers did not describe life as it actually existed in either the present or the past. For their interest they relied on external incidents, piled one upon another without regard to probabilities or even to possibilities. If any thread of cohesion bound together the accumulation, it was of the slenderest. They attempted no delineation of character. Their heroes and heroines were born into the world angels or demons, faultless in virtue or full-blown in vice, without room for growth or development. In either case, their hearts and minds were sealed books.

Among the Greeks and Romans the deliberate composition of imaginative fiction in prose for the entertainment of hearers or readers was a late development. It implied a leisure and a privacy which did not exist in the strenuous public life of the Golden Ages of Greece and Rome. History shows that to write poetry is natural to mankind. Poetry is the first-born of literature. But experience proves that it is less natural to read it. The exact opposite is true of novels. History shows that it is not natural to write imaginative fiction in prose. It is the last-comer in literature. But experience proves that it is natural to read novels and romances. They command an ever-growing market. They supply an immense demand. To-day novels are the most characteristic product of our national literature, and we have become the most novel-ridden people in the world. By what steps have they reached their assured position ? Some answer to the question is attempted in the following chapters.

In the Middle Ages the world went mad for romances in verse or prose. They were one of the principal fields in which the vernacular languages of France and England were trained and exercised. They taught the mass of the people the story of the origin of our nation, the life of Greece, the terrors and treasures of the fabled East, the marvels of a primitive science of natural history. For the leisure of those who could read they were the favourite diversion. Chanted or recited by minstrels, they were the popular entertainment of baronial hall and tavern.

Medieval romances met the same demands as modern novels. Then, as now, children were lulled to sleep, or their troubles soothed, by stories. So Sir David Lyndsay tells, in the Prologue to his *Dreme*, how he used to comfort the boy-prisoner, James V of Scotland, with " feigned fables " of the joy and sorrow of Troilus or of the siege of Troy. Then, as now, men and women found in these products of the imagination the mirror of their own lives or aspirations. So Gower's lover fed his hungry heart with reading of those heroes and heroines of romance who had greatly loved. Then, as now, it was in a story that over-wearied brains sought rest. So Chaucer tells us that in his sleeplessness he charmed the night away by reading a romance. Then, as now, a course of novel-reading was recommended to those whose temperaments were morbidly stern and sour. So Occleve advised the Lollard leader, Sir John Oldcastle, to vary his exclusive study of the Bible by reading " Lancelot du Lac."

The first book printed in the English tongue was the *Romance of Troy*. Printers and schoolmasters proved friends rather than foes to the extension of the influence of romances and novels. From the end of the fifteenth century to the present day the stream of prose fiction has continued to pour itself, in increasing volume, into the ocean of print. In its course it has travelled far from its fountain-heads, but the scenery of its upper waters can never lose its charm for lovers of the picturesque in literature. It has left behind it the knights-errant on their overridden horses, the damsels on their white palfreys, the green giants, the dragons, the dwarfs and the enchantments of medieval romance. It has emerged from the forests, where Robin Hood and Maid Marian, Friar Tuck and Little John, ply their adventurous trade. It has passed beyond the borders of that Arcadia in which princes and princesses, bedizened with ribbons, masquerade as shepherds and shepherdesses, sitting on green hillocks and discoursing languorous music from oaten reeds. No Italian castles now stand upon its banks, echoing with the mysterious footsteps of bandits and monastic villains. The scented mists of moonshine in which Edwin and Angelina vow eternal constancy are dispersed in the broad light of common day. The river has reached the level plain of ordinary life. It saunters among familiar fields and through the heart of great cities. In the headlong rush of its youthful career it had neither leisure nor inclination to mirror the inner workings of the human mind, or the manners and morals of contemporary society. All these are now more or less faithfully reflected in the broad, slow-moving and sometimes muddy stream of the modern novel.

Through many of these successive transformations runs the principle of the growing demand and consequent search for truth. In simple forms it appeared early ; sometimes for long periods in abeyance, or relegated to the remote background, it has been rarely absent. The mind of the Middle Ages was childlike, yet credulous. It desired to have its stories authenticated as facts, yet it was not critical as to the origin assigned to them. In the prose fiction of Greece, the father of romances of adventure and discovery not only elaborately documented his inventions, but carefully explained the recent discovery of his ancient manuscript. Similar devices were adopted by medieval craftsmen to satisfy the demand of their audiences for truth. The three great cycles of medieval romances rested upon forgeries which passed as authentic historical documents.

Thus Charlemagne and his Paladins were founded on the fabulous Chronicle of Archbishop Turpin, and King Arthur and the Table Round on the " very ancient book in the British tongue " from which Geoffrey of Monmouth professed to draw his traditions. So also the story of the *Iliad* was told to medieval audiences, not by Homer, but by two Latin forgers of the fourth century, and the birth, life and death of Alexander the Great were based upon the strange collection of legends and fables swept together from East and West by the false Callisthenes. The spirit of the compromise between avowed fiction and fiction disguised as fact is dear, not only to the Middle Ages, but to the twentieth century. To-day educational reformers banish " Cinderella " and " Puss in Boots " from the nursery ; but they allow *Ivanhoe* and *The Last of the Barons* in the schoolroom.

It was fortunate for novelists that the desire for truth to life persisted, for it eventually proved their salvation. So long as they neglected it, they could not establish a new form of representative art in literature. Poetry held the field of imagination. Romance writers might attempt to vie with it in the ornate language and imaginative extravagances of their prose poems ; but they could not compete with the haunting cadences of musical verse. In exhibiting a dramatic situation, or a mental or moral climax, they could not rival the direct appeal which the stage, aided by the interpretation of actors, made not only to the ear, but also to the eye. Yet novelists felt that there was room for an independent form of the imaginative re-creation of life, which should be different both from poetry and from drama. It was not till they discovered that truth within and without was the essence of their work that they won for prose fiction its position as a distinct branch of representative art.

During the two centuries after the discovery of printing, the interest of the history of prose fiction mainly lies in tracing the halting steps by which writers stumbled towards their true goal. Slowly they learned that no separate kingdom could be carved out of fancy pictures of human beings, raised by heroic romance to the stature of gods and goddesses, or degraded by burlesque to that of dwarfs or pygmies. But before the middle of the eighteenth century, novels of past or present life, as we know them to-day, were still in search of themselves. The art of writing them had yet to be discovered, its scope, form and limitations to be defined. Until fidelity to the realities of life and the exhibition of individuality in character were recognised as goals, no progress was possible. So it was that periods of splendid literary achievement came and went, leaving behind them imperishable treasures of poetry, plays, essays, memoirs, histories, but not a single work of prose fiction which can now be read with pleasure.

Even with the example of *The Canterbury Tales* and the

eternal truth of the human tragedy of Lancelot and Guinevere before them, writers of the sixteenth and seventeenth
centuries still shrank from pictures of the contemporary life
and society of England. They laid their scenes, not only in
imaginary countries, but in bygone ages. Yet they showed
no reverence for historical truth, no respect for geography
or chronology. They may have felt that over distant ages
hung those mists which heighten picturesqueness, and that
the twilight of the past quivered with the mysteries which
are the soul of romance. But history made its strongest
appeal to them by its remoteness from present-day conditions, by the cover that it afforded for their improbabilities,
by the screen which it gave to their imaginative licence.
Before success was attained in reproducing the realities of
the present, inevitable failure awaited the attempt to
revive the past. Thus, though in date it claims precedence,
the modern historical romance owes its present form to the
modern novel of real life and character.

At the beginning of the eighteenth century literary forces
which had long been gathering reached their height. The
reaction against the idealism and imaginative licence of the
previous period led to the violent recoil which Defoe
expressed in prose fiction. His matter-of-fact statements
were designed to produce a belief that his inventions were
actual occurrences. He aimed at the delusion of fact, and he
achieved his object by the verisimilitude of his circumstantial details. But his stories were barren of human
emotion, because he never attempted to describe those
motives, impulses and feelings which underlie and interpret
action. His two great successors inherited his accuracy in
observing and fidelity in reproducing external circumstances ; they combined them with an equal truthfulness in
revealing the mental and moral phenomena of the heart and
brain. The union made the modern novel. It is the subjective, as well as the objective, treatment of life which, for the
first time, is found in the fine analysis and laboured pathos
of Richardson, and in the broader effects, universality and
humour of Fielding. From Richardson and Fielding the
modern novel gained that self-knowledge which it had not
derived from the efforts of their predecessors. With 1750 is

BA

closed the period of its childhood and youth ; though still in the experimental stage, it entered on maturity.

Historical romance waited longer for its development. The spirit of the first half of the eighteenth century was hostile. Contemporaries of Pope despised medieval art and literature. They modernised Chaucer, improved Spenser, patronised and remodelled Shakespeare. They preferred the severe perfection of the classic temple to the aspiration and mystery of the Gothic cathedral. But after 1750 a new spirit was in the air. History began to be understood and written by men like Hume, Robertson and Gibbon. Literature, no longer regarded as beginning with Dryden, was studied as a continuous growth. Medieval architecture was revived. Archæologists and antiquarians grew indefatigable in their zeal. New interest was taken in forgotten sciences like heraldry, and in the forgotten arts of painted glass and illumination. Collections of ancient ballads, coins and armour were formed. On all sides materials for restoring the life of the past rapidly accumulated. It had become possible to apply to historical romance the newly-established principles of the modern novel.

When the hour of the historical novel came, its triumph was for the time even more brilliant than that of its parent. Prose fiction of both kinds profited by the prodigious success of Sir Walter Scott. The position of its writers was immeasurably raised. Novels were recognised as first-rate tests of first-rate abilities. For many years to come they resembled the east wind in spring ; nothing could escape them. Scarcely a bone of our ancestors was left undisturbed ; not a distress or danger of love, lawful or unlawful, escaped description ; few mysteries of fashion remained secrets in the pantry. From the Land's End to John o' Groat's "Apollo's self might pass unheard " ; but every door flew open to novelists. Their art was put to strange uses. If statesmen sought to explain a policy, reformers to expose an abuse, Protestants to reveal the mine over which society slumbered, prose fiction became the recognised channel of communication. Ethical treatises, political pamphlets, social dissertations, scarcely dared to venture abroad without an amatory accompaniment. Travellers who collected their hairbreadth adventures said, with Byron, " I want a hero." Even Dr. Dryasdust played the troubadour, and required a heroine in love to display the costumes of his period.

Of late years novel writers have trespassed less widely beyond the legitimate field of their art. For their main interest they rely on a human struggle ; but its sphere is partly transferred from without to within. No longer concerned only with its external aspects, they reveal the fluctuations of the contest, as well as the composition of the contending forces. The uniformities of modern life have forced them to develop that presentment of character which is one of the essential features of modern fiction. They had begun by distinguishing racial peculiarities, professional idiosyncrasies or social eccentricities. These superficial variations tend to disappear as men's individualities, like pebbles on the shore, round off by contact their rougher edges. Human beings do not differ less than they used to do ; but they differ less prominently. Modern novelists are thus driven to discriminate between the subtle shades of difference which mark off from one another men and women who, in all external points, present the same uniform surface. In doing so, they faithfully express the triumphs of modern science and the introspective tendencies of modern thought. They observe, analyse and classify the problems of human nature in the scientific spirit ; the ideal " Carte du Pays du Tendre " of Madeleine de Scudéri has become the field for their experimental science. They reflect the growing sense of the " mystery in us which calls itself I," the absorption in

> This main miracle that thou art thou,
> With power on thy own act and on the world.

In the hands of modern masters and mistresses the novel has thus become the most flexible and penetrating of instruments for the revelation of character and the exhibition of manners and morals. In this field it has won its greatest triumphs. Here, at least, it has no competitor in the stage ; it has no rival in the film.

The triumph of the novel has continued. In 1886 prose fiction wrested from theology the first place for the year in the numerical output of publications. It has never lost

the lead it then assumed. In 1906 its harvest more than
trebled the yield of its ancient rival. But it has not won its
predominance without a struggle. To the rich literature of
protest against the ascendency of romances such men of
genius as Rabelais and Cervantes have contributed. There
were always those who regarded novel-reading as not only
profitless but mischievous. The prejudice has persisted.

Whether the influence of novels is for good or evil is a
venerable controversy, and the arguments are time-honoured.
It would not have been fought so long and so bitterly if the
subject-matter were unimportant, or if prose fiction had not
played so large a part in national life. Fifty years before
the Christian era the dispute had begun. At Carrhæ
(53 B.C.) the Parthian Surena vanquished the Romans and
slew Crassus. On the battlefield was found, in the " fardle
or trusse " of a Roman soldier, a copy of the Milesian tales
of Aristides. " This gave Surena "—so Sir Thomas North
translates Plutarch—" great cause to scorne and despise the
behaviour of the Romanes which was so far out of order that
even in the warres they could not refraine from . . . the
reading of such vile bookes." Two centuries later the
Emperor Severus could find nothing worse to say of his
defeated rival, Albinus, than that he had grown grey in the
study of such old wives' trifles as the Milesian tales.

No one to-day condemns a soldier for carrying a novel in
his knapsack, or attempts to create political capital out of a
statesman's pleasure in the reading of prose fiction. But
the encouragement of mental and moral effeminacy was
nevertheless one of the charges levelled against novels. As
general propositions, neither accusation can be established.
That prose fiction has powerfully stimulated the imagination
of poets will not be disputed, nor is it surprising that men
like Edmund Burke should have fanned to flame the embers
of the " Age of Chivalry " by frequent perusal of its
romances. Other types of mental vigour were often combined with the love of prose fiction. Samuel Johnson, the
incarnation of sturdy common sense, was, as Bishop Percy
told Boswell, devoted to romances of chivalry, and retained
his love for them throughout his life. Bishop Berkeley was a
hard-headed man and a close reasoner. He was also an

ardent student of the "airy visions of romance," and perhaps
in those unsubstantial regions learned to disbelieve in matter.

Equally difficult was it to establish a general charge of
moral enervation. The most glorious period of the history of
Spain was also the age of her romances of chivalry. When
the conquerors of the New World reached its western shores,
it was from the Spanish romance of *Esplandian* that, to
describe the enchantments and beauty of the country, they
took the name of California. So, in our own Elizabethan age,
romances might turn the brain of Don Quixote or drive a
chambermaid to resolve "to runne out of herself and
became a lady-errant." Yet the same books stirred more
balanced minds to heroic action. They made points of
honour a religion, sometimes a superstition. Sir Philip
Sidney had a poor opinion of *Amadis of Gaul*; yet he had
known men who, even from reading that book, had "found
their harts mooued to the exercise of courtesie, liberalitie
and especially courage." It was on romances of chivalry that
the imagination of the generations, young as well as old,
who hailed the accession of Elizabeth, had been nourished.
The old medieval favourites colour the lines of Spenser's
Faerie Queene; they glow in the pages of Sidney's *Arcadia*
and in the manner of his death at Zutphen; they irradiate
the plays of Shakespeare. Men of action are generally
silent as to their mental processes; but it would be strange
indeed if they had not also translated romances into deeds.

The severest censure on novel reading was based on the
religious grounds suggested by Ascham's experiences:
"I know," he says, "when God's Bible was banished the
Court, and *Morte Arthure* received into the Prince's
Chamber." That side of the controversy has now become
academic. In the days when prose fiction might have been
altogether suppressed, ecclesiastical authorities took no
steps towards prohibition. The Inquisition judged heretics;
it did not try novelists. The Puritans whipped stage
players, but left romance writers alone. In the twelve years
of their ascendency more works of prose fiction were printed
than were published in the previous half century. The
religious argument against novel reading has always had a
double edge. One of the most popular romances of the

fifteenth and sixteenth centuries was written by a Pope, Pius II. On romances were fed the youthful imaginations of the founder of the Jesuit Order, Ignatius Loyola, and of the restorer of conventual discipline, St. Theresa, who, in collaboration with her brother, is said to have written a romance of chivalry. *Astrée* was the favourite reading of St. François de Sales. The faults of Charles I are forgotten in the manner of his death, and it was Pamela's prayer from the *Arcadia* that supported his fortitude. Jeremy Taylor thought it not inconsistent with *Holy Living* and *Holy Dying* to quote Mademoiselle de Scudéri with approval or to point a moral by a tale from Petronius. Nor was a taste for novels confined to Catholics or Anglicans. Among the Puritans, romances still had their devotees. The greatest of Puritan poets, John Milton, was steeped to the lips in the lore of the Table Round, and the sonorous names of " Lancelot, or Pelleas, or Pellenore," fell on his ear like music. The greatest of Puritan prose writers, John Bunyan, who had once loved *Bevis of Southampton* above all other books, did not disdain to cast his immortal allegory in the mould of a romance of chivalry.

With the purely utilitarian argument of waste of time every generation has been familiar. " Don't upbraid me," says the Niece in Steele's *Tender Husband*, " with my Mother Bridget and an excellent housewife." " Yes," retorts the Aunt, " I say, she was, and spent her time in better Learning than you ever did. Not in reading of Fights and Battles of Dwarfs and Giants : but in writing out receipts for Broaths, Possets, Caudles and Surfeit-Waters, as became a good Country Gentlewoman." The Aunt and the Niece survive. But the real question is how men and women would otherwise occupy their leisure. Time is only wasted on novels if it would have been better employed. The general influence of novel reading outweighs the arguments founded on its abuse. No protests have ever convinced the nation that its life is not immeasurably more enriched than impoverished by prose fiction. Novelists have opened new casements in the minds of multitudes of readers, widened their horizons, enlarged their outlook. They have created inspiring characters, who are better known to millions than are the great actors in history or even their own intimate friends. In their pages are preserved the dress, manners, habits, thoughts and ideals of successive generations, and never has the record been presented with such artistic finish, skill in technique, and completeness as in the novels of the last thirty years. The thread pursued in the following pages holds to the end. Truth to the whole truth of life is a distinctive aim of living novelists, and they have proved by not a few examples that real tenderness of feeling may inspire outspoken frankness as well as studied reticence.

CHAPTER II

GREEK PROSE ROMANCES

EVERY country, at every stage of history, has had its popular tales of wonder, told by all sorts and conditions of men. In such tales *Græcia mendax* was rich. But the deliberate composition of prose fiction for popular entertainment was a late growth, which accompanied the decrepitude of her public life and the degeneracy of her literature.

It is not difficult to suggest some reasons for this slow development. In the days of their glory, the crowded life of the Greek States left little space for leisure or for privacy. No need was felt for other distractions than those which the State supplied. Public orations, public readings, public disputations, public games, public festivals, absorbed men's energies. It was not that imagination was starved by its exclusion from the field of prose romance. Rather it was inspired from different sources, and adopted modes of expression more suited to existing conditions. Its highest thoughts flowed naturally into verse. In scenic representations it found the most direct means of communication with an audience. It was warmed by the clear flame of the passion for liberty. It was fed by a devout belief in an all-pervading mythology, which implanted a wholesome fear of the gods and peopled the elements with superhuman beings and spirits of the human dead.

No audience existed for the novel of domestic life. If any prose picture of contemporary characters, manners and customs was painted through the medium of imaginary actors in a love-intrigue, it has entirely perished. The spirit of romance found expression, not in the literary form of prose fiction, but in activities which eventually accumulated rich stores of material for romantic novelists. The conquests of Alexander the Great, for instance, powerfully stimulated a new passion for adventure, and a new curiosity about remote peoples and unknown lands, which created semi-fabulous geographies and histories of Persia and India. At the same time, the extension of their rule brought the Greeks into contact with Oriental countries. It made them familiar with Eastern tales of magic and sorcery, of demons and genii. It added new worlds of wonder to the more native tales of transformation of men into animals or of animals into men, of which in the second century before Christ at least two collections already existed.

As the Christian era was approached and passed, conditions became more favourable to the growth of prose fiction. Poetry throve best when the national spirit rose highest. It was otherwise with the development of the Greek novel. Roman rule gave to the world a semblance of political cohesion ; but it crushed national liberty, or only preserved its forms. Before 30 B.C. Athens had been humiliated, the Macedonian monarchy destroyed, Asiatic Greece mastered. With the loss of political influence disappeared some of the living activities of the Greek people. Rhetoricians and sophists usurped the honours of poets and politicians. Under a suspicious Government, the path of safety lay in frivolity. Society grew more leisured, luxurious, licentious. The old religion lost its hold upon the learned. For them it ceased to be a creed or moral sanction, and degenerated into an antiquarian taste or a superstitious regard for omens and divinations. /

Scepticism and credulity went hand in hand. Wild tales of ghosts, vampires, *succubi*, demons and " incredible natures " were the beliefs of the ignorant, and, in the presence of mysteries of the unknown, even the learned suspended the exercise of their critical faculties. Life was still crowded with cult, ritual, ceremonial. But the chaos of religions grew more and more bewildering, as the old Pantheon was invaded by foreign divinities. Philosophy, degraded into the handmaid of the new worships, occupied herself in dignifying their mystic teaching or in tracing unity through their diversities. The biography of Apollonius of Tyana illustrates the depths of credulity into which the human mind had sunk, just as the work of Lucian, ridiculing every religious creed or philosophical system, indicates the collapse of guiding principles or central purposes in life.

It was under these conditions, and out of these ingredients, that a new form of prose literature was developed. None of the early writers of Greek fiction, with the possible exception of Diogenes, were natives of European Greece. Aristides was a Milesian, Heliodorus a Phœnician, Achilles Tatius an Alexandrian, Eumathius a Byzantine ; Cyprus, Antioch or Ephesus gave birth to the three Xenophons ; Iamblichus and Lucian were Syrians. If anything is certain about Longus, it is that his name is not Greek. The literary impulse came from the cities and islands of Asia Minor and from Egypt. Ionia, highly civilised, indolent, luxurious, pleasure-loving, valuing comfort above freedom, understanding liberty only as the absence of restraint, took the lead in the creation of prose fiction. In Miletus, or in Lesbos, the love-intrigue centred round the courtesan. Was not Aspasia a Milesian ? To the same city belonged Rhodopis, more legendary but scarcely less famous, who built a pyramid by making each of her lovers contribute a stone, who was raised by the loss of her slipper to the throne of Egypt, and, in the romance of *Theagenes and Chariclea,* almost overcame by her wiles the austere virtue of the high-priest of Memphis.

But from Egypt came a different conception, which, as years passed, was powerfully seconded by Christianity. In that country female influence, for good or evil, was powerful. Honoured in the State, venerated in the family, women, free and unveiled, held a position similar to that which they were to occupy in modern Europe. The mutual passion of a man and woman, who hope to marry, becomes the thread on which are strung early romances of adventure. Constancy in love and its reward are employed as mechanical devices to begin and end a story. Like a pair of book-slides, they hold the narrative together. Against the lovers are leaned the perils and adventures which are only connected by the fact that they are encountered either by the hero and heroine or by other persons more or less remotely associated with their fortunes. There is no reason why the escapes, partings, meetings, and other incidents should not be indefinitely prolonged. But when the author feels that his inventiveness or the patience of his readers is exhausted, he uses the second slide to bring his straggling narrative to an end with a wedding. By this expedient novels were for centuries constructed.

It is to the last century before Christ and the first two centuries of the Christian era that the development of prose romance probably belongs. In spite of the advanced stage of civilisation at the time they were produced, no Greek works of prose fiction were introspective studies of human nature. They deal with events rather than with deeds. They treat life externally and objectively. But within the period named appear five distinct forms of fiction : the short story ; the imaginary journey, with its incredible histories of fabulous countries and peoples ; the romance of adventure and love-intrigue, with its succession of improbable escapes from the machinations of jealous rivals, from pirates, banditti, and shipwreck ; the pastoral romance, with its soft and sensuous pictures of Arcadian felicity and primeval innocence ; and the spiritual romance. Each type, in its different way, offered a temporary escape from the realities of a life which was full at once of terror and of despair.

Miletus has given its name to a special kind of short narrative, generally of an amatory character, which reached its highest flight in the beautiful story of " Cupid and Psyche," told by Apuleius as a " Milesian tale." No vestige remains of the *Milesian Tales* by Aristides. Both in its Greek original and in the Latin translation of Sisenna, the collection has so completely disappeared that it is even uncertain whether the stories were written in prose or verse. The work probably belonged to the not uncommon type of histories of towns, in which mythological tales of their fabled founders were mingled with stories of the lives and adventures of their inhabitants. Something of their character may be preserved in the collections of Parthenius of Nicæa and of Conon. Both writers seem to have flourished in the latter days of the Roman Republic and the early years of the Roman Empire. The manuscript of Parthenius was one of the spoils of Napoleon which was restored to the Vatican Library. But the work of Conon only survives in the *Bibliotheca Græca* of Photius.[1]

Parthenius, who is said to have taught Virgil the Greek language, collected abstracts of thirty-six love-stories. Twenty-five are gathered from poets, or from the historians, some apocryphal, of Troy, Pallene, Naxos, Miletus, Sicily, Lydia or Bithynia, whom he cites as his authorities; the remaining eleven are given without any reference to the sources from which they are derived. Told in the baldest outline, the stories have lost whatever amorous detail, graceful embroidery and warmth of colour they may have possessed in their original form. The fate of " Leucone," also narrated by Plutarch, may illustrate the general character of the work :

" In Thessaly there lived a maiden of the rarest beauty, named Leucone. She was loved by Cyanippe, son of Pharax, who pleaded his suit to her parents, and won her hand. Passionately devoted to the chase, Cyanippe passed all his days on the mountains, hunting deer and wild boars. At night he returned to his young wife, so overcome with weariness that often, before he had spoken to her a single word, he would fall into the deepest slumber. Tormented with disappointment and jealousy, Leucone became a prey to the most cruel anxieties. She set herself to discover the secret of the charm which drew Cyanippe to the mountains and thus kept him from her side. Girding her robe to the knees, she escaped from her women, and plunged into the woods. Cyanippe's hounds were hunting a stag. Heated and excited by the fury of the chase, they no sooner scented the young woman than they flew at her. No one was near to beat them off ; in a few seconds she was torn to pieces. When Cyanippe came up, Leucone was a mangled corpse. Overwhelmed with grief, he summoned his slaves by

[1] Soldier, administrator, diplomatist, and eventually ecclesiastic, Photius was also a man of letters. Before he was elected Patriarch of Constantinople (A.D. 857) he had been employed on a mission in Assyria. Thence he sent to his brother, Tarasius, the summaries of the 279 books which he had read, together with comments on their style and construction, which are generally quoted as his *Greek Library*. The work is interesting as the first bibliographical and critical journal ; it is also valuable for its preservation, in outline, of several books which have perished in any other form.

his cries, bade them build an altar of wood, laid upon it the lifeless body of his young wife, offered up his hounds as a sacrifice upon the pyre, and then with one and the same stroke ended both his grief and his life."

No manuscript of Conon's collection survives, but fifty abstracts of his stories have been preserved by Photius. Most of the tales are mythological, and do not illustrate human life, passion or character. One of the narratives has, however, been adapted by Cervantes, though it seems more probable that he derived the story from the *Golden Legend*, where it also appears, than from Conon. The stratagem of the fraudulent banker (No. 38) is discovered in Conon by accident, in *Don Quixote* by the native shrewdness of Sancho Panza. A Milesian, fearing the sack of Miletus by Cyrus the Persian, entrusted his treasure to a banker at Tauromenium. His fears allayed, he sought the restoration of his money. The banker admitted the deposit, but asserted that he had returned it to the owner. The dispute came to trial. Before the tribunal, plaintiff and defendant stood side by side, the banker leaning upon a hollow staff, in which he had concealed the treasure. When called upon to support his assertion by a solemn oath, he gave the staff to the Milesian to hold, while, with both hands uplifted, he swore that he had restored the money to its owner. Furious at the banker's treachery, the Milesian struck the stick violently on the ground. It broke in two, and the fraud was discovered. In *Don Quixote* Sancho Panza himself discovers the trick, having, as he says with a deft touch of characteristic frankness, once heard a story of a similar stratagem.

It is as a Milesian tale that Apuleius gives his Latin version of the *Golden Ass*. In the Greek form, in which the *Luciad, or the Ass* has also survived, the story is a literary masterpiece. Two of the characteristics usually attributed to the Milesian tales are certainly prominent : it is short, and in certain passages amazingly indecent. The book is not only a curious relic of the past. It is also true literature. None of the Greek prose romances can compare with it for the spirit and terseness of the narrative. Whoever the writer was, he is a natural story-teller. Apart from its literary merits, the *Luciad* possesses an additional interest which scarcely belongs in the same degree to any other prose work of Greek fiction. It gives a lively picture of the times.

The transformation of a man into an ass is to modern thought grotesquely impossible ; but in detail the sketches of private life are accurate, and the general impressions true. We see the tremendous gap between wealth and poverty, the contrast between the extravagant luxury of the rich, or the substantial comfort of the well-to-do middle class, and the grinding poverty of the hard-working market-gardener. We see also the insecurity of life and property produced by the apathy of the Government, the licence of the soldiery, the audacity of brigands ; the misery of slaves liable to torture on the slightest suspicion or to cruel punishments for trifling faults ; the religious impostures of the strolling charlatans, who carried into remote villages the image of the Syrian goddess Cybele, and, dripping with blood from self-inflicted wounds, with wild music and frenzied dance, preyed on the superstitious piety of rustics ; the deep-seated moral corruption which could even tolerate the idea of such an exhibition of the ass and the female prisoner as was contemplated in the theatre of Thessalonica.

The *Luciad* probably belongs to the second century of the Christian era. Its authorship is disputed. Photius tells us that he had read the *Metamorphoses* of Lucius, and that the first two books are either copied by Lucius from Lucian's *Luciad*, or copied by Lucian from the *Metamorphoses* of Lucius. He suggests that Lucian stripped off all the unnecessary digressions and embellishments of Lucius, and produced the *Luciad*—as a sculptor chisels a perfect statue from a misshapen block. The theory is not convincing. It is less characteristic of Lucian's genius and professional training to abridge than to expand, and the task of condensing another's composition seems unnatural to a writer so fertile of invention. It is, moreover, uncertain that Lucian ever wrote the *Luciad* which sometimes passes under his name. Two facts seem to be established by the note of Photius. One is that, in its Greek form, Lucius's

longer work on *Metamorphoses* has perished; the other is
that the first two books of that lost work were practically
identical with the existing *Luciad*. Equally uncertain
is the relation of the Greek *Luciad* to the Latin *Golden Ass*.
Which was the copyist—Lucius, Lucian, or Apuleius?
In one sense the answer is unimportant. Undeniably it
was from the *Golden Ass* of Apuleius that Western Europe
learnt the tale, and in the chapter on " Latin Prose Fiction "
the story is discussed in fuller detail.

To the same period as the *Luciad* probably belongs the
Daphnis and Chloe of Longus. Nothing is known about
the author. His name, his nationality, the date at which
he wrote, are all uncertain. Photius makes no mention
of the book. But it would be rash to conclude from his
silence that the story was written after A.D. 857. In the
literary world of the decaying Empire of the East, among
clumsy pedants neglectful of style and careless of form,
the studied elegance of an artificial exquisite like *Daphnis
and Chloe* would have been singularly out of place. Amyot's
famous translation of the work concealed its true character
from readers who only knew it in the French version. In
the original Greek there is nothing artless except the simplicity of the subject. The innocence of two young people
of opposite sexes, conscious of the awakening of mutual
love, yet ignorant of the full purpose of their feelings, veils
the perfection of the art with which the picture is
finished.

Every literary device is freely employed to heighten the
effect; every word is fastidiously chosen to convey with
the utmost precision the most delicate shades of meaning;
every epithet is added with deliberate intention. The
sentences are elaborately constructed, not only to express
the sense with clearness, but to gratify the ear with the
sweetness of their cadence. With remarkable skill the sense
of the tranquillity of country life is impressed upon the
reader. No changes seem to mark the passage of Daphnis
and Chloe from childhood to youth, except the regular
succession of the seasons and the recurrence of the labours
appropriate to spring and summer, autumn and winter.
Rarely has so much artifice been lavished on so primitive

a theme. Its very simplicity becomes a kind of luxury, and its charm is the charm, not of natural grace, but of finished coquetry.

The scene of the story is laid in Lesbos, in the neighbour-hood of Mitylene, but it is unlikely that the writer was himself a native of an island where winter, which he describes as early and severe, is unknown. The roads are blocked with snow; except on the banks of rivers and by the margins of streams, the earth is invisible. Peasants, con-fined to their cottages, ply their winter tasks by blazing fires. The live-stock are brought under cover; oxen are fed with chaff in the stalls, sheep with leaves in the folds, pigs with acorns in the sties. It might be plausibly sug-gested that the author was some sophist of Alexandria—some skilful student of the niceties of the Greek language, such as were many of the scholars who haunted the famous library, under whose shadow, in that busy hive of industry and learning, the weavers, paper-makers, glass-blowers and metal-workers plied their various trades. If this were so, Alexandria might claim a share in the development of pastorals, both in prose and verse. Theocritus, who sang of the Sicilian shepherds, as they pastured their flocks on the slopes of Etna or sheltered from the noonday heat by the side of some shady spring, spent many years of his life at Alexandria. As he was the father of pastoral verse, so the unknown Longus is the father of the pastoral romance in prose.

Daphnis and Chloe is free from the affectations, the wearisome digressions, and many of the cloying unrealities, that are the usual defects of pastoral romance. But it does not altogether avoid the insipidity and monotony that seem inseparable from this style of composition. It is in the atmosphere of country life, in the vivid descriptions of pastoral scenes, and in the descriptions of rural manners and occupations, that its chief attraction lies. The picture is highly idealised; but, in detail, graphic touches abound which are true to nature. The popularity of prose pastorals underwent so many changes that it is difficult to estimate the influence which the book exercised on their development. Though the Greek text remained unprinted till 1598, the

French version of Amyot appeared in 1559, and the translation into Latin verse by Gambara in 1569. It may, therefore, so far as dates are concerned, have influenced, not only the *Diana* of Montemayor, the *Arcadia* of Sidney, the *Menaphon* of Greene, the *Rosalynde* of Lodge, and the *Astrea* of D'Urfé, but the dramatic pastorals of Tasso and Jonson.

The taste of the seventeenth century travelled in other directions than that of its predecessor. But the eighteenth century witnessed a strong reaction in favour of the sentimentalism of pastoral romance. The story charmed men of such different minds as Rousseau and Goethe. Goethe, indeed, says that he read and re-read the book without ever exhausting its beauties. It was the model of Marmontel's *Annette et Lubin*, of Gesner's *Idylls*, and, above all, of *Paul et Virginie* (1788). Longus and Bernardin de St. Pierre belong to two different worlds, and lived under different moral orders ; but the theme of both books is alike. It is the awakening of love in the hearts of two young people, though the earlier book unbares the growth of the senses rather than of affection. Both pairs of lovers remain pure ; but the first is unmoral, the other moral. The innocence of Daphnis and Chloe depends solely on youthful inexperience ; it is safeguarded only by ignorance ; they are unconscious rather than modest. The purity of Paul and Virginia rests on the restraint of virtue, and is protected by the Christian ideal of chastity.

No imitator of the *Luciad* has survived. All could pillage, none could imitate, *Daphnis and Chloe*, to which, perhaps, the touch of a literary artist, like Mr. George Moore, may have given a new lease of life in the twentieth century. Prose fiction turned aside from the composition of pastorals or the presentation of popular fables in the form of Milesian tales. Novelists changed geography and history into romance by weaving love-stories into narratives of imaginary travels or adventures. To the travel class belongs the *Tales of the Incredible Things beyond Thule*, of Antonius Diogenes ; to that of adventure the *Babylonica* of Iamblichus. No manuscript of either work has survived ; they are only preserved in the summaries of Photius. The dates at which

CA

the authors lived and wrote are uncertain. Photius, who held that the *Incredible Things beyond Thule* was written shortly after the death of Alexander the Great, regards Diogenes as the father of prose fiction. Modern critics doubt whether he or Iamblichus wrote before the middle of the second century of the Christian era.

The imaginary travels of Diogenes are inspired, partly by the *Odyssey*, partly by ancient geographies. Early romancers did not assert the omnipresence and omniscience of modern authors, who address the world at large. They manœuvred to secure as narrators eye-witnesses of the scenes that they describe. The *Luciad* is an autobiography, in which the author narrates his own experience. Longus professes to explain a picture by the story of *Daphnis and Chloe*. Heliodorus tells a great part of *Theagenes and Chariclea* by reporting narratives told by one actor to another. Achilles Tatius, in *Clitophon and Leucippe*, seizes on a bystander in a picture gallery, to whom Clitophon tells the tale. In the *Incredible Things beyond Thule*, Diogenes makes Dinias, the Ulysses of his imaginary journey, narrate his adventures to Cambas, the Arcadian legate, and instruct him to have them inscribed on tablets of cypress-wood. The tablets, buried in the tomb of Dercyllis, the wife of Dinias, were discovered by Alexander the Great at the capture of Tyre. So the story is brought to light.

An Arcadian by birth, Dinias leaves his native land in pursuit of knowledge of men and things. He reaches Thule, where he finds Dercyllis, a young Tyrian maiden of noble birth, who, with her brother, was dwelling on the land. She describes to him her flight from Tyre to escape the persecution of an Egyptian priest; her visit to the nether world; her encounter with Astræus; his stories of Pythagoras —which were accepted as truths in biographies of that philosopher; her pursuit and capture by the Egyptian magician; his spell by which she is robbed of life by day and restored to it at night; his violent death, and the breaking of his enchantment. Then Dinias takes up the story in his own person. After telling Cambas of the return of Dercyllis to Tyre, he recounts his own adventures beyond Thule ; what astronomical wonders he had witnessed ; how, as he neared the farthest north, all the mysteries of the moon stood revealed ; and how, finally, he awoke from deep sleep to find himself in the Temple of Hercules at Tyre, where he married Dercyllis and lived a long and happy life.

No modern writer could take more elaborate pains than Diogenes to pass off his fictions as truth. He does not rely on realistic details. The means which he adopts are more mechanical. Not only does he elaborately describe the discovery of his manuscript, he also carefully " documents " each chapter by references to authorities, many of them apocryphal, or supports his wildest fictions by the evidence of tradition, which he claims to have collected at great expense. It is this class of descriptive literature, with its ostentatious pretensions to accuracy, in which he irreverently includes the work of Herodotus, that Lucian burlesques in his *True History*.

Unlike Diogenes, Lucian begins his book by asking his readers not to believe a word of the contents. " In warning them," he says, " that I am not going to speak the truth, I shall at least have spoken the truth once." Not for the last time, the parody, especially in the second book, surpassed the original in wit and invention. Immortalised by the imitation of Rabelais, it afforded a model to Cyrano de Bergerac, Swift and Voltaire. Over one of the first and greatest of English novelists Lucian's influence was strong. Fielding ranked him with Cervantes, Molière, Swift and Shakespeare, who all sent their satire " laughing into the world " ; on Lucian, as he himself says, he " formed his stile " ; and, two years before his death, he offered for subscription a new translation of the works of Lucian by himself and the Rev. William Young, famous as the original of Parson Adams.

Among known writers, Diogenes is the parent of the prose romance of imaginary travels. Iamblichus is similarly the ancestor of prose romances of adventures which, however improbable, are generally possible. The one turns geography, the other history, into romantic fiction The *Babylonica* of the Syrian Iamblichus is gloomy in tone and Eastern in colouring. It is the story of two lovers, Rhodanes and Sinonis. Garmus, the widowed King of Babylon, desired Sinonis as his wife. Because she rejects his suit he causes her to be fettered with chains of gold, and his rival, Rhodanes, to be bound to a cross. Sinonis rescues her lover, and the two take flight together. Pursued by the emissaries of Garmus, they pass through innumerable adventures and make many hairbreadth escapes. Finally, Rhodanes is chosen King of Babylonia in the room of Garmus, and shares his throne with Sinonis.

The story is cast in the same mould as the romances of the sixteenth and seventeenth centuries, in which the hero overcomes all obstacles, weds a beauteous princess, and wins a kingdom or an empire. Existing, as it does, only in a summary, no literary talent is likely to be revealed in an abstract except ingenuity of invention. Judged by this test, Iamblichus was at least resourceful in inventing details. Many of the stock devices of subsequent romancers appear, seemingly for the first time, in his pages. Here, for instance, we find the rout of the pursuing soldiers by a swarm of poisonous bees ; the unintentional release of the heroine from prison by the proclamation of a general gaol-delivery ; the substitution of a sleeping-potion for poison and of death-like slumber for real death ; the discovery by a dog of the buried corpse of the murdered Trophima ; the false inscription on the tomb which induces belief that Sinonis is dead.

It was in the direction of the *Babylonica*, and of the romance of adventure, that prose fiction subsequently developed. Like the authors of the *Luciad* and *Daphnis and Chloe*, Diogenes had no immediate followers. Many trod in the steps of Iamblichus. Between the second century and Heliodorus, who wrote towards the end of the fourth century, a long gap intervenes. Possibly the interval was filled by the *Abrocomas and Anthia* (translated into English 1727) of Xenophon of Ephesus. The prominence of unnatural passion in that story seems to suggest that it preceded the general spread of Christianity, and the elaborate description of the Temple of Diana at Ephesus, which was burnt in A.D. 263, hints an approximate date. If the suggestion is accepted, *Abrocomas and Anthia* is the earliest

Greek romance of adventure of which the manuscript is
known to exist. It is the story of two young people who
had scoffed at love. Meeting by chance in the Temple of
Diana, they became enamoured. But, to appease the God
of Love, whose wrath had been stirred by their jeers, they
were doomed to spend weary years of trial and adventure
before they were united.

Whether Xenophon wrote before or after Heliodorus
may be a question; but of the latter's superiority there is
no doubt. Heliodorus is the true father of the romance
of adventure. By common consent, in the sixteenth and
seventeenth centuries, his *Theagenes and Chariclea* was
regarded as the masterpiece of Greek prose fiction.
Heliodorus, by birth a Phœnician, apparently wrote in the
reign of Theodosius the Great. Ecclesiastical tradition
makes him a Christian and Bishop of Tricca, or Triccala,
in Thessaly. A later legend asserts that, bidden to repudiate
his love-story or resign his episcopal office, he chose to
sacrifice his bishopric. Montaigne, Burton and Boileau
have lent to the story the weight of their authority, and the
case of Home, expelled from the Scottish ministry for
writing " a stage play " entitled *The Tragedy of Douglas*,
affords a literary parallel. But the legend is improbable.
Were it true, the Church in later times made Heliodorus
some amends. Amyot, Bishop of Auxerre, first made
Theagenes and Chariclea known to the Western world in a
modern language, and the translator of a book which cost
the author a bishopric was rewarded by an abbey. Another
French bishop, Huet, Bishop of Avranches, in the seventeenth century, prefaced the *Zaïde* of Madame de la Fayette
with the first critical account of early romances, in which
he praises Heliodorus as the model of all subsequent novelists.

The preservation of the manuscript of Heliodorus is
itself romantic, for it was saved by a German mercenary
from the destruction of the famous library of Matthias
Corvinus during the sack of Buda. Printed in the original
Greek in 1534, it was translated into Latin seventeen years
later by a learned Pole. It is on this Latin version, rather
than on the Greek original, that Thomas Underdown
founded his picturesque, racy, inaccurate translation into

English, which first appeared in 1569. The rediscovered book took the literary world by storm. Here, at last, was a classic model. Art and literature are the finest products of the genius of Greece, but the nation and the conditions which had given them birth had disappeared. Their character was, therefore, permanent and unchangeable, and their literary influence was essentially different from that of any living nation. With all the glamour of this final authority *Theagenes and Chariclea* was invested. Fourteen translations and editions appeared in the sixteenth century alone. Shakespeare did not disdain to allude to an incident in the story. From it Tasso and Ariosto borrowed incidents. It was imitated by Cervantes. It was accepted by Elizabethan romance writers as a model. Sir Philip Sidney took Theagenes as his type of a perfect lover. On Heliodorus Greene and Lodge founded their " love-pamphlets."

Throughout the seventeenth century the further development of a native school of English novelists was checked by the ascendancy of the heroic romances of France. But it was from Heliodorus that the fashionable fiction of the invaders derived a great part of its inspiration. On *Theagenes and Chariclea* Alexandre Hardy, the first French dramatist who definitely wrote for representation on the stage, had founded eight of his forty published plays. Equally striking was the influence of Heliodorus on prose fiction. Gomberville copied him closely in his ponderous *Polexandre*. In her *Grand Cyrus* Madeleine de Scudéri acknowledged her debt to " l'immortel Héliodore " as a master whom all must copy. It was not without good reason that Sorel, in *Le Berger Extravagant* (English translation 1653), attributed to Heliodorus the destruction of the old romances of chivalry. As an illustration of the spell which *Theagenes and Chariclea* cast upon the seventeenth century may be quoted the well-known story of Racine, told by his youngest son. The book fascinated the youthful student at Port Royal. But the sacristan, himself a famous Greek scholar, took it from his pupil and threw it into the fire. A second copy shared the fate of the first. The defiant Racine found means to get a third copy, learned the book by heart, and, having printed it on his memory, gave it to the sacristan, saying, " You can burn it, sir, if you choose."

Nor, even in England, was the influence of Heliodorus confined only to the Elizabethans or solely derived from the French heroic romances. Between 1605 and 1717 the book was twice translated by " Persons of Quality," and seven editions were published. A slight but significant sign of the popularity of the story is to be found in *The English Rogue* (1665–71), where the authors, confident that the allusion will be recognised, burlesqued a well-known episode in *Theagenes and Chariclea*.

In true heroic fashion, Heliodorus plunges into the middle of his story. The opening passage, rendered by an Elizabethan writer, Abraham Fraunce, into English in the form of wretched hexameters, introduces the hero and heroine. At early dawn a band of freebooters climb the brow of a hill, which slopes towards the sea near one of the mouths of the Nile. Below them rides a ship, moored by stern-cables to the land, laden waist-deep with merchandise. On deck no sign of life appears. But the shore is strewn with dead and dying men, and the remains of an interrupted feast. The pirates hurry down to seize their booty.

As they draw near they see, seated on the rocks, a maiden of surpassing beauty, her fair hair crowned with a wreath of laurel, clad in a gold-embroidered robe, a bow at her side, a quiver on her shoulder. Her right arm hangs idly down ; her left hand, the elbow resting on her knee, supports her cheek as she gazes intently on a young man, who lies at her feet, bleeding and sorely wounded. She rises to her full height. Astounded at her beauty, the pirates cower behind the bushes, fearing that in her they behold the goddess who has caused the slaughter. But when she stoops down, raises the young man's head, kisses his lips, and wipes the blood from his face, their fears vanish. The embrace, the action, were human in their tenderness. They rush forward, and the hero and heroine, Theagenes and Chariclea, are prisoners in the hands of pirates. Who they are, whence they come, why they alone survive a bloody fray, what subsequent adventures they encounter, are told in the romance.

In *Theagenes and Chariclea* neither places nor persons are treated individually. The romance belongs to no particular age nor country. The Athens of Heliodorus is neither free nor conquered. His Egypt is the Egypt neither of the Pharaohs, nor of the Ptolemies, nor of the Romans. He attempts no picture of the mind ; he does not even use action to develop the different motives and impulses of his actors. Like all early novelists, he relies for the interest of his romance upon adventures. Capture and recapture by pirates and soldiers are again and again repeated ; peril is piled on peril, escape on escape. By plunging *in medias res* he succeeds in arresting attention. But he creates for himself the difficulty of introducing the previous history of the hero and heroine. He meets it by employing a third person, in the fashion of a tragic chorus, who narrates to a casual acquaintance the events of which his own knowledge is often only second-hand.

Though the main thread of the plot is firmly held, and more than one of the incidents is striking, the mechanical art of constructing a story was evidently still in its infancy. No modern craftsmen would have so weakened the dramatic effect of the conclusion by the premature disclosure of the secret. Prisoners in the hands of the Ethiopians, Theagenes and Chariclea, on the plain outside " sunburnt Meroë," in the presence of King Hydaspes and Queen Persina, are about to be sacrificed to the sun and moon. Only victims who have preserved their purity are accepted as offerings. Both hero and heroine have triumphed over the ordeal of fire which tests their chastity. No way of escape appears. But the reader knows throughout that Chariclea has only to declare her parentage and receive the highest honours.

For nine years Queen Persina had borne no child to her husband, Hydaspes, King of Ethiopia. At length she conceived. In the royal bedchamber the Queen's eyes were always fixed upon a picture of Andromeda, fair and white as are Grecian maidens, rescued by Perseus from the monster. When the child was born she was fair and white as Andromeda herself. Persina was terrified lest King Hydaspes should deem the cause inadequate to the effect. Dreading her own fate and that of her offspring,

" the woful Queene of Blackmoreland," as Lisle calls her in his version of *The Faire Ethiopian* (1631), determined to expose the infant, and to tell the King that his daughter was dead. But to secure kind treatment for the deserted child she placed with her jewels of great price, and round her body bound a silken fillet on which was written in royal or hieratic characters the story of her birth. The child is, of course, Chariclea.

Heliodorus writes like a learned recluse, dependent on the stage for his knowledge of human nature, and in his style reminiscent of earlier poets and historians. It might be suggested that in Calasiris he has portrayed himself. A Mr. Barlow of the fourth century, he is always ready to improve the occasion or to supply explanations of such phenomena as the inundations of the Nile or the roughness of the Ionian Sea, constantly quoting Homer, of whose Egyptian birth he is as zealous a champion as was any Highlander of the authenticity of Ossian. No distinctively Christian sentiments appear. But the moral tone is uniformly high, and the whole story is in praise of chastity for men as well as women.

In moral tone the *Clitophon and Leucippe* (translated into English 1577 ?) of Achilles Tatius, a native of Alexandria, who in date and merit is generally placed next to Heliodorus, is inferior to *Theagenes and Chariclea*. Like his predecessor, Tatius is said to have become a Christian and a bishop. If the legend is true, he was still unregenerate when he wrote his romance. Though virtue finally triumphs, the book is faintly tinged with traces of some of the worst vices of paganism. In many respects Tatius does not suffer from comparison with Heliodorus. His story is shorter, his style more vivid, his narrative, during the first five books, more brisk. His conclusion is less dramatic. His opening is also more awkward. Yet, having once provided his narrator with a listener, his autobiographical method of telling the story is more lively than the second-hand narratives of previous events which Heliodorus so largely employs. The supposed writer is a stranger, sight-seeing in Sidon. He is fascinated by a picture in one of the temples. A bull, swimming out to sea from the Sidonian shore, bears on his back a maiden. It is Jove carrying off Europa. Round him, as he swims, loves sport and dolphins gambol. With fluttering wings, Cupid himself leads the way, torch in hand —Cupid in the guise of a child, with back-turned head, laughing mischievously at Jove, as though mocking him, because, for his sake, the Great God has assumed the form of a bull. As the sight-seeing stranger stands before the picture, he murmurs to himself aloud, " How marvellously doth a puny child lord it over earth and sea, and even heaven itself ! " An unknown bystander, who proves to be Clitophon, overhears the half-spoken thought, and, in illustration of the text, without break or pause, tells him the love-tale of himself and Leucippe.

Clitophon and Leucippe proceeds on the usual lines of the romance of adventure. Shipwrecks, captures by pirates, rescues and escapes are strung to the thread of the identity of the principal actors. As in all Greek novels, the hero is inferior to the heroine. Theagenes is insipid ; Clitophon is not only a mere animal, but a coward. On the other hand, Chariclea shows both firmness and presence of mind, while Leucippe, though a gentler figure than the fair Ethiopian, supports her misfortunes with patience and constancy. Another commonplace of Greek fiction is that the hero is passionately loved by all women, and the heroine by all men. Their fatal attractiveness breeds most of the mishaps into which they are plunged. In Cupid romancers possessed an instrument which the feeblest could employ. It only needed an arrow from his bow to create a fresh complication. But on Tatius it seems to have dawned that some less mechanical and more convincing process was needed, and he makes some effort to trace in Clitophon and Leucippe the stages in the growth of their mutual passion.

The romance of Heliodorus is heroic. We move through temples and palaces among high-priests, Oriental satraps, kings and queens ; Chariclea is a princess, Theagenes is a descendant of Achilles. *Clitophon and Leucippe* introduces us to ordinary Greek citizens in their villas, their gardens, and the routine of their luxurious social existence. Partly perhaps for this reason, the romance is less vague and more particular in its treatment of places and things. The

picture of Alexandria, the birthplace of the author, for
example, has a historical value which is confirmed by modern
excavations. Natural history was one of the studies
pursued by the Alexandrian School, and Tatius gives
spirited descriptions of the crocodile, hippopotamus and
elephant. It is true, however, that he assigns to the hippopotamus a cloven hoof, and describes the fabulous phœnix
with all the confidence and realism of an eye-witness.
Another feature in the romance suggests the influence of
Alexandria. Distinguished as patrons and collectors of
the fine arts, the Egyptian Ptolemies implanted in their
subjects tastes which survived their rule. Of pictorial
art Tatius shows a remarkable appreciation. Besides his
vivid description of the picture at Sidon, he describes with
true feeling two paintings at Pelusium, one representing
Andromeda rescued by Perseus, the other Prometheus
tortured by the vulture.

Both Heliodorus and Tatius, and especially the latter,
were freely imitated, sometimes transcribed, by their
successors. With one exception, the subsequent writers
of Greek prose fiction show a progressive decline. Their
work is that of copyists, and, like engravings struck from
the same plate, the successive impressions grow fainter and
feebler. The *Chæreas and Callirrhoë* of Chariton of Aphro-
disias, written in the fifth or sixth century, alone deserves
to rank with earlier rivals. Its neglect by Western Europe
is probably due to the fact that the manuscript was not
discovered till 1750. In simplicity of construction, and,
assuming the extraordinary attractions of Callirrhoë, in
probability of incidents, the story is inferior to no previous
romance of adventure. It also contains the most satisfactory
sketch of a man which is to be found in Greek prose fiction.
The character of Dionysius, a wealthy and learned landowner, is well drawn and well maintained. He woos
Callirrhoë like a gentleman, and, though she loves Chæreas,
he wins her admiration.

In its respect for chronology, *Chæreas and Callirrhoë* makes
another advance on its predecessors. Though the regard
for history is little more than nominal, and though no
attempt is made to reproduce the manners and customs of

any particular century, it approaches nearer to the historical novel than any previous romance. The scene is Syracuse, and the date is shortly after the failure of the Athenians to conquer the city. The hero and heroine are imaginary persons ; but the names of the subordinate figures are those of contemporary actors in the real history of the period. Thus the author, whose assumed name probably indicates the dedication of his pen to the Graces and to Venus, describes himself as secretary to Athenagoras, the rhetorician, who played a real part in the defence of Syracuse. Callirrhoë is the daughter of Hermocrates, who was one of the actual heroes of the siege, and in history his daughter married a Dionysius. Chæreas is the son of Ariston, who was also one of the conspicuous defenders of the town. When the scene shifts to Persia, the author still consults the history of the times. The contemporary rulers of Persia, both in the novel and in real life, were Artaxerxes and his wife Stateira.

Following closely on *Chæreas and Callirrhoë* came a new type of prose fiction. *Baarlam and Josaphat*, probably written by St. John of Damascus (675–754), was the ancestor of a long line of spiritual romances. Though, in its original form, it was far removed from the religious novel of later times, the book ought not to be entirely unnoticed. It is important, not only for its influence on the religion and literature of the Middle Ages, but for its adaptation of Buddhist legends. The early life of Josaphat is based on the traditional youth of Buddha.

The powerful Eastern potentate Abenner was an idolater and a persecutor of Christians. Childless, he passionately desired a son. When at length Josaphat was born to him, he consulted the wise men of his kingdom on his son's future. All save one foretold that the young prince would excel his ancestors in wealth and power and glory. One sage alone predicted that the boy would become a Christian, and that the only glories for which he was destined were those of heaven. To shield his son from knowledge of the miseries of life, Abenner lavishes all the resources of wealth and ingenuity. But Josaphat rides forth, and, like Buddha, in his rides becomes acquainted with sickness, old age and death.

To Baarlam, a holy monk dwelling in the wilderness of Sennaar, comes the divine command to attempt the conversion of Josaphat. Disguised as a merchant, he obtains audience of the young prince under the pretext of showing him a priceless gem. The jewel is the gospel and the doctrines of the Christian faith. They are put before Josaphat in the series of beautiful apologues and parables on which the medieval popularity of the romance mainly depended. Josaphat, embracing Christianity, is baptised by Baarlam, who forthwith returns to the desert. From that time forward Josaphat lives the ascetic life. Threats, arguments, temptations fail to shake his resolution; a timely vision of heaven and hell puts his most dangerous foe to flight; even the possession of a kingdom does not divert him from his purpose. When his father abdicates in his favour, he resigns the throne and seeks out Baarlam in his lonely cell. There he tends the last years of his master, there buries him, and there, thirty-five years later, finds his own last resting-place.

Through the grotesque machinery of the romance throbs the passion of conviction. For earthly love John of Damascus substitutes a love that is heavenly, for adventures the sufferings of martyrs; his story breathes, not the enjoyment of life's pleasures, but the rapture of their renunciation. He had no imitators among writers of Greek fiction. They still followed the lines of Heliodorus and Tatius.

The last, and certainly the most tiresome, of the prose romances of adventure is the *Hysmene and Hysmenias* of Eumathius, probably written in the twelfth century. It would be charitable to suggest that the book is a burlesque of older works. The exaggerated prominence of descriptions of paintings and of gardens, the capacity of the hero for falling asleep at critical moments, the detailed variety of dreams which follow a succession of heavy banquets, the affectation of confusing the plot by the similarity of the names of actors and places, the part assigned to the heroine Hysmene, who makes love to the unwilling hero Hysmenias —all these are consistent with an exaggerated burlesque of characteristics in earlier romances. If the book is not intended to be humorous, it is a dull imitation of Tatius and, in a less degree, of Heliodorus.　Yet the sixteenth century took the romance seriously.　One Italian translation and two French versions attest its popularity, and its influence may be faintly traced in the pastoral romances of Montemayor and of D'Urfé.

Greek writers of fiction themselves seemed to grow ashamed of their own work.　Conscious of the need of some new attraction, they embellished with verse their faded and imitative finery :

> Carmina non possunt Erebo deducere manes.

The barbarous verse in which the latest romances are written had not the magical power to restore grey ashes to life.　The *Drosilla and Charicles* of Nicetas Eugenianus, for instance, belongs to a later period than the thirteenth century.　In this diffuse, imitative work, two points of interest may be noticed.　The first is the change in the legend of Charon.　No longer the ferryman on the Styx, he is the dark horseman who traverses the earth gathering his convoys for the nether world, carrying the children on his saddle-bow, driving the young before him, and followed by the laggard steps of the aged.　So Cleander meets him in the mountains, and implores him to reveal the doom of his beloved Calligone.　The second point is the praise bestowed on Chagus, the Arab sheikh, as compassionate as he is brave, who restores to liberty the two captive Greeks. It is a tribute to the generosity and learning of the Khalifs of Bagdad, an unconscious recognition of the fact that the intellectual supremacy of the world in medicine and philosophy was passing from Greece to Arabian students.

Strictly speaking, versified romances do not belong to prose fiction.　But it was in these barren sands that the mighty stream of the imaginative literature of Greece was dispersed and lost.　If it be asked how far the ancient prose fiction affected the development of the modern novel, the answer is that its immediate influence was small.　The writers were predecessors rather than ancestors of the novelists.　They did indeed supply models of many forms of prose fiction.　But the romantic literature of the Middle

Ages was, in the main, an independent growth. It is not impossible, it is even probable, that writers like Chrestien de Troyes at the close of the twelfth century borrowed from the prose fiction of Greece the pirates and the magical devices by which they complicated the adventures of their heroes and heroines. But the Middle Ages knew the classical world mainly from Latin sources. After the Crusades the knowledge of Greek almost disappeared from Western Europe. It was not till the Revival of Learning that the literature of Greece was enthusiastically studied in the West, or that her romances were made accessible to an English-speaking public. For a period of nearly a hundred years, from the close of the sixteenth century to the latter half of the seventeenth, Heliodorus powerfully influenced the development of prose fiction. But the domination of heroic romance was short-lived. Its ascendancy in England was decaying at the Revolution ; in France it had already passed away. Greek prose fiction, except in the form of pastorals, had become, what it has ever since remained, an antiquarian interest instead of a living literary influence.

CHAPTER III

LATIN PROSE FICTION : PETRONIUS

In Latin literature prose fiction occupies a narrow space. As early in date, it is more modern in form than the Greek romances. Public libraries in Rome contained collections of short stories of the Milesian type, whether of native growth, or translated, or derived from Greek originals. If librarians had recorded the books most frequently read, these tales would probably be found to have been more in demand than Virgil or Livy. It was with a work of this character that the subaltern crammed his knapsack when he went on foreign service under Crassus against the Parthians. It was a similar kind of literature that Aulus Gellius (flourished A.D. 150), travelling from Athens to Rome, bought at Brindisi to while away the weariness of his journey. But in the Latin language these tales have not survived. As in Greece, so in Rome, the impulse to compose fictitious narratives in prose for the amusement of readers or hearers was not felt till the decay of liberty and of the interest in public life.

Only two works of prose fiction have survived, and both probably fall within the first two centuries of the Christian era. One is the *Satyricon* of Petronius, the other the *Golden Ass* of the African Apuleius. If small in bulk, the product is great in literary value. Each writer opened up new paths, and hundreds of years passed before these were fully explored. Petronius, a first-century Fielding, abandoned the typical and impersonal for humorous and realistic studies of individuals. Apuleius, a Baudelaire of the second century, used language daringly as a colour-box to produce his supernatural atmosphere and the richness of his pictorial effects. The *Satyricon* and the *Golden Ass* belong, in their very different ways, to a higher literary order than the adventurous pages of Heliodorus, or the studied elegance of

Daphnis and Chloe. The modernity of the art of both the Latin writers, as well as their striking personalities, justify detailed examination of their works.

Neither of the Latin writers feels any restraint of decorum. Yet St. Augustine read Apuleius, half believing in the truth of the metamorphosis, and from the pages of Petronius, Jeremy Taylor drew an illustration for his *Holy Dying.* The respectability of such sponsors at least vouches for the general interest of the books. For Petronius, indeed, a defence may be urged. He makes it for himself in lines which may be paraphrased thus :

> Catos ! Why stare at me with disapproving frown ?
> Why damn the strangeness of my work's simplicity ?
> In Latin undefiled—what's done by all the town
> I tell, unsoured by gloom, with frank sincerity.

The *Satyricon* holds up a mirror to a squalid section of Roman society. A picture of the Empire in the days of Nero would be incomplete if the author ignored so conspicuous a feature in social life as the prevalence of immorality, both in its modern and its pagan forms. Petronius accepts vice as a matter of fact, and handles it frankly, without a trace of prurience. He presents it stark naked, with a serene unconsciousness which is a stranger to shame. It is in this sense that Burton in his *Anatomy of Melancholy* speaks of his " pure impurities." The Council of Trent showed sound sense in its decision not to include the *Satyricon* in the list of books which it prohibited. For Apuleius the same defence cannot be urged. He was writing an imaginary work, and was free to omit the subject altogether. He knew the taste of the reading public too well to abstain. The best that can be pleaded for him is that he is less offensive than the writer of the Greek version of his story.

If the *Satyricon* had any literary forerunners in Greek or Latin prose, they have perished. It breaks with all tradition. It opens fresh ground. It stands alone in classical literature, one of the most interesting and curious works that have come down to us from antiquity. It may fairly claim to be, in many respects, the first modern novel. Unlike other ancient works of fiction, it is not serious,

DA

tragic, impersonal, remote from realities, belonging to no particular age or country. Here are no conventional princesses of divine and irresistible beauty, no flower-crowned shepherdesses masquerading in Arcadian innocence. On the contrary, the book thrusts us into the company of three rascally young Bohemians, plunges us into the tortuous by-streets of the half-Greek cities of Southern Italy, forces us into the midst of the squalid realities of the Roman underworld. A keen observer, whom little escapes, Petronius is alive to the comedies as well as the tragedies of life, capable of seeing and understanding both together, and acutely sensitive to the humour of the clash of their contrasts.

So far as appears from the fragmentary form in which the book survives, he makes no attempt at a plot. The connecting thread is slender. But, apart from the construction of his story, his methods are strikingly modern. His figures, strongly individualised, stand up in firm relief against backgrounds which are never too overloaded to be subservient to their purpose. Yet on occasions he does not hesitate to multiply details, and gives them with vivid precision. More than one of his interiors are Dutch pictures in words. When he is not familiarly colloquial, or deliberately slangy, he is the master of a pure, supple style, which has the high finish of simplicity. The coiner of the famous phrase, " Horatii curiosa felicitas," and the framer of the sentence which Landor judged to be the most beautiful " in all Latinity," was no ordinary scribbler. Interspersed with his wildest indecencies and most cynical whimsicalities are passages of fine literary criticism and interludes of verse which often rise to genuine and distinctive poetry.

The date of the *Satyricon* is uncertain, its authorship anonymous ; even the title by which it is generally known is probably not its own. It has come down to us in a fragmentary form ; four-fifths of the whole are lost, and it was not till the middle of the seventeenth century that the longest and most continuous fragment was discovered in the obscure Dalmatian town of Trau. All these circumstances, combined with the possible identification of the author with the famous Roman patrician whose career and

death are described by Tacitus, have made the book the
battleground of critics. Who was this unknown genius
who created a new branch of literature? When did he
write? With what object? No absolute answers can be
given. Manuscripts ascribe the authorship to Petronius
Arbiter. But the evidence which thus connects the book
with the friend of the Emperor Nero is not conclusive,
because the ascription may be the hand of the copyist.
Neither does the title of the book establish the author's
intention to lash the vices of the town. Whether *Satyricon*
or *Satiræ* is accepted as the title—and the best modern
editor adopts the latter—the word probably means, not a
satire, but a miscellany, or hotch-potch of prose and verse.

In the midst of so much uncertainty conjecture is free.
Novelists claim greater licence than critics. Farrar in
Darkness and Dawn, Sienkievicz in *Quo Vadis?* assume that
Nero's favourite was the author of the *Satyricon*. It must
always remain a mystery why, if the historical Petronius
wrote so famous a book, Tacitus did not mention the fact.
Be this as it may, the majority of scholars identify the
anonymous author with the Petronius described in the
Annals as the *arbiter elegantiæ*, whose word was final with
Nero on matters of taste, and who was first the friend, then
the victim, of the Emperor. In the *Satyricon* the author
rigorously suppressed himself; but the few glimpses that
are revealed of his elusive personality are consistent with
the portrait painted by Tacitus. Internal evidence, though
itself inconclusive, suggests the probable date of the book
to be between A.D. 60 and A.D. 65, and so confirms the
identification. The gain in historical interest is great if
the brilliant patrician is accepted as the author of the
Satyricon. No probabilities are violated by the theory,
while many are satisfied. We may therefore imagine the
book to have been composed and read aloud by Petronius
for the amusement of himself and the Imperial Court.

Tacitus tells us that Petronius turned night into day,
and owed his reputation less to his energy than to his
indolence. His contemporaries never confounded him
with ordinary spendthrifts who waste their fortunes in
vulgar debaucheries. They always regarded him as a

supreme artist in all the refinements of luxury.   The graceful air of unaffected naturalness, which characterised his
wildest and most whimsical sayings and doings, caught the
taste of the town.   Yet the man had in him higher qualities.
In public life, both as pro-consul and as consul, he distinguished himself by his vigour and administrative capacity.
His work done, he returned to his former mode of life,
though whether the viciousness of his habits was a reality
or an affectation Tacitus is uncertain.   Chosen by Nero as
one of his few intimate friends, he became the Emperor's
supreme guide in matters of taste.   Nero saw no charm
in luxury except through the eyes of Petronius.   His
superiority in all the science of pleasure provoked the
jealousy of Tigellinus.   Working on the Emperor's dominant
passions of suspicion and cruelty, he accused Petronius of
complicity in a treasonable plot.   A slave was bribed to
inform against him ;   the greater part of his household
were thrown into prison ;   he was deprived of all means of
defence.

At the moment Nero was on his way to Campania.
Petronius followed the Court as far as Cumæ.   There he
was detained.   To linger in suspense between hope and
fear was not to his taste.   He determined to take his life,
but to give his enforced death the appearance of a gradual
and natural end.   He cut the arteries in his arms, bound
them up again, and re-opened them, as the humour seized
him.   Meanwhile he dined, slept, and conversed with his
friends, not on serious topics like the immortality of the
soul, but on light poetry and gay verse.   Many victims
had flattered Nero or Tigellinus in their wills.   Not so
Petronius.   He drew up an account of the Emperor's
monstrous debaucheries, with the names of his male and
female companions, and sent it to Nero, sealed with his
own seal.   Then he broke his signet ring, so that it might
not be used to endanger the lives or fortunes of his friends.
The manner in which the witty and brilliant patrician
quitted life appealed strongly to the cultured aristocratic
Frenchmen of the seventeenth century.   St. Evremond
considered his death to be the finest recorded in antiquity.
He died, not with a Stoic's ostentation of austere fortitude,

but with the gay indifference which Epicureans often affected, but at such moments rarely attained.

The denunciation of Nero, to which Petronius devoted his last hours, may suggest some previous practice in literary composition. To this extent it confirms the theory which identifies him with the author of the *Satyricon*. But earlier critics carried the point further. Though they recognised that the *Satyricon* was too elaborate a work to be the indictment itself, they imagined it to be written in the same vein. They regarded it as a *roman à clé*, in which the actors personated well-known characters at Court, and in which the author scourged the vices of Nero and his friends. The satirist of an Emperor jeopardised his life. A man who, in the cause of morality, faced this danger, must not only possess high courage ; he must also be fired to no ordinary degree by moral earnestness. Men of this type seldom count the cost ; they rarely are at pains to conceal the object of their attack. Yet the champions of the *roman à clé* never agreed on the character which represented Nero. The theory is untenable. Indeed, the gaiety and humour of the *Satyricon* protest against its being regarded as a satire at all. To call Petronius a satirist is to rob him of some of the most characteristic gifts which link him with the moderns and distinguish him among both his predecessors and successors in the prose fiction of Greece and Rome.

In the *Satyricon* there is no trace of the high scorn, the passionate indignation, the moral fervour, of the satirist. Petronius is at once too accurate an observer, too artistic and too humorous to play the part. He sees both sides of human nature represented in each individual ; like Fielding, he detects a vein of gold, however thin, running through the basest ore. He has not the one-sided concentration of vision which enables the satirist to see and use only one colour, and that the blackest. He knows the artistic value of gradations of light and shade. His most disreputable or broadly comic characters show flashes of higher feeling. Encolpius, ripe for any rascality, is a scholar and an educational enthusiast ; Eumolpus passes from disgusting confessions to poetry and sound criticism ; the contemptible and wheedling Giton has the grace to maintain the laws of

hospitality ; Trimalchio himself is not the monster of the
satirist, but a many-sided living man.

It is in the rapid play of contrasts between the two sides
of human nature, in the sudden clash of opposing motives
or sentiments, in the abrupt transitions from grave to gay,
or from high to low, that Petronius finds the fount and
inspiration of his humour. On these lines he etches his
figures and handles his situations. Over the whole plays
his peculiar irony—the tragic echo which accompanies
and mocks the most boisterous comedy. Aristocrat to
the finger-tips, he never pities or sympathises with his
actors. They are not of his world or surroundings. His
irony has in it almost a touch of condescension. Rarely
bitter, seldom playful, it is light, tolerant, bantering, the
amused tone of the disillusioned man of the world, of letters,
affairs and pleasures. It strikes the note which ripe
experience, with every advantage of birth and education,
might sound towards those whose opportunities have been
fewer and horizons more limited.

The *Satyricon*, then, is not a satire ; it is rather a humorous
commentary on human life. It contains much that would
gratify, little that could displease, the Emperor Nero. Of
the Court, or the fashionable world, nothing is said. On
politics it is equally silent ; they were in the danger zone.
It does not allude to the Constitution : the forum is only
mentioned as the midnight market for stolen goods : no
emperors would resent the gibe at the Senate, which they
alternately cajoled and threatened. The theatre is dis-
creetly omitted ; Petronius, as a man of independent mind,
could not, without gross flattery, approve the degradation
of the imperial dignity by Nero's appearances on the stage.
On the other hand, the literary criticism of Lucan's poetical
innovations in the *Pharsalia* was calculated to please the
Emperor, who prided himself on his mythological learning.
So, too, the elaborate portrait of the millionaire freedman
Trimalchio, could only have been welcome to Nero, who
was proud of his birth, detested the memory of the Emperor
Claudius, who had encouraged the freedman class, and
dreaded its rapid rise to wealth and influence. Nor can the
other ingredients of the book have been less to the Emperor's

taste. The desire for knowledge of life among all classes drove Nero to roam the streets in midnight masquerade. In the *Satyricon* he found some of the materials that he sought, observed with photographic fidelity and presented with dramatic power and humorous gaiety.

The contents of the *Satyricon* show no trace of any intention to satirise Nero. It is a novel of manners, the scenes of which are laid among the freedmen, traders, and small officials of a provincial city like Naples. With many tantalising gaps, historians have reconstructed for us the world of official and fashionable Rome under the Empire. The value of the *Satyricon* is that it reveals something of the minds, prepossessions, and ordinary conversation of a different section of the community. Making due allowance for literary licence, the most striking effect of the picture is the impression which it produces of moral decadence. To discover in the *Satyricon* a serious purpose would be to break the charm of irresponsible gaiety which pervades this wayward and whimsical work. It is also dangerous with an author, whose personality is so carefully concealed, to distinguish between his own opinions and those which he attributes to his actors speaking in character. But, after his own whimsical fashion, Petronius gravely discusses two social features which contributed not a little to the decay of public and private morality. One is the vicious artificiality of Roman education, the other is its consequence —the hollowness and unreality of mental life.

Like Rabelais, Petronius seems to be in earnest on the subject of education. Characteristically enough, he chooses as a spokesman one of the three beggar-students, whose adventures are the peg on which the story hangs. Encolpius, who is, throughout, the narrator, is an ancestor of Gil Blas, but with a more definite character of his own. Still quite young, he has crowded into his short and wandering life unnumbered rascalities. Well born, well educated, without a scruple or a penny, he is, when the story opens, a wanderer, " wanted " in every town, shivering at any contact with the majesty of the law. Bold to plan, ingenious to execute, he is physically a coward. But his gaiety is imperturbable. He takes his beatings with a shrug and a tag from the classics, and sets himself to devise some new shift by which he can cadge a meal. This young rascal, the rhetorician, Agamemnon, and the poet, Eumolpus, are the mouthpieces of Petronius's views on education and mental life.

Rhetoric was still the chief avenue to power at Rome. As such it was the coping-stone of the educational system. Encolpius has just listened to a declamation by Agamemnon. Taking him aside, he preaches to him the gospel of Carlyle. Everything is words—words, cant—cant. Schools of rhetoric succeed only in one thing ; they turn out fools. Boys are trained in exercises so remote from real life that, when they appear in public, they are liké stuck pigs. Eloquence has no substance ; it is merely a jingle of empty phrases. As with oratory, so with philosophy, logic, astronomy and, above all, literature. None are real ; their life is strangled by a bastard Hellenism. Agamemnon admits the charge against the schools of rhetoric. But teachers must live. Fishermen might as well expect to catch fish with a naked hook as a master to get pupils if he teaches what parents do not want. It is parents who are to blame. They refuse to have their children brought up under discipline. Entirely without intellectual or moral enthusiasm, Agamemnon acts up to his own sordid view of his art. To him teaching means only a livelihood, a method of securing an invitation to the rich man's table.

The whole tendency of Roman education was artificiality. To the artificiality of education and of literature the Stoics added another element of unreality. Their philosophy contained some of the strongest elements which made for the regeneration of society, but it had lost touch with humanity. Its tendency was to regard men and women as abstractions, dominated by pure reason. In its contempt for the passions, it neglected the natural sources of human conduct and action. Against this mental attitude Petronius revolts. He and the Stoics stand poles asunder. Whatever are the faults of the *Satyricon*, it is neither artificial nor unreal. It throbs with vitality ; it has too much, rather than too little, flesh and blood. In effect, its realistic methods of treatment seem to say to a hollow, artificial

age : Get back to the elemental truths of life, and you recover
its reality and substance. Study human nature at your,
doors, and you cease to be imitative and artificial. Learn
that Romans are not impersonal types dominated by pure
reason, but creatures compounded of good and evil, governed
by natural impulses and desires, and you will find the
materials of a sane education and a native art and literature.

His well-known criticism of Lucan's *Pharsalia* appears,
at first sight, to contradict this view of Petronius. Lucan,
still almost an infant prodigy, had produced the first three
books of his epic poem on the struggle between Cæsar and
Pompey. Determined to rely on the true facts of history,
he discarded the superannuated machinery of Greek
mythology. Through the mouth of the poet, Eumolpus,
Petronius champions the extreme artificialities of the older
school against Lucan's attempt at more realistic methods.
On these lines he re-writes Lucan's *Pharsalia* in his poem
on *The Civil War*. The question is whether Petronius is
speaking for himself or whether Eumolpus is speaking in
character. In the latter case, the poem is a parody, designed
to reduce to an absurdity the extreme classical theory ;
Petronius is true to himself, laughing both at revolutionary
and reactionary.

It is generally held that the poem is serious, and that it
proves Petronius to have been a classical conservative.
But it is submitted, with some confidence, that this view
is incorrect, and that the poem of Eumolpus is a skilful
parody. In deciding the question, both the literary tendencies of Petronius and his distinctive poetic gifts should
be borne in mind. The imitative and artificial methods of
the poem find no parallel in the vivid realism of the prose
portions of the *Satyricon*. Neither are they at all reproduced in the minor pieces of poetry in which Petronius
undoubtedly speaks for himself. These little compositions
reveal, to a striking degree, an artist's delicate sense of
form, colour, and finish. Their ease and grace give Petronius
a distinct place of his own in Latin poetry. But he holds
it by none of the qualities which appear in *The Civil War*.
Apart from the originality and realism of his literary tendencies, it is difficult to imagine that his fastidious taste

would have tolerated the flamboyant artificiality of Eumolpus. It seems far more probable that the poem is a parody written to turn into ridicule the theory of the critic, and the school to which he belonged.

The place, however, of the *Satyricon* in the history of prose fiction does not depend on the identity of the anonymous author or on his views of education or poetry. It rests on its humorous, realistic pictures of Roman life in the days of Nero. Here it stands alone in classical fiction. It strikes a new and original note. It makes no appeal to the marvellous ; its incidents are possible, if not probable, its methods of treatment surprisingly modern. The feast of Trimalchio may serve as an illustration. It is the longest and most continuous fragment that has survived, and it contains little to which moral objection can be taken.

Encolpius and his two companions are invited to the party by Agamemnon. On their way to the house they see an ugly, bald-headed, elderly man, in a russet tunic, playing at balls with a crowd of lads, but too proud to pick up the balls that he drops. It is their host Trimalchio. They pass through the lodge, where lounges a gorgeous porter, busy shelling peas into a silver bowl. The courtyard is surrounded with frescoes depicting Trimalchio's rise from slave to millionaire. Everywhere there is magnificence—troops of officials, regiments of servants, and, in the dining-room, costly lamps and ponderous plate. Encolpius takes his place at a table. On his left is a frequent guest who knows the house and its inmates. When all the guests are seated, Trimalchio enters, heralded by a flourish of trumpets, and takes the place of honour. The sight of his bald head peeping out of his scarlet mantle, bolstered round with cushions and scarves to keep off the draughts, is almost too much for the gravity of Encolpius.

The feast begins, each course being introduced with some fantastic machinery. The description of the surprises is tiresome ; but, as the reality bored Encolpius, the effect may be intentional. The composition of a banquet, which was carefully studied in fashionable Rome, often followed the lines of the stage. At the end of each course the curtain, as it were, fell, and rose again on a new course in a fresh scene. The point which Petronius means to be ridiculous is not so much the theatrical surprises as their tastelessness or puerility. Another ridiculous feature is the excess of music. The servants sing as they enter or leave the room or perform their services. Encolpius begins to wonder whether the waiters are not a company from a low music-hall, instead of the trained servants of a well-ordered household.

Trimalchio is cast in the heroic mould. His life is the epic of the self-made man, or, in modern phrase, the pro-fiteer. He tells his guests the story of his rise. Born a slave, he came out of Asia no bigger than this candlestick. A Ganymede to his master, no Joseph to his mistress, he won their confidence. At their deaths he found himself his master's heir, and the owner of a senator's estate. Money begets the need of money. He speculated in ships, and in cargoes of food and wine, which were necessaries and scarce. Once his vessels foundered. His wife, Fortunata, sold her jewels and clothes and brought him the money. There she showed her heart ; but, after all, she only gave him a pig from his own sow. He rebuilt his fleet, bought cheap, sold dear, and prospered. Money gathered money like a snowball. He turned his hovel into this magnificent house, with its twenty bedrooms, the apart-ments for himself and his wife, its two marble porticoes, its gallery above stairs, its four dining-rooms capable of accommodating a thousand guests, its excellent porter's lodge. If a man has a penny in his purse, he is worth a penny. We are all taken at our cash value. And so your friend, who was once a frog, is become a king. It is no wonder that his three household gods, which, together with a statuette of himself, are carried round for the worship of his guests, bear the titles of Business, Luck, and Lucre.

From the first, Trimalchio dominates the conversation. He patronises his guests. At the beginning of the feast, displaying his rings and bracelets and picking his teeth with a silver toothpick, he says, " I did not intend, gentle-men, to come to table myself so early. But, rather than keep you waiting, I have sacrificed my own convenience." When his century-old wine is brought round, he pronounces

it " sound Opimian," and adds, " I did not put such wine
on the table yesterday, though my company was much
better quality." " Be merry," he urges them elsewhere ;
" time was when I was no better than yourselves, but by
my own industry I am what I am." He is ostentatious of
his wealth to the point of arrogance. He boasts of his
collection of silver plate : but, when a slave drops a silver
dish, he orders him to leave it to be swept up with the
rubbish. When his wife's ornaments are admired, he
sends for the scales to advertise their weight. A boy who
accidentally strikes his arm instantly receives his freedom, in
order that no man should say that Trimalchio was bruised
by a slave.

With his servants he is at once harsh and familiar. On
one of his estates a slave has been crucified ; he threatens
to have another burnt alive. On the other hand, he puns
on the name of one, nicknames a second, takes a bet with
a third. " After all," he says, " slaves are men ; they have
sucked the same milk as ourselves " ; and he invites his
own to take their places at the tables. However much the
sentiment may appeal to the Stoics or to ourselves, Petronius
does not intend it as praiseworthy. Roman patricians
might tolerate the severity ; they would have been outraged
by the familiarity.

As the feast proceeds, Trimalchio interprets the bill of
fare, so that his guests may know what they eat and drink,
acts little comedies with his slaves over the surprises at the
banquet, moralises, versifies, strikes out an epigram, and
enters it on his note-book as an impromptu. His efforts
are received with applause by his guests, and none are noisier
than those who have heard it all before, and hope to hear it
again. At one stage he gives the talk an intellectual turn.
" We must," he says, " use our brains as well as our jaws."
In reality he betrays himself in every sentence ; his grammar,
his pronunciation, his history, are all at fault. A patron of
letters, he says that he has two libraries, one of Greek
books, the other of Latin ; but he calls them " librairies "
(*bubliothecas*). He has read Homer as a boy, and appeals
to Agamemnon whether he also remembers the twelve
labours of Hercules and the story of Ulysses. He himself

had seen the Cumæan Sibyl hanging alive in a bottle, and, when the children asked her, " What would'st thou ? " she answered, " I would die." He flounders in his history and mythology. He places Hannibal, " a mischievous crafty fellow," at the siege of Troy, and confuses Cassandra with Medea.

Interested in declamation, he asks Agamemnon what is the theme for the day. " A poor man and a rich were at enmity," begins the rhetorician. Trimalchio breaks in with the question, " What is a poor man ? " " Spoken like a true gentleman," says Agamemnon, with his eye to another dinner ; but, before the explanation is complete, it is again cut short with, " If it is a fact, there is no dispute ; if it is not a fact, there is nothing in it." He expounds the signs of the Zodiac, and the type of men born under each. " Under Sagittary are born the squint-eyed rogues who stare at the cabbage, and steal the bacon ; under the Fishes those who fill men's bellies and minds—caterers and rhetoricians." The guests loudly applaud his exposition, and agree that not even the Astronomer-Royal could show more learning.

Trimalchio's table-talk is often pretentious and ignorant. He is too thick-skinned to suspect that he may be a laughing-stock to the guests whose applause he purchases with a meal. But, though his literary affectations are ridiculous, they spring from a natural appreciation of higher things than material enjoyment. With all his follies and vulgarities are blended rough humour and native shrewdness. Though it may tend to his own glorification, his hospitality is genuine. There is tact, as well as kindliness, in the way he stops a quarrel. Some absurdity has set Ascyltos and Giton giggling. Their laughter infuriates an older guest, who gives them the rough side of a very rough tongue. " Gently, there ! " says Trimalchio ; " let us all be pleasant, and do you, Hermeros, leave the lad alone. His young blood is hot. Play the soberer man. He who withdraws first from a quarrel withdraws the conqueror."

He tells a story admirably. There is a genuine touch of Gothic horror in his weird tale of the corpse of the beautiful boy, stolen by the night-hags from the house of mourning.

He is not entirely deceived by his flatterers. " No one in the company," he says, as he throws a roll to his favourite dog, " loves me like this poor beast." Through all his pride in his wealth runs a curious vein of scoffing irony. His Opimian suggests to him the reflection that " the life of wine is longer than the life of a paltry man." As he plays with his jointed skeleton of silver, he moralises in verse :

> What a truly contemptible trifle is man—
> Just a bundle of bones at the end of life's span !
> So we all will make merry as long as we can.

Even in the delight of rehearsing his own funeral, he wonders sombrely whether in death he will enjoy the spikenard as much as he does in life.

Till almost the end of the feast the hostess remains in the background. Trimalchio's attachment to his ugly, scolding wife is to his credit. He is grateful for her help in past struggles, proud of her dancing the " kli-ki-can." *His* Fortunata, as he affectionately calls her, is the chief heiress under the will, which he reads aloud with choking voice. Her statue is to adorn the monument that he minutely describes. He loads her with costly clothes and ornaments. But she has not risen with her husband. The ordering of her household is her passion and her life. Her eye is everywhere ; nothing escapes.

Encolpius had already noticed a woman bustling backwards and forwards. His neighbour tells him that she is Fortunata, the wife of Trimalchio. While the meal is being served, she will not sit down. " Till she has checked the plate," says Trimalchio, " and served out the broken meats to the servants, neither bite nor sup will pass her lips." It is not till an important guest, arriving late, and bringing his wife with him, refuses to sit down without his hostess, that she joins the company. Trimalchio has read his will aloud, and for the thousandth time given his instructions for his mausoleum. Suddenly, with one of those rapid contrasts which Petronius loves, a storm bursts. Fortunata, catching her husband in some act of familiarity with a slave, rails at him as a disgrace to an honest woman. Beside himself with rage, he throws a cup at her head, and

follows it up with a torrent of the vilest abuse. As the
only punishment adequate to her offence, he orders that
her statue is not to be placed on his monument, and that
she shall not be suffered to kiss his corpse. At last his
friends pacify him. He apologises humbly to the company
for his violence. But he does not so readily forgive Fortunata. The storm still rumbles in the distance, and
" bandy-legs," " dunghill-scraper " and " viper " are some
of his endearments. Finally his vanity culminates in the
rehearsal of his own funeral. As he lies in state, he bids
his trumpeters blow, and his friends prepare to pay him
compliments. With so lusty a blast did the trumpets
sound that the night watchmen mistake the noise for a
fire-alarm. They burst into the room, and in the confusion
Encolpius and his friends escape from the house and stagger
home to their lodging.

Scarcely less vivid than the portrait of Trimalchio are
the sketches of some of the guests. For a brief interval
the host retires from the banquet. No sooner is his back
turned than a flood of conversation pours across the tables
from the humbler company. Encolpius can only report the
talk of the nearest group. It is typical of the rest. With
the vivacity and gesticulation of the South, each with his
particular trick, like the " D'ye see ? " of Encolpius's
neighbour, they pour out a stream of proverbs, oaths,
popular sayings, words racy of the soil, idioms fresh from
the mint of the market.

The range of subjects and ideas is limited. The guests
talk of what they have most at heart. Food and sport—
and money, as the means of both—stand first. Other
subjects are their neighbours, the weather, suspicion of
profiteering by officials and retailers, and the passionate
desire, doubly strong in these former slaves, to give their
sons a better chance than their fathers. Towards education
their attitude is half envious, half contemptuous. They
are jealous of the advantages it gives in the race for wealth.
They resent the distinctions founded upon it, and the
superior airs of scholars. They resent them the more, because
in practical life they can give points to the professors.
" Book-learning apart," says Echion to Agamemnon,

" we know you for a fool." What he says in a good temper, Hermeros, the mason, says in a rage. He has never studied geometry ; but he knows all that wants knowing about stones and metals, and thanks God for his trade. A vocational training, not a liberal education, is what they want.

The first speaker complains of the cold ; he could not get hot even in the bath. But a good bellyful of wine keeps out more cold than the stoutest broadcloth. Then he confesses that he has drunk his whack, and relapses into incoherence. The next speaker takes up the subject of the bath. He does not hold with too much bathing. Water stews the juices out of a man's blood. He took no bath that day, because he had been to a funeral. Old Chrysanthus is gone. He was a good sort. I was with him only the other day and seem to be talking to him now. We men are blown-out bladders, strutting on two sticks. We are of less account than flies ; they have something in them ; we are only bubbles. Anyhow, he had a handsome burial. Only his wife did not cry as if she would miss him much. Well ! and what if he did not treat her very well ? Women are vultures. Men are fools to show them kindness ; they might as well chuck it down a well. Phileros interrupts with, " Let's talk about the living," and then proceeds to abuse the dead man. He is one of those who boast of their plain speech. Chrysanthus, he says, got his dues. He had nothing when he started, and to the day of his death would have picked a farthing out of a dung-heap with his teeth. He died worth the Lord knows what—all ready cash. But he was a foul-mouthed, rough-tongued, quarrelsome fellow. He had words with his brother, and left his money to somebody's love-child.

The fourth speaker, Ganymede, is a pessimist and a Churchman. He complains that their talk is about things that concern nobody. Nothing matters but the scarcity of food. He has not been able to fill his belly for a twelve-month. A plague on these food controllers and bakers ! They play into each other's hands. Wink at me, and I'll wink at you. No wonder that the poor man has to work double shifts, if he has to keep the great jaws of these fellows

going. When old Safinius was alive—he used to live just
by the old arch—things were different. Corn was as cheap
as dirt. You could buy more bread for a farthing than any
two men could eat in a day. But now we go from bad to
worse, and grow, like a cow's tail, downwards. And why
so? We have a rascally market-clerk, who thinks more of
feathering his own nest than of keeping us alive. No wonder
he laughs in his sleeve. He scrapes up more money in a
day than many an honest man's whole estate. If we had
any real men among us, he would laugh the other side of
his mouth. But nowadays people roar like lions at home,
and baa like sheep in the street. My clothes are gone in
food already. If corn keeps at its present price, I shall have
to sell my shanty and everything. I really believe that
it is all a judgment from heaven, because nobody believes
that there is any such place, or would give a pin's head
for Jupiter. Time was when our married women, with
pure hearts, their feet bare, and their hair down their backs,
prayed to Jupiter for rain, and rain it did—in buckets.
Now we have no religion, and our fields lie . . .

Don't be so dismal, interrupts Echion, more prosperous
and an optimist. Better luck next time, as the country-
man said when he lost his speckled pig. What doesn't
happen to-day may happen to-morrow. That's the way
the world wags. Heaven is just as far off, wherever you
live. If you lived somewhere else, you would say that
here porkers ran about ready roasted. That reminds me.
We are going to have some real good shows these holy-days.
Titus will see to that. He's true-bred—no mongrel—
and has the money. He won't put us off with a lot of old
doddering hirelings that you could blow flat with a puff.
Not he! His men will be freedmen, and the theatre will
be like a butcher's shambles. Glyco is sending his steward
to the beasts. He caught him in bed with his mistress.
And what sin was the slave doing? As like as not he only
did as he was bid. It is the slut of a wife who ought to be
gored by the bull. But if you can't hit the ass, you must
thrash the saddle. And what business had Glyco to expect
anything better from the daughter of Hermogenes? He
would have cut the claws of a flying kite. Snakes don't

EA

father halters. I see, Agamemnon, that you are saying to yourself, " What is this dull fool maundering about ? " I only talk because you, who can, won't. I know that you are above our sort, and look down on us common folk. But, outside your book-learning, we know you for a fool. Take a walk into the country, and see us in our little cottage. We won't starve, I warrant you—a chicken, some eggs, and such-like. You'll find my little Cicaro, who is growing up to be your scholar. The boy takes kindly to his books. I tell him that, if he gets learning, the devil himself cannot take it away from him. It is a man's bank, and there's always a living in a trade.

Here Trimalchio returns, and again takes command of the conversation. The brief, condensed paraphrase necessarily sacrifices the spirit and vivacity of the original. But it may serve to illustrate the method of treatment, to vindicate the claim of the *Satyricon* to have created a new kind of literature, and to justify its title to be considered the first of modern novels. It is regrettable that, so far as the general public is concerned, its indecency has condemned a work of genius to comparative obscurity.

The book first reached England at the moment when heroic romances were at the zenith of their power. There was little room for its humorous realism. A detached fragment was translated into English by Walter Charleton under the title of *The Ephesian Matron* (1659). But no complete version appeared till 1694, when Burnaby published his translation of *The Satyr of Titus Petronius Arbiter, A Roman Knight*. The tide was turning from idealism to realism. In the next forty years the book was frequently republished, and " several hands " contributed to render it into English. It is difficult to suppose that such a masterpiece of realistic art did not affect the movement which culminated in Defoe, and the subsequent course of its development. No proof of such an influence is forthcoming. But in the twentieth century there is direct evidence of its power from at least three eminent writers of widely varying minds and different nationalities. Nietzsche, Merejkowski, and Anatole France have acknowledged the influence of Petronius.

CHAPTER IV

THE second of the works of prose fiction which have survived in Latin literature is *The Golden Ass* of Apuleius.
Its fate was widely different from that of the *Satyricon* of
Petronius. In originality the two writers can hardly be
compared. By the side of Petronius, Apuleius may seem
to be little more than an ingenious decorator of borrowed
material. Yet for centuries the literary world neglected
the humorous realism of the *Satyricon* for the picturesque
romanticism of *The Golden Ass*. Few, if any, works of prose
fiction have enjoyed so great and continuous a popularity
as the Latin romance ; none have entered more largely
into serious and momentous discussions.

More fortunate than the *Satyricon*, *The Golden Ass* has
been handed down in its entirety. It owed its preservation partly, no doubt, to accident; partly to its intrinsic
interest as a story ; partly to the local celebrity of its
author as an Admirable Crichton of learning and eloquence ;
partly, and most of all, to his reputation as a wonder-working magician. His miraculous powers were ranked in
popular estimation with those of Apollonius of Tyana.
They were the boast of the champions of paganism. In
his own person—for Apuleius identified himself with the
adventures of his hero—the author had been transformed
into an ass and recovered his human shape. Christianity
itself could vaunt no greater miracle. On these and other
grounds, *The Golden Ass* has played a part in theological
controversy from the third to the eighteenth century, and
exercised the minds of champions of Christianity from St.
Augustine to Bishop Warburton.

By its narrative power and pictorial richness *The Golden
Ass* took by storm the romantic world of the early and the
late Renaissance. Boccaccio drew from it some of his

inspiration. It was one of the first books to be printed (1469). From it, in all probability, Cervantes borrowed. Translated into the principal languages of Europe, it was made known to English readers by the admirable version of William Adlington (1566). On the one hand, it appealed by its erudite preciosity of elaborated phrase to the Euphuists ; it attracted the notice of men of letters like George Gascoigne, who, in his *Posies* (1575), wrote upon the book " three sonets in sequence " :

> For Lucius thinking to become a foule,
> Became a foole, yea more than that, an Asse.

It may even have suggested to Shakespeare his immortal Bottom. On the other hand, it called down a special out-pouring of the wrath of Puritan writers like Stephen Gosson. In later times, students of religious observances and ritual have recognised the value of its description of the worship of Isis. Historians have ransacked its pages for vivid details of the manners and customs of the provinces in the second century of the Roman Empire. Melancthon thought that the language of Apuleius resembled the braying of his own ass ; but philologists have never ceased to explore the collection of archaic, obsolete, vernacular and newly coined words which are so carefully gathered and patiently compounded into his elaborate Asianic style. Perhaps above all, the " most pleasaunt and delectable tale of the Marriage of Cupide and Psyches," which enthralled on winter evenings, as Burton tells us, the inmates of English country-houses in the days of Charles I, has delighted lovers of folk-lore, and fascinated the imagination of painters, musicians and sculptors, of masters of prose like Walter Pater, and of a long line of poets which ends with the present laureate.

The early life of Apuleius is known in outline from the speech which he delivered in his own defence against the charge of magic, supplemented by such biographical details as may be safely gathered from *The Golden Ass* and his other works. Born about A.D. 125[1] in the highly Romanised

---

[1] The dates are those accepted by Messrs. Butler and Owen in their edition of the *Apologia*.

city of Madaura, in Africa, he was the son of a wealthy magnate from whom he inherited a considerable fortune. In the schools of his birthplace he learnt his rudiments. At Carthage he advanced to rhetoric. In the University of Athens he studied philosophy, especially Plato, and cultivated the Nine Muses, as he says himself, " with more will than skill." His mind inclined strongly to the investigation of the channels of communication between the seen and unseen worlds, between the gods and their creatures. These were the mysteries which his romantic temperament delighted to explore. All those psychical phenomena which would now be described as telepathic, auto-suggestive, hypnotic, or subliminal fascinated his imagination. They stimulated his curiosity to enquire into divinations and augurics, the predictions of soothsayers, and all the occult powers which wizards and witches claimed to exercise. Probably these researches inspired his extensive travels in Asia Minor; they certainly suggested his initiation into many mysterious rites of religion, and especially into those of Isis and Osiris at Corinth and Rome.

Still under thirty years of age, he returned to settle in Africa, bringing with him vast stores of miscellaneous if superficial learning, and a curiosity to penetrate the mysteries of existence which time and study had rather stimulated than satisfied. A facile, showy speaker, he speedily made his name as an advocate, but still more as a popular lecturer, travelling from city to city and attracting large audiences. On one of his journeys he fell sick at Tripoli. There he remained many months, and there (about A.D. 155) he married a wealthy widow named Pudentilla, the mother of a fellow-student at Athens. So far as the lady was concerned, there was nothing extraordinary in the marriage. But her relations resented the possible loss of her money to the family. Some three years after the wedding they tried to set the marriage aside, on the ground that Apuleius had procured it by the exercise of magical powers. In a similar fashion, probably, the witch-finders of Würzburg or Cotton Mathers of New England used popular superstitions to further private ends.

The charge was serious. Put upon his trial, Apuleius

conducted his own defence. He had no difficulty in dispos-
ing of the specific accusation, and in exposing the motives
of his accusers. But he did not attempt to meet the more
general charge. On the contrary, he did not conceal that
he was deeply interested and had even dabbled in matters
akin to the subject of the accusation. He confesses his
faith in divinations and the powers of magicians. He
admits a knowledge of the use of a medium, and does not
disguise his belief that human beings, in temporary trances,
may be so divorced from the trammels of the flesh as to
return to their divine immortal nature and foretell future
events. Among the charges against him was the possession
of mysterious " somethings " which he carefully concealed.

In reply, he acknowledges that he jealously guarded from
the eyes of the profane the sacred emblems of the religious
mysteries into which he had been admitted. On such
admissions, in the seventeenth century, it would have gone
hardly with Apuleius. The second century was more
enlightened or more indifferent. He carried the court
with him when he took the war into his opponent's camp.
Surely, he urged, the reverence of things divine is better
than the mockery of the prosecutor—a man who never
entered a temple, never uttered a prayer, never acknowledged a shrine with a kiss of his hand, and on the whole
of his land had neither anointed stone nor garlanded
bough.   His speech appears to have secured his triumphant
acquittal.

Throughout the whole course of the trial, neither Apuleius
nor his accuser mentions *The Golden Ass*.   In some respects
the book seems to be a youthful work, though the argument
which is drawn from the exuberance of the style is ineffective.   At any period of his life Apuleius would probably
have adopted the same literary device to raise the level
of the story.   But, if the book had been in existence, and
published, at the time of the trial, it seems difficult to explain
why it was not used against the author.   The silence becomes
the more inexplicable when it is remembered that Apuleius
identifies himself with the hero of his story.   On this strong,
but purely negative, evidence is based the opposing view
that the book was written, or at all events published,

later than the trial; that is, at some period subsequent to
A.D. 158.

Henceforward Apuleius seems to have fixed his head-
quarters at Carthage. There he expounded, with lavish
exuberance of balanced phrases, his philosophical theories
of intermediate spirits. At the University of Athens he
had been known as the Madauran Platonist. But he had
strayed far from Plato's idealism. His true spiritual
ancestor was Plutarch. From him he borrowed, and it
was his theory which he modernised. As he conceived of
the universe, there could be, and there was, no contact
between the One Supreme Ultimate God, or the celestial
Deputies who were His emanations, and the mortal dwellers
upon the earth. Yet the affairs of men were ceaselessly
cared for by the gods. There were links between the divine
and human elements. If there was no contact, there yet
were channels of communication. Between the two
extremes of existence were intermediate powers of a mixed
nature, mediators between gods and men, carriers between
heaven and earth, bearers from one to the other of prayers
and bounties, supplications and blessings. Stronger than
mortals, these powers partake both of the divine and the
human; they are capable of rising into gods, and are
recruited from the spirits of men. They are disembodied
souls, susceptible to human passions, pains and pleasures,
some good and kindly, others evil and malignant.

The whole material world of men and things is eloquent
with souls; the air quivers and vibrates with sympathetic
intelligences. Nor are they mere abstractions. In ordinary
conditions the human vision is too clouded and the human
ear too dull to behold or hear this celestial company. But
in certain circumstances of the mind and body these spirits
are visible to the eye; and it is they who reveal the future
to mortals by dreams, signs, oracles, visions, miracles. No
possible channels of communication, therefore, should be
neglected; all should be investigated and explored.

It was from this point of view that Apuleius studied the
obscure phenomena of human existence. Psychical problems not only excited his emotional curiosity; their
manifestations formed part of his philosophy. His early

life, as well as the evidence at his trial, shows the depth of
his interest in these obscure subjects. Their mysteries
attracted and fired his imagination. But his temperament,
at once romantic and superstitious, was not that of a man
of science. He wished to strengthen beliefs, not to establish
proofs. His mind, receptive rather than original or independent, had not the critical or analytic detachment of the
investigator. At no special pains to discriminate between
truth and falsehood, he suspends his critical faculties, and
lets himself go. The influence of this spirit world, it may
be suggested, supplies the key to one of the chief charms
of *The Golden Ass*.

No other book in Greek or Latin conveys so impressive
a feeling of atmosphere. In English literature, it was not
till the publication of *Wuthering Heights* that, in this peculiar
quality, Apuleius found a rival. He is so steeped in the
supernatural that it has become a part of his being. His
conviction that mortals are surrounded by hosts of unseen
intermediaries, both good and evil, was strong and genuine.
On this side, at any rate, his affectations, his artificialities,
his supreme literary consciousness, as it were, slip off him.
He becomes spontaneous, natural, primary.

It is the strength and sincerity of his belief that contribute
to the story the sense of mystery and the touch of strangeness which are the soul of romance. From the moment
when Lucius, riding by night through the hills of Thessaly,
hears the grim story of Socrates, the air is heavy with
sorcery ; it thrills with witchcraft. Since the flight of
Medea the country has been the home of Black Magic.
There, as Plutarch records, witches are able to bring down
the moon herself out of the heavens and make her their
instrument. Every breath that Lucius breathes is laden
with spells and enchantments. In Hypata, the midmost
town of Thessaly, we almost feel, with the hero, that nothing
is really what it seems ; that stones and chirping birds,
and trees and running water, are human beings transformed ;
that oxen and other dumb beasts might speak and tell
strange news. It is quite possible, and even probable, that
Apuleius mocks at those who meddled too closely with these
dangerous obscurities. But it is none the less true that he

himself shared the insatiate curiosity of his hero, Lucius, to explore the mysteries by which we are surrounded.

Apart from the impression of the supernatural atmosphere, *The Golden Ass*, in its own class of romantic fiction, is superior to its Greek rivals. But an original story it is not. Its idea, framework, and many of its incidents and details are derived, either directly or indirectly, from a Greek work which has perished—*The Metamorphoses* of Lucius. On this lost book is also founded *The Luciad, or the Ass*, once attributed to Lucian of Samosata. But from whatever source Apuleius borrowed his materials, he has so enriched them as to make them his own. A master-hand at telling a story, he narrates episode after episode in the adventures of Lucius in the best and most lively manner of the Italian *novelle*.

The comparison seems less of an anachronism because the fantastic luxuriance of the methods of Apuleius appears to be centuries removed from the statuesque severity of the classical era. Keenly sensitive to the artistic value of words, he ransacks the spoken and written vocabulary to find vivid picture-making phrases, pushing the elaboration of his style beyond the verge of literary foppishness. His love of colour, heightened, perhaps, by his African parentage, shows itself in the richness and warmth of his pictorial effects ; jewels, tissues, marbles glow with variegated and distinctive hues. Both style and colour are appropriate to the romantic story ; they harmonise with its incidents. The subject is so bizarre that it needs a bizarre setting. Incidents, which would appear intolerably fantastic if told with greater restraint and depicted in more subdued tones, lose the effect of extravagance from the gorgeousness of the language and the blaze of colour.

By the side of Apuleius, the best of the Greek romancers, Heliodorus, is cold, insipid and lacking in distinction. Yet the difference between him and his Greek rivals is rather one of quality than of kind. Apuleius brings before us a picturesque group of every degree in social life. But none of his figures is realistic in the same sense as the strongly individualised characters in the *Satyricon*. Goddess and donkey-boy, high-priest and waiting-woman, the baker's wife and the great lady of a provincial city, are all euphuists of the second century. All speak the highly ornate and artificial language of the African rhetorician.

The Golden Ass is, as has been said, borrowed from a Greek original. It is a copy, and often a very close one. But Apuleius is not always content to borrow. He adds innumerable incidents, details and episodes of his own. Among his longer additions are the story of Socrates and the witches, the tale of the noseless man, the assassination of the wine-skins, the mock trial of the assassin and the picturesque and vivid description of the worship of Isis. Above all, he has introduced the immortal irrelevance of the story of Cupid and Psyche. It is in the robbers' cave that the crooked old hag, who keeps house for the bandits, tells the tale to solace a captive maiden, and the Ass, " not standing farre off, was not a litle sory in that I lacked penne and inke to write so worthy a tale."

The story seems to be, in various forms, one of the oldest in the world ; none is more widely disseminated throughout the human race. Had it been current in Italy at the time of Ovid, he would assuredly have put it to use. Where Apuleius found it is uncertain. He may have brought it back with him from his Eastern travels ; and possibly the suggestion of the jealous sisters that the unseen lover is a serpent may point to its Indian origin. Artistically, the introduction of the story may be a blemish in *The Golden Ass*. If so, its beauty more than atones. Apuleius decorates the simple story with all the adornments that his rich fancy suggests. But in his own fashion he tells it exquisitely, with a delicate idealism which is in striking contrast with the coarseness of many other passages. By identifying the unseen lover with Cupid he links the story with mythology. His choice of the name Psyche gives him at once definiteness and symbolical meaning.

If in his vivid narrative of episodes in the adventures of Lucius he may be compared with Boccaccio, in his handling of the fairy-story he may be contrasted with Hans Andersen. Psyche fails in the test of obedience. She cannot resist the natural impulse to see the face of her unseen lover, the father of her child that is to be. The bride of Love himself, she loses him by her fatal curiosity. As she wanders in search of her lost Cupid, she suffers grievous trials at the hands of his jealous mother. Nature conspires to help her to triumph over the tests. The ants sort into their different kinds the heap of mingled grain. The reed by the water's edge tells her how to win the wool of the golden sheep. The eagle brings her the vessel filled with water from the spring that is guarded by sleepless dragons. Even the tower, from which in her despair she is about to cast herself, finds voice to reveal to her the secret of passing to and fro from the house of Proserpine. There comes at length a happy ending to her troubles. Reunited to Cupid, pardoned by Venus, she drinks from the hand of Jove himself the cup of immortality.

The Golden Ass itself is a story of strange adventures. Consumed by a passion to investigate the miracles of witchcraft, Lucius has travelled to Thessaly as to the Mecca of magic. At Hypata he lodges with the miser Milo and his wife, Pamphile. Their pretty servant, Fotis, becomes his mistress. One evening Fotis comes running to tell Lucius that Pamphile is preparing to change herself into a bird, in order that she may work her sorceries where she lists. Through a chink of the door at midnight he watches the witch at her work. First she stripped herself stark naked. Then, taking from a chest a box, she rubbed herself with ointment from the crown of her head to the soles of her feet, muttering to herself over her lamp, and jerking and shaking her limbs. Presently soft feathers began to clothe her body. Her nose hardened and curved into a beak; her fingers crooked into claws; Pamphile had become an owl. She uttered a screech, made trial of herself by little leaps from the floor, and then, in full flight, flew through the open window and was gone.

Lucius, eager to attempt the same change, prays Fotis to procure him the ointment. She goes into the witch's chamber and brings him a box from the coffer. He hurries back to his room, rubs himself with the ointment, and is transformed, not into a bird, but into a " plaine Ass." Fotis consoles him by telling him that, if he eats a rose, he will recover his human shape. The adversity will endure only for the night ; at daybreak she will bring him the roses.

He is led to the stable, where he is kicked by his own horse
and cudgelled by his own groom. In the night robbers
break into Milo's house, load Lucius with their booty, and
drive him up the mountains to their cave. Robbers, in
fear of pursuit, forget that " an ass will bear his own burden,
but not a double load." Each successive owner through
whose hands he passes is equally forgetful. Overladen,
overdriven, menaced with mutilation, cruelly beaten, Lucius
pays dearly for his curiosity. Bitter experience teaches
him that roses do not strew the path of a beast of
burden.

Unlike Bottom, he is not bewildered by his translation.
He clearly understands the nature of the metamorphosis,
and how it has happened. His human mind and brain
remain. But he has lost the power of human speech, and
has not obtained in exchange the tough hide or digestion
of the ass. He cannot, like the practical weaver, take
kindly to his strange provender, with " a good hay, sweet
hay, hath no fellow." It is his natural craving for human
food which, in the end, secures him the comforts of life, and
indirectly procures his restoration to human shape.

The story of the Ass is full of thrills. Never was a robber
cave more exciting than that of the Thessalian hills, never
a robber captain more chivalrously gallant than Lamathus.
There are horrors of every kind. There are passages of
indecency derived from the Greek original, and, to the
credit of Apuleius, somewhat modified in the process.
Intermingled with the polychrome ingredients of the story
are many lighter touches. There is humour in the way in
which Lucius speaks of himself as " my ass," and in the
detached attitude which he assumes to the animal whose
form he inhabits. He is half amused at his failure to
pronounce the complete formula which would summon all
citizens to his aid. His " O " is sonorously sounded, but
" Cæsar " refuses to be brayed intelligibly. He consoles
himself for the length of his ears by the reflection that they
enable him to overhear the whispers of the baker's wife.
On the other hand, he forgets them to his undoing. Hidden
from the soldiers by the gardener, he peeps slily out of the
room in which he is concealed. But his huge shadow on the

wall betrays him ; and " The Ass and his shadow " became
a proverb.

The beginning of the penultimate scene is true comedy.
Passing from owner to owner, the ass has been sold to two
brothers, one of whom was the cook, the other the baker,
of a wealthy Thessalonian. They stored the dainty food
which remained over from their lord's table in the chamber
which they shared with the ass. Whenever they were out
of the room, he was not " so muche a foole, or so very an
Asse to leave the deintie meats and to grinde my teeth upon
harde hey." The stores of food disappear. At first the
puzzled brothers suspected one another of being the thief.
But at last, seeing that the ass grew day by day fatter and
sleeker, and that his provender lay untouched in the manger,
they began to suspect him. They watched, and caught him
in the act of devouring their chickens and cheesecakes.
Like Sterne, they hugely enjoy the jest of seeing " how an
ass would eat a macaroon." But, as they cannot themselves
afford to finance the diversion, they call in their master.
Highly delighted with the sight, he makes a pet of the
four-footed epicure. His fame spreads. The ass becomes
a lion, and is ridden to Corinth to be exhibited in the
amphitheatre at the public games.

Up to this point, with the exceptions noted, Apuleius has
closely followed the Greek original. The story is practically
the same in its incidents as *The Luciad, or the Ass*. Now,
and henceforward, the note is changed. While preparations
are being made for the disgusting exhibition in which he is
to figure, the ass slips out of the gate and escapes to the
seashore. There, by moonlight, he prays fervently to the
Queen of Heaven to release him from his animal form.
While he sleeps, he beholds in a vision the goddess rise out
of the sea. She reveals herself to him under her " true
name, Queen Isis," as the Mother of Nature, essentially
one in her godhead, worshipped throughout the whole world
by many titles, under diverse aspects and with many different
rites. She tells him that, at to-morrow's celebration of her
mysteries, her priest will bear in his right hand a garland of
roses, flowers mystically associated with the honour of women.
If Lucius crops them, he will regain his human shape.

All passes as Isis has foretold. The day itself seemed to rejoice. " For after the hore-frost," so Adlington translates the passage, " ensued the hot and temperat Sunne, whereby the little birdes, weening that the spring time had ben come, did chirp and sing in their steven melodiously." The solemn procession sweeps through the streets. The ass, eagerly waiting in the crowd, watches for the priest, who, admonished by the goddess, thrusts out the garland of roses. And, as Lucius eats, the ass's shape slips from him, and he is restored to human form.

Thenceforward he consecrates his life to the service of the goddess, dedicates himself to chastity, and becomes enrolled as a soldier in her warfare. Many visions are vouchsafed. From the lips of Queen Isis, or of the " Soveraigne Father of all the Goddes," Osiris, the reformed Lucius learns the will of Heaven. He journeys to Rome, where he passes from stage to stage of initiation into the sacred mysteries. He approaches the borders of Hell ; he treads the very threshold of Proserpine ; he is rapt through all the elements ; at midnight he sees the bright shining of the sun; in its dazzling light he beholds gods of the heaven above and gods of the earth below, and in their sight and presence he worships. He bears the heavy expense of his ascent in the religious hierarchy with cheerful readiness, for Osiris himself has promised to the " poore man of Madaura " the temporal blessings of rich forensic triumphs. Undeterred by the cost, he continues his advance from degree to degree, until at length, as one of the shrine-bearers of Osiris, with closely shaven crown, he joyfully performs his sacred duties in the ancient " Pallace " of Sulla. So ends *The Golden Ass*.

The conclusion of *The Golden Ass* is added by Apuleius himself to the original story. In the arduous services of religion the reformed Lucius finds his salvation. By the sudden turn which Apuleius thus gives to his tale, he lifts it to a higher plane. The abrupt change and the unexpected elevation of the tone suggest the question whether the book is only a brilliant piece of nonsense, or whether a thread of serious purpose runs through the humorous absurdities, the burlesque terrors, the animal coarseness of *The Golden*

Ass. It is impossible to answer such a question satis-
factorily, because so little is known of the true beliefs of
the author. But the narrative of the passion of Lucius for
Fotis, his metamorphosis into a brute beast, his accumulated
sufferings, his recovery of a human shape through the intervention of the goddess, and his consecration of the remainder
of his life to her service, obviously lend themselves to allegorical interpretation. Midway in the book comes another
addition by Apuleius.

Imbedded in the strange setting of his wild tale of adventure is the fairy-story of " Cupid and Psyche," through which
runs a similar vein of allegory. Both may be interpreted
as the purification and ascent of the human soul. In both
cases, fortunately, the tale itself triumphs over its symbolic
interpretation. Apuleius is too good a story-teller to allow
his attention to be distracted by any subordinate purpose.
His artistic sense would have repelled him from such a
division of aim. Nor is this all. To suggest that he is a
deliberate allegorist would be to claim for him a piety of
intention which the general tone of the book belies. Yet it
seems probable that throughout he allows himself to play,
not indeed with allegory, but with the idea of a higher
meaning.

In this connection the first few lines of the book may be
significant. Lucius introduces himself as being, on his
mother's side, of " the line of that most excellent person
Plutarch." This strange piece of genealogy, which is
another addition made by Apuleius, is put conspicuously
in the forefront. The statement may, of course, only mean
that Apuleius, who identifies himself with Lucius, acknowledges his spiritual descent from Plutarch as the father of
his theory of demonic intermediaries. Or it may also
indicate that, as is here suggested, the story will be handled
after the manner of Plutarch, with a due regard to its
ethical value. At first sight no two men seem more dissimilar than the African rhetorician and the Greek
biographer. A kindly, simple-minded country gentleman,
Plutarch was content to live in a decayed city of a depopu-
lated Greece, spending a busy and useful public life
in local administration, and, innocent of all rhetorical

artifices, writing his garrulous, rambling, immortal *Lives*. All this is in startling contrast with the career of Apuleius. But in their interest in the relations between divine and human natures the two men meet on common ground.

To the ancient ancestral faiths Plutarch was bound by every tie which attached him so closely to the land of his fathers. For him every mystery of polytheism, every ritual form, every ceremonial observance, every popular myth or legend, however gross or perverted they might be, yet enshrined some essential truth inspired by the gods. It was on this line of defence that paganism was entrenching itself against attack. It is difficult to imagine that Apuleius approached these questions from Plutarch's starting-point of reverent conservatism. But, by whatever road he travelled, he had reached the same position. The most fantastic rite of the religions into which he had been initiated might be a real means of access ; every ceremonial, however gross, by which the simplest country-folk invoked the interposition of the gods, might be a true channel of communication ; oracles, divinations, auguries might prove to be open avenues of inspiration and revelation. No myth or tradition, however extravagant, was wholly without a core of divine truth. If any ritual or observance was, from its cruelty or obscenity, wholly indefensible, it might be the work of the malignant or revengeful demons who were among the host of intermediaries.

So here, in Plutarch's manner, he applies to the materials of his romance the same methods, and brings to bear the same habit of mind. In some lost Greek manuscript he has found the wild legend of a popular belief which is credited far and wide. In his wanderings he has heard, perhaps from the lips of some ancient beldame like the robbers' housekeeper, a fairy-story, which circulates throughout the world. He seizes on the ethical value both of the popular legend and of the fragment of folk-lore. He retells both as in outline he had found them ; he leaves them structurally unchanged ; he obtrudes no interpretation. But with the deft touch of a literary master—in the one case by the choice of a name, in the other by the consecration of his hero's life—he suggests their deeper meaning, and claims for both the expression of a moral truth. Only in this limited and remote sense can *The Golden Ass* be regarded as an allegory. It remains what it was meant to be—a story, and a story so brilliantly told that a farce is transformed into a romance.

CHAPTER V

MEDIEVAL ROMANCES

THE Crusades brought Western Europe into contact with the decadent Greek writers of romance. But it was not till the latter half of the sixteenth century that the progress of prose fiction in England was to any extent affected by the fictitious narratives of Greece. Meanwhile a vast literature had been created which, broadly speaking, was independent of earlier models. In dealing with its growth in this country, however superficially, it may seem rash to ignore the imaginative efforts of the people on whom the Norman Conquest had imposed an alien rule. But, apart from the derivation of some of their finest materials, medieval romances were in form and character essentially the literature, not of the conquered, but of the conqueror. They were Norman-French, and not British or Anglo-Saxon.

The stage of literary history at which fictitious narratives in prose or verse for popular entertainment were first developed among both the Greeks and Romans on the one hand, and among the younger nations of Northern Europe on the other, is strikingly contrasted. The Golden Ages of Athens and of Rome knew nothing of the novel or romance. Long before the birth of either, the language of both countries was matured, their literary style perfected, their finest literature created. Material was not lacking. It was offered to a novelist in as rich an abundance as it was used by dramatists or by satirists. At Rome, under Nero, for instance, the luxury and licence of society, the note-book of a fashionable physician like Musa, the scandals of such health-resorts as Baiæ or Sinuessa, the *causes célèbres* which exercised the ingenuity of lawyers, the crowd of picturesque adventurers who fringed the borders of great cities, must have afforded abundant scope for novelists. The humorous realism of Petronius proved the richness of the opportunity. But he had no predecessor and left no successor.

In the Greek States or the Roman Republic the composition of prose or metrical romances was a late development. It grew out of political and literary decay. It was not till public activities were suppressed by a suspicious Government, not till society, losing its old interests and ideals, was growing more leisured and more private, that the imagination of Africa and Asiatic Greece devised new forms of literary entertainment in the ideal extravagance of romance.

Very different was the growth of romantic fiction in France and Norman England. With its development their literary history begins, instead of ending. Under the late Byzantine Empire it was in the dreary sands of versified romance that the majestic stream of the imaginative literature of Greece frittered and disappeared. It is with the metrical romance of *Roland* that the profane literature of France in the vernacular language begins. In our own profane literature, the first book printed in the English tongue was the romance of *The Siege of Troy*, and the first work in English prose which is still widely read is Sir Thomas Malory's romance of *Morte d'Arthur*. In both France and England romantic fiction belongs to the spring and not to the late autumn of national life. It is not the child of decrepitude ; it is the firstborn of youth. It did not grow out of the decay of literature and of liberty ; on the contrary, it accompanied and fostered the progress and expansion of both. It did not wait for the maturity of language or the perfection of literary style. It was one of the first exercises in which the English tongue was trained to literary expression and a standard of prose composition established.

Few of the conditions which checked the growth of romantic fiction in Greece or Italy retarded its development in our own country. Neither in public interests nor in drama had romance any serious rival. Except at the great festivals of the Church, when the Creation of the World or the Passion was enacted on the stage, there were no dramatic representations. The rigour of a northern climate prohibited the open-air life of the cities of Southern Italy or Asiatic Greece. The severity of winter enforced longer hours of comparative leisure, spent within doors in such privacy as the Middle Ages allowed. Amusements were few. Social intercourse was rare. The nation was in the childlike stage, credulous, athirst for tales of wonder or of incident.

In their monotonous isolation, splendid or squalid according to their means, and weary of one another's company, men welcomed the arrival of some professional wayfarer. Pilgrims with their licensed exaggeration, friars with their tales of the saints outwitting the Devil, gleemen, jugglers, and all the tribe whom *Piers Plowman* denounces as " Satan's children "—even pedlars and itinerant drugsellers, with their lively patter—were distractions and diversions. They were links with the outside world, the newspapers of the day, purveyors of rumour and gossip, carriers of idle fables, transmitters also of not a few new thoughts and fresh ideas. Above all, perhaps, the minstrel met a social need. He was the circulating library when there were as yet no readers. But he was more than a medieval Mudie. He was the publisher of the Middle Ages. Through him the work of the *trouvères* reached the public. As he drew his bow across his *vielle*, or swept the strings of his harp, and in droning chant prayed audience for some romance of chivalry, the bickerings and boastings of the common hall were silenced ; the hoarse murmur of the market-place or the rough chatter of the ale-house was hushed.

At the end of the eleventh century, when France was beginning to assume her domination over the vernacular literature of Europe, a new world was in the making. As in the heroic age that was passing, so in the dawning age of chivalry, there was leisure. In both it was filled by the aid of minstrelsy. When, in the Anglo-Saxon epic of *Beowulf*, the hero sits in the splendid hall of King Hrothgar, the minstrel sings the deeds of famous men. When men are " festid and fed," says the medieval romance of *Alexander the Great*, they would fain hear some love-lay, some tale of knighthood or feat of arms, or stories of the saints. The office of the minstrel, though he had fallen from his high estate, remained the same. But his themes had profoundly changed. The epic had passed into the romance. No visible gap of centuries separated the two, as in the literature

of Greece.   New literary records were required to satisfy
the tastes of the world that was in the making.

The old *chansons de geste*—the songs of feats of arms which
clustered round Charlemagne and his paladins, and of which
Roland is the oldest and purest example—could not meet the
new needs.   Though they continued to be multiplied throughout the twelfth and thirteenth centuries, they belonged, in
structure and in character, to the age that was passing.   They
were composed exclusively for singing.   Their background
is historical ;   their substance is legend.   Their prodigies of
valour may be wildly incredible ;   Charlemagne may, like
Joshua, make the sun stand still ;   his sword, like that
of Roland, may be invincible ;   a snow-white stag may guide
his army through the passes of the Alps.   Yet, in spite of
these and similar marvels, they convey a vivid impression of
truth to life.   They depict a lawless, ferocious, pious race,
living in a rude, simple society.   Apart from the architecture
of the Palace of Aix-la-Chapelle, there is little trace of either
arts or refinements.   Religion is rudimentary.   Love is a
natural instinct, as brutal as it is strong.   Hunting is a
necessity as well as a recreation. War is the business of life.

It is true that the motive of the fighting is more impersonal
and complicated than it is in epic poetry, and that men
fight for ideas—for the Cross, for France, for their oath of
fealty.   But, apart from this greater complexity of motive,
Roland is more akin to the *Iliad* than it is to the coming
romances of chivalry.   The *chansons de geste*, in their pure
forms, are survivals of a stage of society, of a phase of
national history, of a type of national character which are
already extinct.   Travellers are often arrested by the sight
of some Druidic monolith standing among the rich, smiling,
highly cultivated fields of France, a grim sentinel of a past
civilisation.   With something of the same aloofness the
chansons de geste appear among the ornate, brightly coloured
romances of chivalry as rude relics of a bygone age.

A new world was being born.   It is not enough to say
that society grew richer, more luxurious, more refined and
artistic.   It changed profoundly in structure, ideals and
thought.   It changed in structure.   The dependence of
followers upon chieftains assumed the legal form of feudal

lord and vassal. The prosaic interests of life ceased to be common enterprises. Divisions of labour multiplied, and out of them classes were formed. Idlers despised workers. Warriors disdained traders. Codes of conduct, conventions of behaviour, niceties of speech strengthened the new barriers. On the one hand, they helped to transform class distinctions into castes ; on the other, they helped to soften manners, to refine and humanise life. In this direction they were the manifestation and expression of the changing ideals of society. The spirit of chivalry was astir. It was born of the same horror of the violence and savagery of the world which had bred the Peace of the King or the Truce of God; like them, it was in close alliance with religion. By subtler means, and with wider application, it aimed at similar objects.

Chivalry was a generous recognition of the human tie between strength and weakness. It was the civil as well as the military code of Christianised feudalism. It defined the rules of knightly conduct in both war and peace. The man who gained admission to the order of knighthood had been trained as page and esquire not merely to use his weapons skilfully, to sit his horse surely, to fly his falcon or hunt the deer. He had been also trained to service, to obedience, to courtesy and reverence towards women. The ceremony of admission was religious. The sword which was girt upon his thigh was the sword of righteousness ; the bathing of his body symbolised his purification from evil thought and action. He swore, and confirmed his oath upon the Sacraments, not only to uphold his honour in any perilous adventure, to pursue the infidel, to abjure ease and safety. He swore also to speak truth, to maintain right, to protect women, to succour the poor and the distressed. Lamentably as practice fell short of ideal, the ideal itself was invaluable. During the twelfth and thirteenth centuries, when many of the medieval romances were being framed, chivalry was a living force—especially when it had behind it the ecstasy of devotional feeling which inspired the Crusades, and the delirium of the spirit of adventure which they in turn engendered. Nor must it be forgotten that it was the afterglow from the sunset of chivalry which illumined the pages of Spenser and quivered to the beat of the drum of Drake.

Society had changed in structure and in ideals. It was also changing intellectually. The great swelling undercurrent of new thoughts was gathering strength and volume. On one side, there were the insatiable thirst for knowledge, the eager curiosity, the craving to recover the old springs or to discover new sources of intellectual and imaginative enjoyment. On another, there were the dim yearnings and unsatisfied longings of religion, its mystical idealism, its spirit of rebellion against the harshness and ugliness of the realities of life. On yet another, there was the growing awe of the supernatural. Into the mind of medieval Europe were flowing the ideas and beliefs of many civilisations other than its own. This vast influx carried with it pagan and Oriental mythologies which were irreconcilable with the Christian faith. The Bible forbade polytheism; it fostered belief in the dualism of the powers of good and evil. Passed through the crucible of an inspired revelation, the greater gods and goddesses of Greece and Rome emerged as emissaries of Satan. As the medieval world realised their ubiquity and influence over human destinies, its sense of the omnipresence of diabolic agencies deepened, and it shuddered at the power of wizards, witches, magic, spells and enchantments. Yet, on the other side, the minor deities of earth and air and water, of mountain, wood and mine, retained their milder sway, and joined the creations of their own native superstitions and fancies to swell the graceful rout of the *Midsummer Night's Dream*.

It was with romances of chivalry that a host of literary craftsmen, some known, many nameless, strove to satisfy the changed needs of society. Patronised by the great, and notably by our own Anglo-Norman rulers, they had, by the dawn of the thirteenth century, fashioned the framework of the three great groups of romance which their successors expanded, amplified and embellished. This great output of literature, practically all of which was originally in the French language, formed the stock-in-trade of our medieval minstrels. For centuries it constituted one of the chief sources of entertainment and eventually of the light reading of our medieval and Tudor ancestors.

Every literary text-book quotes the line from *Les Saisnes*, in which Jean Bodel, the thirteenth-century *trouvère*, who died a leper, divides romances of chivalry by their subject-matter into the three *matières* of " France," of " Bretaigne," and of " Rome la grant." Of these three groups, the oldest, from the use made of the existing *chansons de geste*, is that which deals with Charlemagne and his Paladins, with France and the deeds of Frenchmen. But the same methods which the romance writers applied to the old songs of feats of arms they almost simultaneously applied to the heroes of classical antiquity and to the legends of King Arthur and his Table Round. The change in society may be illustrated from the transformation of the structure and character of the *chansons de geste*. The new romances are not written exclusively for singing ; they are composed also for recitation and reading, in prose as well as verse. The austere simplicity of the older forms is overlaid with a riot of romantic fancy ; their compactness of structure is lost. The romances are swollen to a prodigious length, in which incident is threaded to incident, adventure strung to adventure, and encounter piled on encounter.

Descriptions clog the action. History ceases to be an object and becomes a pretext. War is a pastime pursued in the capricious spirit of knight-errantry. Women hold a new and assured position. It is the adoration of these new deities which inspires the most perilous adventures. Love becomes a romantic passion, elevated by constancy and tinged with tenderness, dissected with some of the delicacy of observation which characterises its famous thirty-one Rules, and distinguished by not a few of the casuistries that influenced the decisions of its still more celebrated Courts. Religion plays an essential part. It contrasts a Galahad with a Tristram, opposes to the licence of the Court the ideal of chastity and the asceticism of the cloister, and closes the blare of trumpets with a psalm. At every stage in the drawn-out story complications are created, solved, increased or continued by the intervention of fairies or the machinations of magic.

Admittedly the romances of chivalry violate many of the canons of literary art. It is not so much that their incidents are wildly improbable or frankly impossible.

By generations which stood so close to the Norman Conquest that defect might well be pardoned. Men who had
almost seen the son of the tanner's daughter of Falaise win
a kingdom at a blow might be excused for suspending their
critical faculties, and thinking that the marvels of fiction
could not transcend the miracles of fact. Other faults
which the romances show are natural to the stage of literary
development at which the stories were written. They have
little unity of design. They rarely attempt delineation of
character. Instead of development of plot they give us
accumulation of incident. For growth they substitute
accretion. Again and again they miss their own points,
and fail to utilise the situations they have created. They
become wearisome from repetitions and surplusage, which
are probably more obvious to readers than they would be
to hearers. As general pictures they are false to the realities
of medieval existence. But, unreal and artificial though
they are, they are true to the life which a large section of
society aspired to live, and which a few individuals may
have actually attained. It is this truth to ideals which
makes them one of the golden keys to the tumultuous heart
of the Middle Ages and of the Tudor times.

Even when the critical brain wearies of romances of
chivalry, the eye is irresistibly fascinated by their blaze of
colour. Over the shadowy figures of a Charlemagne, an
Alexander the Great, or a King Arthur, the romance writers
have worked intricate patterns, embellished with all the
ornaments that the fertility and quaintness of medieval
fancy could devise, embroidered with episodes of the
romance and constancy of love, adorned with pictorial
pageants of fighting, sport and adventure, enriched with
elaborate scenes of feasting in magnificent halls, bright
with the jewels and sumptuous robes of gay lords and ladies.
The imaginative treasures of the known world have been
ransacked to furnish variety of colour. Here are inter-
mixed brilliant silks from the Far East, gold and silver
threads from classic literature, sombre skeins from the
superstitions of Northern Europe, tissues glowing with the
lyrical passion of Provence, and here and there rough
strands from the hair-shirts of cloistered penitents. The

fabrics woven by these medieval craftsmen are not so much
literature as gorgeous tapestries, set in the richly decorative
framework of feudalism and chivalry.

The influence which romances of chivalry exercised for
centuries over successive generations of our ancestors was
prodigious. They had no rivals in the shape of newspapers.
Except among an infinitesimal minority of the people,
they had no educational competitors in schools or colleges.
They coloured the medieval and Tudor conception of
history and biography, of science, geography and natural
history. They opened to the unlearned the treasures of
classical antiquity, and made Medea and Jason, Hector
and Helen household words. They educated the vulgar
in the faiths of other nations. They were powerful popular
preachers of the Christian religion. How many anxious
souls, perplexed by the war of dogmas, may have found
solace in the simple creed of Roland or the theology which
Oliver expounded to the giant Ferumbras ? They elevated
the manners of successive generations, inspired their ideals,
warmed their enthusiasms. They stimulated discovery by
their revelations of the wonders of the mythical East—its
castled elephants, its unicorns, its ivory-gated cities, its vines
of gold and grapes of pearl, its cliffs studded with diamonds,
its dark valleys tenanted by the mysterious basilisk. Their
chief actors passed into the proverbial currency of speech as
the representatives of particular vices and virtues.

Scenes and figures from their stories have been painted
on the walls of castles and convents, pictured in the windows
of cathedrals, carved on the panels of doors or on the
capitals of pillars, traced on the compartments of treasure-
chests, woven into famous tapestries, preserved in the
popular names of the features of natural scenery. On their
manuscripts were lavished the loving skill of illuminators
and binders. They were among the choicest treasures
bequeathed in medieval and Tudor wills. They figure
largely in the catalogues of monastic libraries, and in the
book collections of all sorts and conditions of men and
women, from Captain Cox of Coventry to Mary Queen of
Scots. For many years they were the principal products
of our printing presses. Their influence provoked a literature

of protest to which a Rabelais and a Cervantes did not disdain to contribute. They kindled the imaginations of poets and dramatists. Though Chaucer might caricature them, he was steeped to the lips in their lore ; when sleep forsook him, it was to a romance that he fled for relief ; and it was from romances that he and a long list of writers, from Spenser and Shakespeare to Tennyson and William Morris, have quarried some of their choicest treasures.

Each of the three groups of medieval romances is represented in our own vernacular literature. But their influence and popularity varied. Least to the liking of an English audience was the " matter of France." The old songs of deeds of arms were favourites in the halls of the great, if the number of them that were included in the bequest (1317) to Bordesley Abbey by Guy Earl of Warwick may be taken as proof of popularity. Yet vernacular versions of them are rare. A fragment of the *Song of Roland* exists. But it almost seems as if the songs that chiefly appealed to the English people are those which, like *Sir Otuel* or *Sir Ferumbras*, celebrate the prowess of Saracen knights or giants against such paladins as Roland or Oliver. Much more popular were the expanded romances of chivalry, which had travelled far from the form of the original *chansons*. Of these, *Sir Bevis of Hampton*, valued by John Bunyan, in his unregenerate youth, above the Book of Books, was the chief favourite. The choice was not undeserved. The story of Sir Bevis, who wooed Josian, the fair daughter of the King of Armenia, tamed the giant Ascupart, and slew the dragon of Cologne, is one of the best.

In the century of translations, Caxton translated and printed the *Lyf of Charles the Grete*, which tells, among other feats of arms, the death of Roland at Roncesvalles. He also gave us a version of the *Four Sons of Aymon*, perhaps with a *flair* for the taste of a horse-loving people, for the true hero is not Renaud of Montauban, but his black horse Bayard,[1] whose leap is commemorated on the Meuse at

[1] The name is given by Langland, in his *Piers Plowman*, to the horse that was carried off by Wrong : " He borwed of me Bayard—he broughte hym home neure " (i.e. " He borrowed my horse, and never brought him home ").

Dinant, whose whinnyings may still be heard in the forest of the Ardennes, and who supplied to his famous namesake, the fearless and stainless knight, the proud retort that a Bayard of France yields not to a German cart-stallion. *Ogier the Dane*, the " Ancient Knight," who returns from Avalon in France's hour of need, supplied the groundwork for the ballad of *Thomas the Rhymer*, and lives for us in Morris's *Earthly Paradise* (August). Through *Macaire*, the original of *Sir Triamour*, have come the dog of Montargis and a cant name for a Frenchman. To yet another romance we owe a far greater debt. It was by the aid of Oberon, the son of Morgan le Fay and Julius Cæsar, that *Huon of Bordeaux*, who survives in the Tudor version of Lord Berners, achieved his enterprise of fetching " a hair from the Great Cham's beard." But the permanent contribution of the Charlemagne group to English literature is not large. It is summed up in the proverb, " A Roland for an Oliver " ; in Ganelon, who takes his place by Judas Iscariot as the type of traitor ; and in Oberon, the King of the Fairies.

The temporary influence on English thought of the romances of the classical world was greater, and can scarcely be exaggerated. They helped to sweep us, with the Latin nations, into the movement of the Early Renaissance. Through vernacular versions they made the heroes of classical antiquity familiar to a wider public than has ever known them since, turned the sympathies of the English people against the Greeks, strengthened their belief and pride in the Trojan ancestry which they shared with France. Curious and interesting though these romances are as products of the medieval mind, their hold on literature scarcely endured beyond the close of the sixteenth century. They gave us the once popular phrase of " honest Trojan." But their most permanent gift has been the episode of Troilus and Cressida, originally told by Benoît de Sainte More in his huge *Roman de Troie*, which was successively seized upon by Boccaccio, Chaucer and Shakespeare.

There remains the third group which centres round King Arthur and the Table Round. Its fame was world-wide ; it reached, as Dante tells us, the far-off walls of Rimini. In our own country, its vast popularity is attested by the number of vernacular versions of the different branches of the story. But even here, though the " matter " is that of " Bretaigne," and though British hands helped to mould its structure, its oldest forms, whether in verse or prose, are Norman-French. Many literary craftsmen, some known, more of them uncertain or anonymous, contributed to build up, enlarge and embellish the story. Every stage in its growth bristles with controversy. If a man would speak with convincing authority on its origins, he must have reached the age of Methuselah in their study. He must be a second Mezzofanti in his knowledge of languages and dialects. He must be a philologist, a palæographer, a master of half a score of kindred sciences. Even so equipped, he is a bold man and a hardy who attempts to ride by the Way Perilous, so dour and hard-bitten are the warriors who guard its critical passages. Humbler wayfarers will be content to take the story where Sir Thomas Malory left it in 1470.

It was a huge literature in French and English which Sir Thomas Malory, translating, transcribing, extracting, condensing, omitting, and perhaps adding, welded into that masterpiece of English prose, the romance of *Morte d'Arthur*. His choice of this particular group of romances of chivalry may have been influenced by motives partly of patriotism, partly of religion. But assuredly it was also guided by a true literary instinct. The Arthurian group has in it the elements of vitality. It alone has the compactness of a plot, for through it runs the quest of the Holy Grail and the sin of Lancelot. In fuller measure than in either of the other groups its actors stand out as human beings, the tragedies of whose lives are eternal verities of human nature. In the shadowy legends on which had brooded the passionate, idealistic, imaginative Celt, is preserved more of the mystery, the aspiration, the emotional suggestion, the touch of strangeness, which are, and always must be, the soul of romance. Through it run also the inward spiritual meanings, the capacity for allegorical interpretation, the mystical symbolism, which remain living and lasting influences, because each successive generation can appropriate them to its special needs and circumstances.

A guilty passion had wrecked a noble enterprise. King Arthur was dead ; the Table Round was broken up. Alone, for eight days in the chill and gloom of the close of the mystic year, Lancelot had ridden westward towards the home where Guinevere had found refuge from the world. "At the last he came to a nunnery, and then was Queen Guenever ware of Sir Launcelot as he walked in the cloister, and when she saw him there she swooned thrice, that all the ladies and gentlewomen had work enough to hold the queen up. So when she might speak, she called ladies and gentlewomen to her, and said, Ye marvel, fair ladies, why I make this fare. Truly, she said, it is for the sight of yonder knight that yonder standeth : wherefore, I pray you all, call him to me. When Sir Launcelot was brought to her, then she said to all the ladies, Through this man and me hath all this war been wrought, and the death of the most noblest knights of the world ; for through our love that we have loved together is my most noble lord slain. Therefore, Sir Launcelot, wit thou well I am set in such a plight to get my soul's health ; and yet I trust, through God's grace, that after my death to have a sight of the blessed face of Christ, and at doomsday to sit on his right side, for as sinful as ever I was are saints in heaven. Therefore, Sir Launcelot, I require thee and beseech thee heartily, for all the love that ever was betwixt us, that thou never see me more in the visage ; and I command thee on God's behalf, that thou forsake my company, and to thy kingdom thou turn again and keep well thy realm from war and wrack. For as well as I have loved thee, mine heart will not serve me to see thee ; for through thee and me is the flower of kings and knights destroyed. Therefore, Sir Launcelot, go to thy realm, and there take thee a wife, and live with her with joy and bliss, and I pray thee heartily pray for me to our Lord, that I may amend my misliving."[1]

Through the chill of Guinevere's self-renunciation still burns the fire of her love for Lancelot. The tragedy of the two lives is eternal in its truth and freshness. As the simple beauty of the sentences falls upon the ear, it creates a sense of wonder that no novelist for more than three centuries should have taken up the thread of the work which Malory had done so excellently. The romance of *Morte d'Arthur* was completed in 1470. Why had we to wait for nearly three hundred years before the novel of real life and character was developed? The wonder is increased when the work of Chaucer is added to that of Malory.

[1] The passage is quoted from *English Prose Selections*, edited by Sir Henry Craik, vol. i., 1893, p. 75.

CHAPTER VI

THE ROMANCE OF TROY

IT is tempting to wander at large over the picturesque highlands from which sprang the stream of English prose fiction ; but in a book of this scope loitering is forbidden and selection is necessary. If any single romance of the Middle Ages is to be selected for more detailed examination than was given to the three great collective cycles, obvious reasons point to the choice of *The Romance of Troy*.

Its subject is compact and definite. Unlike other romances which sweep together a mass of tradition round some historical or semi-fabulous hero, its origin is easily traced to its source. It illustrates with striking force some sides of the medieval mind, although the aspects which it presents are more commonplace than the mystic yearnings of the Arthurian legends. Its history is so curious that in itself it is a romance of literature. More powerfully than any other single romance, it influenced for four centuries popular knowledge and opinion. Finally, it is the romance which Caxton selected to be the first work that he printed in the English language under the title of *The Recuyell of the Historyes of Troye*.

The child-like mind of the Middle Ages, eager for tales of incident and credulous, longed to have its stories authenticated as true. The craving had to be satisfied. Deft craftsmen, who supplied the literary entertainment of the medieval public, sought or created historical backgrounds for their romances. Where they could penetrate to some Latin source, they probably believed in its genuineness as devoutly as their hearers or readers. Where no such source could be discovered, they did not hesitate to shelter their inventions under the imaginary authority of some real or fictitious person. Of this process no more striking examples are to be found than the accepted authorities for the immense

86

romantic literature which interpreted classical antiquity to the medieval world, made its heroes household words, and established Hector and Alexander the Great, in the minds of thousands before and after Caxton, as two of the three best and worthiest of Paynims.

The history of the birth and life and death of Alexander is mainly based on that strange collection of traditions, legends and fables which the unknown author, commonly known as the false Callisthenes, swept together from the Western World, from Egypt and from the Far East, and which was interpreted to Europe in the Latin tongue by Julius Valerius. Similarly, Dares the Phrygian and Dictys the Cretan were for centuries the accepted authorities for the true history of the Trojan War. They, and not Homer, wrote the medieval *Iliad*. Few literary forgeries can have enjoyed a triumph so complete and lasting. It was not till the eighteenth century that their authority was overthrown.

The histories of Dictys the Cretan and Dares the Phrygian purport to be contemporary records of the Trojan War. In their Latin form they really belong, though their dates are disputed, to a much later period. The favourite opinion now seems to be that Dictys really wrote in the fourth century A.D. and Dares in the sixth century A.D., or possibly later. Whether the original language of either or both was Greek, or whether they embody new facts drawn from sources which have perished, are questions which have been much discussed. In their extant shape, both books are elaborately " documented " in order to establish their authenticity and account for their late discovery. A letter and prologue to the *Ephemeris Belli Trojani* explain that the work was composed by Dictys, who accompanied Idomeneus to the war ; was inscribed in Punic letters on tablets of linden-bark, enclosed in a tin case, and buried with the author in his sepulchre at Gnossus.

There it remained for centuries undisturbed. But in the thirteenth year of the Emperor Nero an earthquake broke open the tomb and disclosed its contents. The manuscript was taken to Rome, where, by the Emperor's orders, it was transliterated, or translated into Greek.

GA

From this version it was faithfully rendered into the extant Latin text by Septimius, who sends it to his friend Aradius. The *Daretis Phrygii de Excidio Trojæ Historia* is less elaborately and more plausibly " documented," but it invokes more illustrious names in support of its authenticity. In the *Iliad* the name of Dares occurs as that of a priest of Hephæstus at Troy, and to him or to a namesake antiquity attributed a lost Phrygian *Iliad*. This hint the forger utilises. In the prefatory letter Cornelius Nepos explains to Sallustius Crispus that he had found the manuscript at Athens, written in the handwriting of Dares himself, and that he had now translated it into Latin in order that readers might judge which was the more reliable authority on the Trojan War—Dares, a Trojan, who kept a journal of what he himself saw, or Homer, a prejudiced Greek, who was born years after the siege and was condemned at Athens for his folly in making the gods fight with men.

In these critical days the elaboration of the deception would arouse suspicion. But similar devices to secure authority for literary inventions were both ancient and various. To the device adopted by Antonius Diogenes to explain the origin of *The Incredible Things beyond Thule* reference has already been made. An almost exact parallel to the Dictys story is supplied by the contemporary history of the alleged discovery of the Gospel of St. Matthew in the tomb of St. Barnabas under a cherry-tree in the island of Cyprus. These solemn literary frauds amused and delighted Rabelais. Was not the genealogy of Gargantua himself discovered by Jean Audeau in a meadow which he had near the archway, under the olive-tree, as you go to Narsay ? In digging a ditch, the spades of the diggers struck upon a tomb so vast that its ends were never discovered. In the middle of the tomb, under a row of bottles arranged like ninepins, was discovered a manuscript, " smelling strongly but no sweeter than roses." It contained the genealogy of Gargantua, inscribed, not on paper, or parchment, or wax, but on the bark of an elm-tree.

But the Middle Ages were not the Renaissance ; and men of the twelfth century were less critical than Rabelais. The genuineness of Dictys, and still more certainly of Dares, was devoutly and even enthusiastically received. Satisfied that in the two impostors they possessed the testimony of real actors in the actual scenes that they described, medieval writers criticised the *Iliad* by the test of the accuracy of its facts. More intent on matter than on form, they had not the literary sense which distinguishes between a fine work and a poor one. They treat Homer as a historian rather than as a poet, reproach him for his poetic licences, condemn the improbabilities of his account, and reprove him for the falsification of history. For centuries Dares and Dictys were regarded as the trustworthy authorities on the events of the siege of Troy.

Chaucer in *Troilus and Criseyde* ranks Dares and Dictys with Homer as historians of the " Trojane gestes," and in the *Hous of Fame* Dares and Dictys both appear among those who bear up the burden of the fame of Troy. At the close of the sixteenth century Sir Philip Sidney discusses, in his *Apologie for Poetrie*, whether poetry or history is the " more doctrinable." He opposes the " fayned Æneas in Virgil " to the " right Æneas in Dares Phrigius," without any suspicion that no contrast existed, because both were equally " fayned." None of the thousands who accepted the authority of Dares and Dictys doubted their authenticity. Still further were they from suspecting that many of the statements attributed to their mythical guides were not made by them at all. But that belongs to a later part of the story.

The pretensions of Dares and Dictys were accepted. It was the universal opinion that they gave accurate and impartial accounts of the Trojan War. Their own literary merit contributed nothing to their success, for Dares, at any rate, has none whatever. Written in bad Latin, his chronicle is a bald, dry statement of details. Beginning his story with Jason and the Golden Fleece, he describes the first capture and plunder of Troy by the Greeks, the slaying of King Laomedon and the abduction of his daughter Hesione. Priam returns to find the city in ruins and his sister a captive. After rebuilding Troy with more than its former magnificence, he holds a council of chiefs. There it is determined to send an embassy to demand the restoration of Hesione. When his insulted ambassador returns with a curt refusal, an expedition is fitted out under Paris to harry the Greek coasts. The abduction of Helen is thus represented as a fair act of reprisal. The war begins.

A description of the principal actors precedes the story of the actual struggle. The portraits are feebly drawn. But, on the assumption that they were based on the notes of an eye-witness, the Middle Ages were interested to learn that Hector stammered slightly and had a squint—a defect which must have added terror to his swordsmanship ; that Æneas had merry black eyes ; that Helen had very shapely legs, a tiny mouth, and a mole between her eyebrows ; that Polyxena had a long neck, tapering fingers, straight legs, and the smallest and most beautiful feet in the world. Once embarked on the siege, Dares is as meagre and dull as possible. With mechanical precision the identical sentences recur : " The time had now come to join battle ; so-and-so led forth the armies ; terrible was the slaughter ; night put an end to the conflict."

Circumstantiality of detail is the strong point of Dares. Hector is the hero of the siege, as prudent and moderate in council as he is gallant in the field ; in Troy the most beloved by man, woman and child, and in the Greek camp the most feared. Second only to him is Troilus. The character of Achilles is blackened. He is represented as an unfair fighter, and, for the sake of Polyxena, a traitor to the Greek cause. Throughout, Dares will have nothing to do with the intervention of gods and goddesses. Every event is rationally explained or attributed to human agencies. He will not even allow the mechanism of the horse. The Greeks are treacherously introduced into the city through the Scæan gate, over which is painted a horse's head.

Dares profited by his literary defects. The very baldness of his chronicle seemed to give internal evidence of strict adherence to the truth. The Middle Ages to some extent suspected the superior style and composition of Dictys. They could not resist the dry and precise circumstantiality of Dares. For their literary purposes, his meagreness of statement was a merit. He supplied, not only historical facts, but a complete epitome of the war, together with a

Table of Contents and an Index of Proper Names. Romancers could take his canvas, set it in the gorgeously decorative framework of chivalry, fill in his outlined figures, and group them in the haphazard fighting which suited the fashion and taste of the day.

It flattered the national pride of Western Europe to regard Homer as prejudiced and Dares as impartial. Their championship of the cause of the " thrice-beaten Trojans " was more than a chivalrous sympathy with the vanquished. It was founded on their own history. As a Trojan, Dares belonged to the race from which Western nations boasted their descent. Filial piety prompted them to prize his contemporary record as the most ancient of their national archives. The claim to Trojan ancestry was not a poetic fiction or a literary affectation. To a Frenchman, a Norman, or an Englishman it was as much an article of patriotic faith as it was to an Italian, that the founders of their race and power were Trojans. The desire to link themselves with Rome was reinforced by the Latin tradition in literature and by the ascendency of the Church.

Politicians, even if they attached little value to the belief in itself, recognised that it might serve a useful purpose. It helped the process of amalgamation. No alien race had conquered England ; Saxon and Norman both claimed Trojan descent. So also, through the long wars with France, both the English and the French Kings, who ruled the divided territory, traced their lineage back to common ancestors. In England, traditions of a Trojan origin long survived the growth of a more exclusive national spirit, and lingered into the sixteenth century.

Apart from literary utility and patriotic pride, the works of Dares and Dictys appealed strongly to the Middle Ages on the side of religion. Both rationalised Homer by attributing divine interventions to human agencies. For Christian nations it was difficult to accept the historical truth of the Homeric poems on any other lines. They were unable to reconcile gods and goddesses with the revelation of the Bible. To them the polytheism of Greece was devil-worship. They personified the Power of Evil. Out of the eternal conflict between Heaven and Hell they evolved a new mythology, which, in certain of its aspects, was as grotesque as it was grim, menacing and sinister. Nothing tended more strongly to overthrow the authority of Homer as a true chronicler of history than his treatment of the intercourse between gods and men. On the other hand, scarcely anything contributed more largely to the enthusiastic acceptance of Dares and Dictys as accurate historians than the exclusion from their narrative of all but human agencies.

When all these circumstances are taken into consideration, it is not altogether surprising that Dares and Dictys, the products of a late and decadent literature, should have been enthroned by the Middle Ages as the contemporary authorities on the Trojan War. But in the middle of the twelfth century neither they nor their story were known to the multitude whose judgment makes or mars the fortunes of books. They had yet to be thrown into the popular forms which reached the widest possible public. Mere translation into the vulgar tongue was not enough ; it would have left their histories dull and unintelligible. The great mass of people could not conceive of other types of individuals or of other conditions of society than those with which they themselves were familiar. The world was too young and self-centred to make the effort. Even if any medieval writer had possessed the learning to piece together the minute details required for the reproduction of Trojan times and feelings with scrupulous exactitude in costume, habits, customs and conditions, his labour would have been wasted. For his contemporaries the result would have been lifeless.

Shakespeare might make the Greeks and Romans known to the Elizabethan age by seizing on elemental truths of human nature which are universal and independent of time. But the medieval romancer was only in rare moments a genius. In dealing with classical antiquity, he chose the easier task of transplanting the Trojan story into the world of the Middle Ages. His originality lay in the skill with which he transformed classical heroes into medieval knights, or cast the society of Greece and Rome into the mould of feudalism, or steeped the whole romance in the picturesque idealism of chivalry. He knew no other way—in the circumstances there probably was no other way—in which to give vividness, actuality, interest to his story.

Whatever may be thought of his methods, the romancer was a true pioneer of the Renaissance. His quaint anachronisms are committed with an unconsciousness of his crimes which gives them the charm of child-like simplicity. Neither he nor his hearers distinguished stages or degrees in antiquity. To-day was to them vividly present. But in the dim region which lay behind their daily life, their memories or their own traditions, the ages were confused. All the actors in the history of the remote past were classed together as the Ancients, whether they were pagans, Jews or Christians. No incongruity was felt when, in the *Roman de Troie* of Benoît de Sainte More, Calchas is represented as Bishop of Troy, or when Troilus carries a shield with his heraldic bearings of two lions *rouge* on a field *argent*, when Neoptolemus receives the arms of his dead father and is made a knight, when all the clergy of the bishopric attend the funeral of Hector, or when Diomede fights with the sleeve of Cressida fastened to his helm, or conducts her to the magnificent tent of her father which had belonged to the rich Pharaoh who perished in the Red Sea.

Somewhere between the years 1175 and 1187, Benoît de Sainte More seized upon the dry chronicles of Dares and Dictys. Careful to acknowledge their contemporary evidence as his source, whether he borrowed their facts or invented his own, he wove them into his metrical *Roman de Troie*. In the Teubner edition Dares occupies 52 pages, and Dictys 113. The poem of Benoît consists of 30,108 lines—five times the length of his two original authorities put together. For three-quarters of his version he relies on Dares. In the last six thousand lines, as he is careful to state, he supplements him with Dictys. Similar expansions of material characterise many medieval romances.

Benoît has more than his full share of the fertility of fancy and of the ingenuity of invention which were needed to convert the bare hint of a name or a detail into hundreds of lines of a romance. He also possesses to a marked degree a graceful ease of versification. He may not, perhaps, be compared with the unknown author who conceived the simple, austere dignity of *Roland*, or with the genius, be it of one or of many, which endowed the Arthurian legends with their human interest and imperishable soul. But he stands in the front rank among his fellow-craftsmen, and it was in a moment of true inspiration that he created the character of Cressida and told the tale of her fickle love. His *Roman* was prodigiously popular in all European languages. Copies of it multiplied. It was adapted, rendered into prose, dramatised. It founded a school. It was expanded by the grafting of fresh developments like the *Enfance d'Hector* in the fashion of other popular romances. It coloured the imagination of the Middle Ages. In literature it left an enduring mark, for it influenced the work of Boccaccio, Chaucer, Caxton, Henryson and Shakespeare.

The credit for none of these things fell to Benoît de Sainte More, the text of whose poem was printed for the first time by M. Joly in 1870. Yet the *Roman de Troie* deserved a more kindly fate. It is a vivid commentary on the medieval mind. Benoît was well aware of what his public wanted, and set himself to meet the demand. He knew their scientific curiosity, and there is a touch of Marco Polo in his quaint geography and the phantasies of his natural history. He locates with definite particularity the territory of the Queen of the Amazons ; he invents the " dindialos," trapped in the East by a dog-headed people called the Cynocephales, of whose skin, glowing with every colour of every flower, is made the mantle of Briseide, hemmed by the fur of the still more mysterious beast that lives by the river of the Earthly Paradise.

He knew the passion of his contemporaries for the marvellous. Unable to use divine interventions, he finds a substitute in the mechanical inventions of the " wise poets." Neither magic nor enchantments nor fairies are prominent, though Morgan le Fay flits across the canvas as a lover of Hector and the giver of his horse Galatea. On the other hand, there are, in the spirit of the *Arabian Nights*, the eagle made of gold which flies as naturally as if it were alive, the magic mirror, the growing tree with golden trunk and leaves of gold and silver, the ever-burning lamps that are never trimmed or extinguished, the instruments which of themselves discourse sweet music.

Benoît knew the taste of his public for luxury and magnificence. He gratifies it by descriptions which in their Oriental splendour recall memories of the Crusades. The armour and the weapons are cunningly chased, the trappings of the horses gorgeous—rich prizes for the victors. Still more magnificent is the apparel of the knights when they have doffed their mail—the feathered hats of the Greek Ambassadors adorned with the plumage of rare birds from India, or the silken robe, embroidered and bejewelled and woven in Saragossa, which Hector wears when he rides Galatea to meet Achilles in the Greek camp.

He knew also the medieval passion for building. In restoring Troy from ruins, or in rearing a shrine for the body of Hector, he gratifies their love of beauty in civil and religious architecture. The centre of the new Troy, the circumference of whose walls, pierced by six gates, is a three days' journey, is the castle of Ilium, with its keep, its wells, its chapel, cloisters and vaulted chambers, and its great hall with the dais at the end. Troy is a feudal fortress ; the ranks of its society are feudal ; its defenders and assailants breathe the feudal spirit, tempered on occasions by the ideals of chivalry. The heroes fight, not from chariots, but on horseback. Fighting is the main business of their lives. Though it is interrupted by intervals of truces which are used to vary the subject, it is necessarily monotonous, and often becomes tiresome. Yet here and there, in the wilderness of repetition, occur touches which dimly suggest the picture-making power of Villehardouin.

In his love episodes Benoît finds another absorbing interest for his public. The scenes are cleverly distributed, dispersed through the poem in such a way as to break its monotony. Four principal types seem to be distinguished. There is the hot, temperamental passion of Medea for Jason, the deep affection of Andromache for Hector as the father of her children, the coquetry of Cressida, and the virginal love-at-first-sight of Polyxena for Achilles. It is Cressida, or, as he calls her, Briseide, who is Benoît's most original creation. Her subsequent fame gives his treatment of the story a special interest.

Dares mentions Briseide among the principal figures in the Greek camp. But apart from her description[1] he says nothing about her. In all probability he meant her for Briseis, the girl of whom Achilles was deprived by Agamemnon. But he does not tell that story, and so robs Achilles of the excuse for his sulkiness. The name of the girl occurs only in her portrait. Benoît leaves her, as he found her, in the Greek list, though in his version of the story she is Trojan-born, and, when the siege began, living in Troy. He follows with some closeness the description of Dares, though he makes significant changes. Briseide, he tells us, was beautiful, neither too little nor too big; her skin was white as the lily or as the snow on a branch. Her eyebrows had the mischance to meet at their birth. *Her wit was sprightly and nimble.* In figure she was graceful, and in her countenance modest. Well was she loved, and well could she love; *but her heart was inconstant.* She was of a simple, kindly nature, and *in almsgiving she was generous.*

The changes (in italics) are few. But they are skilful. The girl in Benoît's hands becomes ready of speech, open-handed and fickle. Some eight thousand lines intervene between her portrait and her first appearance in the story. At the end of what seems to be the seventh battle, a truce is agreed. The Greeks and Trojans parley for the exchange of prisoners. Calchas, the renegade Trojan priest who, in consequence of the oracle's prophecy that Troy would fall, had joined the Greeks, demands that his daughter, Briseide, should be sent to him from the city. Priam consents. Then for the first time we learn, not only the parentage of Briseide, but that she lived in Troy, and that she and Troilus loved each other. They spend their last night together in tears, despair and happiness. They swear eternal constancy. Briseide prays that she may die rather than leave Troy, which held all that she loved on earth. In the enemy's camp, among the hated Greeks, she will ever be true to Troilus.

---

[1] Here are his words: " Briseidam formosam, non alta statura, candidam, capillo flavo et molli, superciliis junctis, oculis venustis, corpore aequali, blandam, affabilem, verecundam, animo simplici, piam."

With the breaking of day comes the hour for parting. Perhaps only with a romancer's love for an inventory, perhaps with an instinctive truth to human nature, or perhaps with conscious art, Benoît describes minutely how the girl arrays herself in her finest robe and her famous mantle, and, as he is careful to add, packs up *all* her apparel. The heavy-handed plagiarist, Guido delle Colonne, mars the grace of the story. Except by weeping, the Briseide of Benoît had no desire, even in her grief, to disfigure herself. But Guido turns her into a passionate Sicilian woman, who tears out her hair, and furrows her cheeks with her nails till the blood runs in streams, like lilies and roses mixed. According to Guido, also, it is by the order of Priam that she arrayed herself in her best clothes. More true to the character which he is creating, Benoît dispenses with any royal commands, and relies on the instinctive wish of a young and beautiful girl to make a favourable impression.

The Trojan ladies grieve for the departure of the weeping Briseide. Troilus rides moodily at her side to meet the Greek escort. With quaint simplicity, and with less art than Shakespeare, who lets a hint of the future fall from Ulysses, Benoît warns his audience that Briseide will prove inconstant. He moralises on the character of her sex. Soon will the girl be comforted. A woman's grief seldom lasts. If she weeps with one eye, with the other she laughs. Rarely, as Solomon well knew, is a faithful woman to be found. But Benoît is not a preacher. There is no hint that he desires to change the charming constancy to fickleness which he alleges against women. He does not, like Guido, sermonise.

Briseide is handed over to the Greek escort. Now it is Diomede who rides by her side. The contrast is well chosen. Troilus is truly of the breed of Hector, second only to his brother in prowess, courtesy and generosity. Diomede is a fine fighter, but false to his promises, a bad master to his servants, rough and violent in temper. He at once falls a ready victim to Briseide's beauty. As he is escorting her to her father's tent, he speaks to her of all his deeds, and declares his love. She answers that she can neither refuse him nor agree to him at that time. Not otherwise could her heart answer. Then Diomede rejoices that he has not been utterly rejected.

Arrived at the tent of Calchas, as he helps her to dismount he captures one of the gloves which she was holding in her hand, and she suffered him sweetly. Face to face with her father, Briseide upbraids him for his treachery to the Trojans, and entreats him to return with her to his own fellow-countrymen. He refuses, becauses he knows that the city is doomed. The Greek leaders make much of Briseide. They are struck by her beauty ; they question her of those within the city ; they promise that she shall be to them as their own daughters. Flattered and excited, recognising that her father's decision is final, she begins to reconcile herself to her new surroundings. Day by day Diomede's passion grows hotter. He can neither sleep nor eat. Many times he requires of her her love. She answers wisely, giving him hope, yet without certainty.

Meanwhile the battle has been renewed, and Troilus again and again seeks out his rival. Their fortunes vary. Once Troilus is unhorsed, and Diomede sends the captured steed to Briseide as the prize of victory. But at last Troilus has his revenge. He strikes Diomede to the ground, taunts him with Briseide's fickleness, and leaves him wounded nigh to death. The stricken Greek is borne to his tent. There, for the first time, Briseide visits him, nurses him till his wound is whole, and then, with a sigh for Troilus, yields herself to the passion of Diomede. Her name does not occur again in the poem, and Troilus, who, after the death of Hector, becomes the Trojan hero of the siege, meets his fate at the hand of Achilles.

It is this episode which suggested to Boccaccio and to Chaucer the subject of a poem, to Henryson a continuation in which the hideous penalty of leprosy punishes the girl's inconstancy, and to Shakespeare the subject of a play. In Benoît's sketch nothing is said of the wooing of Briseide by Troilus; they appear on the scene as lovers who possess each other's love. The interest centres on subsequent developments. It is otherwise with his great successors. With the hands of masters they cast Benoît's faint suggestion into moulds of their own making. Boccaccio's *Filostrato* is an impassioned chapter of autobiography. His Griselda, whom, like Chaucer, he makes a widow, is an impersonation of his own beloved and faithless Fiammetta. He himself is the "love-destroyed" Troilus. The points in which Chaucer and Shakespeare resemble or differ from the original sketch in the *Roman de Troie* are too familiar to require to be indicated here.

The credit for what was in its day a great work passed from Benoît de Sainte More to Dares and Dictys, or to Guido delle Colonne. The first part of the loss was mainly the fault of Benoît himself. He was at once over-honest, and, in his anxiety to establish his veracity, not honest enough. In the preamble to his poem he explains his method, and why he has adopted it. Homer, he says, was a marvellous clerk, a man of great learning and worth. But he was born a hundred years after the gathering of the Greek host. It is not, therefore, surprising that he made mistakes. He was not at the siege. But he falsified history, and his representation of the gods and goddesses as fighting for or against mortal men was an untruth (*desverie*), and *marveillose folie*.

This was recognised at Athens, and it was only the high honour in which Homer was held that saved his book from formal condemnation. But there was an authority which was trustworthy because it was the work of an eye-witness. Dares wrote, on the spot and day by day, the events of the war in which he himself took part. His manuscript record was found by Cornelius, nephew to Sallust, while he was studying at Athens, and when he was rummaging in a chest —here Benoît outdoes the forger in particularity of detail— in search of a grammar. This manuscript Cornelius faithfully translated into Latin. Dares then is the guide whom Benoît will carefully follow. But he warns his hearers that he will not deny himself the pleasure of adding *alcuen buen dit*, or any pretty fancy that occurs to his own mind.

This is clear enough. Benoît does, in fact, follow closely the outline drawn by Dares. He also cites him as his authority sixty-three times—the calculation is that of M. Joly—for dates, numbers, facts, events, speeches. Sometimes, though one word may be expanded into a hundred

lines, the reference is correct. But in nearly half the cases
it is his own inventions which he authenticates by references
to imaginary statements of Dares. One instance, which
Shakespeare has made famous, will suffice. Benoît, with
the Centaur in his mind, invents the dreadful Sagittary, a
monster covered with hair like an animal—in its upper part
a man, from the navel downwards a horse. Its eyes blaze
like the openings of fiery furnaces ; it deals death with its
darts ; and, like our own tanks, it strikes terror into the
Greek host. For this creation of his own imagination
Benoît refers to Dares ; but not the faintest hint of it is
anywhere to be found in that author. The same process
is repeated again and again. No one who reads the *Roman*
without any knowledge of the Latin writer would suppose
that Dares was the baldest and driest of epitomisers. In
the Middle Ages men did not verify references. They took
Benoît at his word, and when they copied his poem they
thought that they were copying Dares.

As Benoît dwindled, Dares waxed. The final extinction
of the *trouvère* was brought about in 1287 by Guido delle
Colonne, who translated the *Roman* into Latin prose, and
sent it into the world as his own version of Dares and Dictys.
Guido abridged some portions of the original, and added a
few unimportant points. But nine-tenths of his *Historia
Trojana* are taken, without any acknowledgment of the
debt, directly from Benoît de Sainte More. No doubt the
offence was far less heinous than it would be to-day. Men
were little interested in the personality of a writer : they
were only concerned with what he had to say. Moreover,
translation was almost regarded as authorship, and it is
barely possible that, in the manuscript from which Guido
worked, the name of Benoît had already been removed from
the passages in the poem where it occurs.

One thing seems probable. Guido had not before him
the Latin works of Dares and Dictys. If he had, poor
Latinist as he is, he could hardly have repeated the many
errors of Benoît. He hands on, to take a single example,
the mistake of making Cornelius Nepos the nephew of
Sallust, and Lydgate follows him. Still more difficult is
it to believe that, with Dares before him, he could have

accepted the many false references by which Benoît authenticates his own inventions. Not only does Guido pass them, but he adds to their numbers. It is Guido, for example, who fathers on Dares Benoît's description of the Hall of Beauty.

Dull though it is, Guido's Latin version of the Norman-French romance added immensely to the popularity of the Trojan *Iliad*. It was translated into all the languages of Europe, including French. It was from Raoul Lefèvre's French version of Guido, as Dr. Sommer has established, that Caxton worked. Here, at last, Guido met with retribution. Lefèvre makes no mention of his name. But Guido's fame was already firmly established, as well as that of the two impostors whose reputation he had greatly enhanced. He was the " maister " whom Lydgate englished into verse ; he was the " wise clerk " on whose rendering of Dares and Dictys is founded the *Gest Hystoriale*; by Chaucer he was enrolled in the *Hous of Fame* among those who bear up the burden of the fame of Troy ; to three great masters of literature he suggested a subject which fired their creative imaginations ; by his work was indirectly inspired the impassioned verse of Robert Henryson's *Testament of Cresseid* ; by Caxton he was honoured in the first English book to be printed. His literary success and his popular influence were great ; yet, except as a translator, he had no claim to either. The honours justly belong, not to the Sicilian lawyer, but to the Norman *trouvère*, Benoît de Sainte More.

CHAPTER VII

EARLY TUDOR TALES

THE first book printed in the English tongue is Caxton's *Recuyell of the Historyes of Troye* (1474). The oldest book in English prose which is still read in England—with the possible exception of Mandeville's *Voiage and Travaile*, itself rather a romance than a guide to the Holy Land— is Sir Thomas Malory's *Morte d'Arthur*. Printers and schoolmasters did not kill the romance of chivalry. On new terms they gave it a fresh lease of life. Only the method of publication was altered. Minstrels yielded place to printer-publishers and ballad-singers.

Throughout the first half of the sixteenth century the mass of prose fiction which issued from the Press consisted almost exclusively of English versions of old medieval favourites—in prose for the widening circle of readers, in verse to be sung as ballads to audiences still inaccessible to printers. During the next fifty years stories of a different type passed into circulation. The great majority of them were translated, either directly or through French versions, from the originals in Greek, Latin, French, Spanish, German and, above all, Italian. A few were more original in character. They were the imitations, the adaptations or the inventions of native writers experimenting in the process of nationalising foreign models. In them may be dimly traced the lines on which English novels ultimately developed.

As a stage in the growth of the novel or historical romance, the interest of the sixteenth century lies rather in experiment than in achievement. In training the English tongue to literary expression translators and writers of prose fiction helped to accomplish much. It is not only that they enriched the vocabulary by preserving vernacular idioms, words and phrases. The resources and suppleness of

English prose owed something to Malory's direct simplicity or Caxton's business-like workmanship, to the colour, richness and archaic charm of Lord Berners, to Lyly's ornate mannerisms, to Greene's fluent ease, to the racy vigour of Thomas Nashe.

In other directions little progress was made. It was through the spoken word that literature became national. For one reader there were fifty spectators. Novelists were overwhelmed by the triumph of the dramatists. They had not yet divined the secret of competing with scenic representations. Dimly conscious that the multiplication of readers was creating new needs, and that poetry, tragedy and comedy did not exhaust the literary means of representing the truths of thought and feeling, observation and experience, they were vaguely searching for a new form of imitative and interpretative art. But the scope and structure of that form were as yet concealed from their eyes.

Unlike the poets and dramatists, novelists had no models or standards transmitted to them from the golden ages of Greece and Rome. They were adrift on an uncharted sea, without beacons to guide their voyage of discovery. Beyond the pale of criticism, bound by no rules of prosody, disciplined by no unities, they were literary outlaws relegated to the liberties of Alsatia. If freedom for the time proved fatal, they eventually found in it their salvation. But for nearly two hundred years, bewildered by its own lawlessness, prose fiction remained in search of itself, groping its way blindfold, more often off than on the true road, towards the definite and assured position into which, in the eighteenth century, it seemed suddenly to leap.

In their study of dramatic literature, students have ransacked Tudor romances and tales for hints of plots of plays, or for dramatic parallels and coincidences. Few searchers have turned the pages to discover what contribution, if any, they make to the development of the novel, which is to-day the most characteristic product of the literary efforts of the nation. The neglect is not surprising. Romantic fiction shows few examples of any freshness of observation or directness of impression; it makes few attempts to delineate contemporary society, to individualise

HA

character, to penetrate from action to its hidden springs. Yet it was only in these regions that a separate kingdom could be carved for the novel of real life. That the field was so rarely entered is the more remarkable because Chaucer in verse had already trodden the path. His Canterbury Pilgrims, acutely observed, sharply individualised, humorously presented, ride in broad daylight along familiar English roads. They are his own contemporaries, ordinary men and women painted to the life, each distinguished by his or her own personal characteristics.

It was not till the course set by medieval romances was reversed that the faces of novelists were turned in the right direction. For many years to come the old tales of chivalry proved too strong for any change. They remained the fashion among a people more interested in national than in individual life. Their gallery of heroes and heroines consists of puppets pulled by wires, unreal figures moving through unreal scenes in imaginary countries. Superficially the stories are romantic in their remoteness from ordinary life—romantic, also, in the strangeness of their happenings, though the edge of surprise is blunted by repetition. But through the best of them and of their immediate offspring there runs a truer vein of romance. They represent an aspiration and a quest for an ideal, whether of knightly conduct or of human society. Their writers are seekers and explorers. In this sense *Morte d'Arthur* and Sidney's *Arcadia* belong to the literature of revolt.

For prose fiction of some kind there was a market. That at least was certain. A man of business as well as of letters, Caxton studied the taste of his limited public. He catered more for the amusement of his readers than for their instruction. He did not consult the needs of scholars by editions of the classics, or of theologians by the works of the fathers and doctors of the Church. To historians he was more generous, as became one who was himself a skilful chronicler. Devotional literature was strongly represented. But poetry and prose fiction were the main products of his press. That he correctly gauged the wants of his public is suggested by comparing the list of his publications with the contents of the libraries of manuscripts or books collected by country

gentlemen like Robert Thornton (1440) and John Paston
(1470), by a great noble like Gerald Earl of Kildare (1525),
by literary artisans like Captain Cox, the mason of Coventry
(1575), or by royal ladies like Mary Queen of Scots (1587).
In all these miscellanies of works, grave as well as gay,
romantic fiction is prominent, if not predominant.

Similar evidence of the kind of literature that was bought
by English readers is furnished by the day-book for 1520
kept by John Dorne, an Oxford bookseller.   Apparently a
Dutchman by birth, he plied a brisk trade in the University
city.   He enters his sales of books, with their prices, from
time to time casting up his accounts, and not forgetting
his *Deo gratias*, *Amen*, even when the addition is inaccurate.
Of the 1851 entries, the bulk were Latin books, mostly
printed abroad, consisting of missals, breviaries and service
books, volumes of theology and of Civil or Canon Law,
texts of the classics, and grammatical or other works connected with the studies of the University.   Significant
among them are the entries relating to the New Learning
and the gathering storm of theological controversy.

The English books are comparatively few.   Miscellaneous
in character, the list is almost as interesting for its omissions
as for its contents.   No book either of history or of poetry
is sold.   Only one entry relates to travel and discovery—
The New Fonde Land, a tract on Portuguese navigators
printed at Antwerp and sold for 1*d*.   Science is represented
by one copy of *Husbandry* (1*d*.) and three copies of *Medecens
voer hors* at 2*d*. each.   As science, also, purchasers probably
bought the 106 almanacks and prognostications.   Domestic
life and education are not neglected.   Four books on
cookery, at 4*d*. each, and three on carving, each at 1*d*.,
appear in the entries.   Out of the fourteen copies of the
well-known treatise on good manners at meals, *Stans puer
ad Mensam*, only one is in English.   More hopeful are the
eighty-eight *A B C's*, " fore to lern red," printed, with the
Lord's Prayer, on paper (1*d*.) and on parchment (2*d*.)

The greatest number of the English entries relate to
devotional literature and to fiction.   From the invention
of printing to the present day they have been rivals in the
output of the press.   The most costly of the religious books

is *The Rules of St. Benet*, with a sheet of carols thrown in, at 1s. Ten copies of various Lives of the Saints, of whom St. Catharine is the most popular, and nine copies of such tracts as *The Miracles of our Lady*, *The Lamentations of our Lady*, and *The Complaint of St. Mary Magdalen* are sold mostly at 1d. each. The fifteen Christmas carols, some on one sheet at 1d., some on two sheets at 2d., must also be classed as devotional. On the border-line stand the three copies of the *Gesta Romanorum*, sold at 8d. each, of which one is in English. This great medieval storehouse of anecdotes, swept together from all ages and countries, might be equally bought for its moralisations and for its entertainment.

The remaining entries definitely belong to the literature of fiction. There are 195 ballads, sold, for the most part, at ½d. each, or thirteen for 6d. Of these, Captain Cox, it may be remembered, possessed a bundle wrapped in parchment and tied round with whipcord. Only three of the ballads are named. The *Nut-brown Maid* is sold at 1d.; *Undo your Dore*, of which two copies are entered, and *The Sege of the Kid* (? Cid) seem both to have disappeared. *Roben Hod*, sold for 2d., is probably the " little geste " of over 1,500 lines printed by Wynkyn de Worde in 1510. There remain seven romances of chivalry—*Sir Isumbras*, two copies at 2d. each; *Sir Eglamour* (3d.); *Robert the Devil* (3d.); *King Pontus* (8d.); *Æneydos* (2d.), probably Caxton's romance, written for him that " understondeth in faytes of armes, in loue and noble chyvalrye "; and, bound in parchment, at 1s. 8d., *The Four Sons of Aymon*, " no les pleasaunt to rede then worthy to be knowen of all estates bothe hyghe and lowe."

John Dorne's day-book confirms the evidence of the contents of private libraries. There was a sale for romances of chivalry. The printer-publishers who succeeded Caxton followed his lead. Of the mass of romantic fiction which they printed, scarcely anything was new or original. From the signs of the " Sunne," the " Hands and Starre," or the " George " in "Flete " Street, from the " Brazen Serpent " in " Powles Churchyard," or from the " Marmayde " in " Pater Noster " Row, issued a host of medieval favourites.

In full armour, with plumes flowing, Sir Huon of Bordeaux, Sir Guy of Warwick, Sir Bevis of Southampton, the " excellent and myghty Prince and hygh renowned Knyght, King Ponthus," Helyas of the " Swanne," and a score of other knights-errant, ride their sturdy horses, east and west and north and south, on their adventurous wanderings. Where did they find a resting-place? Who were their readers? Who their buyers? Dwellers in baronial halls and manor-houses perhaps welcomed them as inmates with the greater warmth because their idealised pictures of the past harmonised with their own wistful regrets for a vanishing social order. But they also found a home with a literary artisan like Captain Cox. " An od man . . . very cunning in fens and hardy as Gawin," he took part in a pageant before Queen Elizabeth at Kenilworth. He had " great oversight in matters of storie," and had formed a curious library. He cannot, perhaps, be regarded as typical of the Elizabethan workman. Yet, as education spread and readers multiplied in every rank of life, the spirit of chivalrous romances appealed to a widening circle. How tenacious was their hold is shown by their continuous republication, by the direction that they gave to the development of prose fiction, by the success of Spanish knights like the Knight of the Sun, or Palmerin of England or Amadis of Gaul, or by the triumph which Richard Johnson, aided by the book's appeal to patriotism and religion, attained with his *Seaven Champions of Christendom* (1597).

Two centuries later, in the debased form of chap-books, knights-errant still roamed the country among the laces and ribbons of the pedlar's pack. Puritans denounced them as " idle babblements," or worse ; humanists like Ben Jonson scorned them as fitter for the maid than the mistress ; a Democritus like Burton ridiculed the country gentleman for reading—if they read anything at all—*Huon of Bordeaux*. Yet, for all that and more, the medieval romances were the pioneers of popular literature. They helped to preserve chivalry as a living standard of conduct from the crash of the shattered framework of feudal society. They fanned the heroic enthusiasms of the Elizabethans ; they wove round them the magic spell of adventure ; they fostered the glorified vision of life and the splendid illusions of the greatest period of our literature. In them were mingled " vertue and synne." But all were free to follow Caxton's counsel : " Doo after the good and leve the evyl, and it shal brynge you to good fame and renommee."

Before 1560 medieval romance held the field of prose fiction. England, except through Chaucer, knew little of Boccaccio and his Italian and French followers. Few translations of their novels were made in prose or verse. Henry Parker, Lord Morley, left behind him in manuscript a prose version, dedicated to Henry VIII, of Masuccio's tale of the Pope's betrayal of Frederick Barbarossa to the Soldan of Babylon. Sir Thomas Elyot, in the *Governour* (1531), translated into English prose Boccaccio's story of " Titus and Gisippus " as an example of " perfect amitie." The same story, and another from the *Decameron*, were versified by an obscure poet, William Walter (fl. 1520). If other translations in prose or verse were made during the first half of the sixteenth century, they have been thumbed out of existence.

One formidable rival to romances of chivalry had indeed appeared. It was a prose translation of a tale of unlawful passion, written in Latin in the middle of the fifteenth century with all the warmth of the school of Boccaccio. It proved to be, as its advertisement claimed, " very pleasant and delectable to the reader." The *Goodli History of the most noble and beautifull Lady Lucres of Scene in Tuskan and of her Lover Eurialus* (1550) was more than once reprinted in this country. The book found a place in the library of Captain Cox and, a century later, in that of Samuel Pepys. Abroad, it passed through many editions in several languages. Its authorship probably contributed to its success. It was written by a Pope. " Æneas Sylvius, an ancient divine," afterwards Pius II, was " past forty years of age "—so says Burton—when he " indited that wanton history." The Pope lived to regret his mature indiscretion. Yet the conclusion of the story, at any rate, makes for edification. It shows how the moral blindness of passion destroys the two persons whose vision is obscured by the obsession.

The story is said, like most of the Italian novels, to be founded on an actual occurrence at Siena. It is well and briskly told. Lucretia, the young wife of a rich Sienese nobleman, and Eurialus, a Franconian knight high in the favour of the Emperor Sigismund, fall in love at first sight. Running hairbreadth risks of discovery, Eurialus contrives to meet his mistress and yet to keep secret the fulfilment of their passion. Weeks pass. The Emperor is on the point of proceeding to Rome, with Eurialus in his train. Lucretia implores him to take her with him. Her lover gives her prudent counsel. He advises her to remain with her husband, enjoying her unblemished reputation of a virtuous wife. Half blinded with tears, Lucretia watches Eurialus ride out of the city. Then, all joy of life departed, she pines away and dies. Eurialus, following his master to many countries, carries with him the memory of his mistress. Wherever he journeys, the form of the dead Lucretia robs him of sleep. Though the emperor gave him to wife a " ryghte excellent Ladye," he took no joy in his marriage, but " pitifully wasted his painful lyfe."

Except by *Lucrece and Eurialus*, the sway of medieval romances remained undisputed. On them the younger, as well as the older, generation who hailed the accession of Elizabeth had been bred. But their exclusive domination could not long withstand the wave of curiosity which swept over Tudor England as the sixteenth century advanced. The intellectual treasures of every country, ancient as well as modern, were ransacked to nourish and enrich the English genius. Two hundred years in advance of England, the influence of Italian civilisation for many years reigned supreme. To speak or read Italian became no rare accomplishment among women as well as men. Next to Greek and Latin, Ascham loved it " above all others." Queen Elizabeth was a mistress of the language, and in it more than one of her ministers corresponded. Young courtiers crowded the Italian church to hear the spoken tongue. Without some sojourn in Italy an English education was incomplete.

Books in Italian were printed and published in England, while, for those who could not read the originals, there were,

between 1547 and 1600, some two hundred English translations of Italian works. Their range of subject was wide.
Protestant theology owed something to leaders of the
Italian Reformation like Peter Martyr and Ochino. In
courtly manners the world was Italy's pupil; no better
book on what Dr. Johnson called "good breeding" was ever
published than the *Courtyer* of Castiglione. Young Englishmen studied the science of horsemanship from Grisone and
Corte, as they learned the tricks of fencing from "Signior
Rocko." Others beside Touchstone regulated their "honourable quarrels" by the rules of Saviolo.

Italy supplied the plots to the majority of Elizabethan
plays. She furnished most of the material for jest-books
like the *Hundred Merry Tales*, from which Beatrice was
charged with borrowing her wit. Her doctors and
anatomists were our masters in medicine and surgery. In
astronomy Italians were our teachers; in architecture, or
the laying out of gardens, our tutors; in the art of war, in
tactics, in gunnery, our instructors. Italian historians set
a new standard to our native writers. Records of Italian
voyages and discoveries fired the imagination and stirred the
emulation of our navigators. To the daring spirit of
Giordano Bruno England offered an asylum, and for his
speculations her printing presses. In the science of government and of politics, "murderous" Machiavelli, Nashe's
"Muster-master of Hell," stood to the Elizabethans as the
incarnation of satanic force and statecraft.

On all these subjects, from theology to cookery, Italian
books were translated into English. Yet nearly half the
translations from the Italian consisted of poetry and fiction.
Widest of all was the influence of the tellers of short stories
in prose. In them was most clearly sounded the note of
the return to nature which was not less a part of the Renaissance than the return to classical antiquity. Their pictures
were painted from real life in all the heat and glow of Italian
passion. They were examples of the possibilities of action
to which men or women, in pursuit of any passion, might
be driven by that force or *virtû* of the will, restrained neither
by law nor conscience, which fascinated the imagination
of many of the Elizabethan dramatists. Totally different

in subject, structure and treatment from medieval romance, they took English readers by storm. Their triumph was the more complete because of their novelty. This country knew nothing. like the short popular stories of Northern France, in which the emancipated townsmen and the rising Third Estate protested against the aristocratic idealism of romances of chivalry. A stranger to the French *fabliau*, England welcomed the Italian *novelle* as a new-found land of realism and as one of the richest revelations of the Renaissance.

In the unknown compilers of the *Cento Antiche Novelle* Boccaccio had his predecessors. He left behind him many followers. But in literary skill and finish, in the artist's eye for composition, in the lightness of touch which often saves indecency from grossness, he had no rival. He and his successors worked on lines opposed to those of the incoherent, rambling writers of romance. Each story has a beginning and an end. Each has a plot developed by natural events, rarely relying on the supernatural, and with a rigid economy of superfluous detail. Most of the stories might or did happen in the experience of their audiences.

In the substance of their tales there is little to distinguish Boccaccio from his six followers who were best known to Elizabethan England. Nearest in point of time is Masuccio, whose *Novellino* was printed in 1476. His moral indignation and Neapolitan provincialisms are strongly contrasted with the gay indifference and linguistic purity of his model. Of the *Pecorone* (1550), attributed to a shadowy personality, Ser Giovanni Fiorentino, more than half consists in extracts from the Chronicles of Villani. The *Pleasant Nights* of Straparola (1556) are remembered for their fairy stories rather than for their enigmas, and their author is most famous as an ancestor of Madame d'Aulnoy and of Perrault. More important in their influence on English literature are Bandello (1554), the Queen of Navarre (1558), and Cinthio (1565). The immediate popularity of the last two Italians was at least as great as that of Boccaccio.

The setting of the *Decameron* is a literary masterpiece. Singularly effective is the contrast between the gay masquerade of life and its grim realities. In the plain, the terrified citizens of Florence cower within the walls of the plague-stricken city. On the hills above, in luxurious palaces and terraced gardens, the graceful company of youthful lords and ladies pursue their pleasure in story, dance and song. Neither Masuccio nor Bandello adopt any framework for their collection of stories. Their tales are separately addressed to some friend or notability. The others follow Boccaccio in inventing a setting. Straparola gathers his company of lords and ladies on the island of Murano during the Carnival at Venice. Cinthio embarks his refugees from the sack of Rome on board a ship bound for Marseilles. The Queen of Navarre detains her company on their return from the Baths of Cauterets by the repair of a broken bridge. Quaintest and coldest of all is the setting of the *Pecorone*. For twenty-five days Sister Saturnina and Brother Auretto meet to tell a story and sing a canzonet in the convent parlour of Forli. There Sister Saturnina tells how Messer Ansaldo of Venice, to save his godson, Gianotto, enters into a bond to pay a pound of his flesh to a Jew of Mestri ; how the bond is forfeited ; how the Jew claims its execution ; how Ansaldo is saved by the wit of the Lady of Belmont disguised as a doctor of laws of Bologna ; how she asks as her only fee the ring which she had herself given to Gianotto. Well might Auretto say, " In truth your story is one of the finest I have ever heard."

The invasion of England by the Italian novelists is roughly dated by a well-known passage in Ascham's *Scholemaster*, a book which he began in 1563 and left unfinished at his death in 1568.

> " Ten *Morte Arthures* (he says) do not the tenth part so much harme, as one of these bookes, made in Italie, and translated in England. . . . And that which is most to be lamented, and therfore more nedefull to be looked to, there be moe of these ungratious bookes set out in Printe within these fewe monethes, than haue bene sene in England many score yeare before."

Ascham's condemnation of Italian novels is the more note-worthy because he was neither a pedant nor a recluse, but, in modern phrase, a sportsman—an archer, a cock-fighter ; even, as some said, a gambler. Had he lived another ten years, he would have been still more aghast at the popularity of these " forreine reapportes " of the enchantments of Circe. Before he began his book the change was in progress. Two metrical translations from Italian novels had already appeared, one of which was Arthur Broke's *Tragicall Historye of Romeus and Juliet* (1562), a version of the story told by Masuccio, Luigi da Porta and Bandello. But it was the publication of two collections of prose novels in 1566 and 1567 which specially roused Ascham's wrath. One was William Painter's *Palace of Pleasure* (vol. i., 1566 ; vol. ii., 1567). It contains, with the additions made in 1575, a hundred and one " pleasaunt Histories and excellent Nouels," mostly drawn from the Italian masters, and especially from Bandello, the Queen of Navarre and Boccaccio. The other collection was that of Geoffrey Fenton, whose *Certaine Tragicall Discourses* (1567) contain thirteen translations from Bandello. Pro-bably neither Painter nor Fenton knew Italian ; both used the French versions of Belleforest.

Neither of these writers was particular about exact translations. Painter cannot refrain from preaching. A story of the triumph of honour, which he borrows from the *Pecorone*, affords a good example. Galgano refuses to " dishonest " the willing wife of his friend. Ser Giovanni puts one brief sentence into his mouth ; Painter adds a moral rhapsody of nearly twenty lines in length, delivered in circumstances grotesquely inappropriate to such oratory. More effective is the naïve comment of Sister Saturnina, to whom the tale is told in the convent parlour by Brother Auretto : " Had I been in his place, I know not what I should have done." Fenton, a writer of greater distinction, is an even worse offender. He checks the rapidity of Bandello's narrative with classical allusions, rhetorical speeches, and moral reflections. A Puritan, he drags in the Bible, abuses the Pope, protests against dancing or sermonises on the proper dependence of women, who must be conscientiously chastised into obedience by their husbands. Almost as studious of his manner as he is of his matter, he is an euphuist before Lyly. He not only liberally employs the artifices of antithesis and alliteration, but commands for metaphorical use an assortment of animals which is a promising instalment towards the more miscellaneous collection of the author of *Euphues*. Interesting as Fenton is as a stylist and a personality, he has not mastered the secret of the short story.

Other translations, imitations or adaptations from the novelists appeared in collections of prose and verse under such picturesque titles as *The Forrest of Fancy*; *The Rocke of Regarde*; or *A Posie of Gillowflowers*. The stories in George Pettie's *Petite Palace of Pettie his Pleasure* (1576), though the title is imitated from Painter and the material is handled in the Italian style, are more original, and are drawn from classical sources. In *Cymbeline*, it was over " the tale of Tereus " and Philomel that Imogen fell asleep, and the second of Pettie's twelve stories is that of " Tereus and Progne." Among metrical versions of the *novelle*, two may be mentioned. One is Christopher Tye's translation (1569) of Boccaccio's story of the spectral huntsman and his " hell-dogs," which, in Dryden's rendering, haunted Byron in " Ravenna's immemorial wood " ; the other is George Turberville's *Tragicall Tales* (1587), the first of which is a translation from the *Decameron* of the story that inspired Keats to write *Isabella, or the Pot of Basil*.

CHAPTER VIII

ELIZABETHAN NOVELS AND ROMANCES

In numbers of English works the Italian masters were translated, imitated, adapted ; but they founded no native school of writers of short stories of real life in England. For this neglect the translators themselves were partly to blame. Another and a stronger reason why English writers of prose fiction did not at once apply Italian methods to contemporary society at home lay in the taste and fashion of the day. Authorship was becoming a profession, and romance-writers kept an eye to their living. They wrote for a courtly public. Till almost the close of the century, Elizabethans were less curious about themselves than anxious to read of unfamiliar surroundings and of events remote from facts of their own experience. Those who imitated or adapted the Italian novels set themselves to meet the demand by laying their scenes in Italy or in imaginary countries, and by inventing incidents which were possible rather than probable. Among the most interesting of those who worked on these lines are George Gascoigne, Barnaby Rich and Robert Greene.

Gascoigne professes to translate his *Pleasant Fable of Ferdinando Jeronimi and Leonora de Velasco* (1575) from the " Italian riding tales of Bartello." Elsewhere, he identifies his alleged authority with himself, and the story is, therefore, an original work in the Italian style. Longer than the ordinary length of the *novella*, it has its compactness of structure. It has a clearly outlined plot, which is brought to a definite conclusion by natural events. A country gentleman of Lombardy lives at his castle of Velasco in the company of his daughter, Franceschina, and his daughter-in-law, Leonora. To make his story more " perspicuous " to his " countriemen," Gascoigne calls the two young ladies Frances and Elinor. The neighbourhood of Velasco swarmed

with game. Ferdinando, a young Venetian, well born,
rich, agreeable, fond of field sports, is invited to bring his
servants and horses and spend three months at the castle.
It is hoped he will fall in love with Frances. Unfortunately,
he prefers Elinor. No tedious soliloquies or lengthy
speeches interrupt their love-making. It proceeds with the
rapidity which might be expected from an ardent youth
and a beautiful young married woman, who is willing to
meet him more than half way. The conversations are
natural, and the narrative is enlivened by interesting details
of ordinary life in a country house. Elinor gives her lover
all that he desires. But she is, at the same time, carrying
on an old intrigue with her secretary. Ferdinando's jealousy
provokes a quarrel. Elinor dismisses him contemptuously.
Disillusioned and soured, he returns to Venice, where he
ruins his health and fortune in low dissipations. The
interest of the story centres in Frances. She knows Elinor's
secrets, but is too loyal to betray them. Yet she has given
her heart to Ferdinando, while he, absorbed in his passion
for Elinor, gives her only his trust and friendship. His
departure leaves her broken-hearted. In the two wrecked
lives, Gascoigne pays his belated tribute to morality.

Gascoigne's scene is laid in Italy, and in this respect
Barnaby Rich consults the prevailing taste. In the con-
cluding address to the readers of *Riche his Farewell to Mili-
tarie Profession* (1581) he gives local colour to Machiavelli's
story of " Belphegor " by marrying his devil to the daughter
of a citizen of London and providing him with an escape from
his wife by migration into the body of a King of Scotland.
Otherwise he lays his scenes in the countries frequented by
the Italian novelists. Less original than Gascoigne, he is
either a translator or a borrower. His story of " Duke
Apolonius and Silla," which Shakespeare may have used in
Twelfth Night, is freely translated from Bandello. Even
where he allowed himself greater latitude, and " forged "
stories " onely for delight," he follows his masters with a
closeness which he defends by pleading the success of his
models. But he was capable of more independent work.
Passages in the introduction and conclusion to the *Farewell*
show his keen eye for realistic detail. The popular dances

of England, the dress of young men about town, the sumptuous hospitality of Sir Christopher Hatton, are closely
observed and vigorously described.

A more arresting figure than either Gascoigne or Rich
was Robert Greene, whose peaked red beard was familiar
in the Bohemian circles which were now beginning to form
in London. His literary facility was extraordinary, his
inventive faculty varied. Writing for his bread, he poured
out a stream of novels and romances, in which he blended
all the ingredients that seemed most calculated to attract
popular favour. He even turned the Bible to account. In
his *Mourning Garment* (1590) he " moralised " the " Divine
historie " of the Prodigal Son. Susannah and the Elders
are treated in a similar fashion in the *Mirrour of Modestie*
(1584).

His most distinctive romances were not written in the
style of the *Decameron*; but in a considerable group of his
works he was a close follower of Italian masters, and especially of Boccaccio, though he never imitated their licentious-
ness. He wrote moral tales in praise of honest love, in
warning against pride, inconstancy or want of reticence,
in condemnation of love's disloyalties, in proof that married
happiness depends on a wife's chastity, obedience and
modesty. He set his collections of short stories or moral
dissertations in frameworks which were modelled on the
Italians. Thus in *Morando, the Tritameron of Love* (1584-7),
the widowed Panthia, her daughters, and other guests
assemble to moralise on love at a " grange " in Bononia,
belonging to their host, Morando. In the *Farewell to Follie*
(1591), Jeronimo Farnese, a nobleman of Florence, escapes
from the factions of the Guelphs and Ghibellines to his
farm near Vienna, where he, his wife, three daughters and
four young gentlemen pass their time in " friendly con-
ferences " on follies.

In other books the imitation is not only of form, but of
substance. *Perimedes the Blacke-Smith* (1588), for instance,
is set in a pleasant framework of a cottage home at Memphis
in an unknown era of history. The blacksmith and his
wife, Delia, spend their days in the forge together, " he
at his hammers, and she at the Bellowes, for boy they had

none." Their labours ended, they sup and pass the evening
in talk. Greene professes to "rehearse" three of their
"nights prattle." In their main features and incidents
the stories are strongly reminiscent of Boccaccio. Another
instance is *Ciceronis Amor, Tullie's Love* (1589), a very
popular tale, frequently reprinted. It is largely borrowed
from his favourite master. Thus Fabius the fool is the
Cymon of the *Decameron*, and the transformation which
love works in the one is faithfully reproduced in the other.
So also the pleading of Cicero with Terentia on behalf of
Lentulus is a reproduction of the similar situation in
Boccaccio's "Titus and Gysippus."

English writers of prose fiction were slow to learn from
Italian masters the secret of the art of narrative—its
economy of details, its selection of incidents, its concentration on the desired effect. Still slower were they to feel
the need of truth to nature. There was, as yet, no demand
for the realistic presentation of English life, society or
character. At Court, the tide of fashion set strongly in
the opposite direction. Medieval tales of chivalry had
retained their popularity, rather because, than in spite, of
their remoteness from everyday life. For their literary
entertainment Elizabethans preferred illusions to realities.
They had outgrown their taste for magicians and enchantments; they banished giants and dragons to their native
fastnesses; they were weary of aimless fighting, especially
of single combats whose issue was always foreseen. Purged
of these obsolete elements, a new type of romance was
created, mainly on the old lines.

Written for private reading, the stories are less marred
by repetition, and the manner of telling them becomes no
less important than their matter. In other directions
little advance was made towards the modern novel. Writers
of the new school still lay their scenes in imaginary countries.
Their incidents remain improbable. Their heroes and
heroines are indistinct shadows, uniform in pattern. Their
treatment of history, chronology and geography continues
as fantastically absurd as before. Love becomes the central
feature of their plots. But writers of the new romances
do not, like the Italian novelists, dwell on the shifts and

stratagems of its infidelities. It is its constancy that they hold up to admiration and make the pivot of their stories. To this change both Greek and Spanish romances contributed.

In 1569 appeared Underdown's translation of the *Theagenes and Chariclea* of Heliodorus. Clothed with the glamour of Greece, the book became immensely popular. Numerous references to it occur in Sidney, Francis Meres, Greene, Lodge and others. Shakespeare seized on one episode in the story. It is the attempt of Thyamis, the robber chief, to kill Chariclea, lest she should fall into other hands than his own :

> Why should I not, had I the heart to do it,
> Like to the Egyptian thief at point of death,
> Kill what I love ; a savage jealousy
> That sometimes savours nobly ?

But the point which most impressed English writers and readers was the loyalty of the lovers to one another through every form of adversity.

The same note of constancy in love is struck by the Spanish romances of chivalry. They did not reach England in an English dress till the last two decades of the sixteenth century—a moment when the products of Spain were unwelcome to the nation. The first to arrive was *The Mirrour of Knighthood*, partly translated by Margaret Tyler (1578) from the Spanish original. The book never lost the advantage of its early start. It remained the most popular of its class. From it Lyly, in his *Euphues in England*, took the names of two of his minor figures. One of its heroines, Lindabrides, though a daughter of the Emperor of Constantinople, became an English synonym for a light woman. Its twin heroes, Rosicleer and the Knight of the Sun, Falstaff's " wandering knight so fair," were better known to English readers than any of the heroes of the *Palmerin* series (1581–1602), *Amadis of Gaul* (1589–1619), or *Don Belianis of Greece* (1598), than whom none was " more slashed and slashing."

Survivals or revivals of the Middle Ages, Spanish romances of chivalry arrived fifty years too late. By the critical and cultured classes they were coldly received. The incessant

clash of arms was wearisome. Enchanted islands and
magical weapons were out of date. Even had circumstances
been more favourable, they were unfortunate in their
translators, and in the piecemeal method and inverted
order of their publication. Yet, in spite of these drawbacks,
they were widely read. References to them in plays,
though usually contemptuous in their tone, show that
dramatists expected their audiences to catch the allusions.
In the following century they prepared the way for the
ascendency of the French school of heroic romances. But
they also contributed to the development of the new style
of Elizabethan fiction. It was their idealised treatment of
love and its fidelities which appealed to the English public.
Amadis and Oriana were types of constant lovers ; Palmerin
remains true to Polinarda, Rosicleer to Olivia; even the more
fickle Knight of the Sun remembers, at the last moment,
his troth to Claridiana. Thousands of Englishwomen read
them as love-stories. They agreed with the innkeeper's
daughter in *Don Quixote* :

> " It is not (she says) the blows that my father likes
> that I like, but the laments that the knights utter when
> they are separated from their ladies ; and indeed they
> sometimes make me weep with the compassion I feel
> for them."

On the pattern of Greek and Spanish fiction were moulded
the new romances of love's constancy. Their coming was
preceded by two important books, written almost at the
same time by two youthful contemporaries. One was
Lyly's *Euphues* (part i., 1579 ; part ii., 1580) ; the other
was Sidney's *Arcadia*, posthumously published in 1590,
but written nine or ten years earlier. The first broke new
ground, and then withered ; the second, though almost
reactionary in tone and method, flourished and bore fruit.

Lyly owed a great part of his prodigious but brief popularity to his innovations in style. His bestiary, his herb-
arium, his cabinet of minerals, his aviary, his collection of
fishes, supplied him with a store of similes, which he pours
out with exasperating persistency in monotonously constructed sentences. Euphues became a name to conjure

with, and euphuism a fashionable craze. But Lyly was not of the new movement, and his book was more remote from the coming love-romance than from the modern novel. There is neither plot, nor stirring action, nor delineation of character. It is not so much a story as a series of moral reflections on such subjects as religion, marriage, education, manners, travel. The spokesman is Euphues, a self-satisfied, virtuous and didactic prig, but intensely in earnest.

Turning his back on the old romances of chivalry, Lyly had struck a new vein. He appealed to the serious qualities which underlay the frivolities of English society. For the most part, the materials are derived from North's *Diall of Princes*, itself translated from the Spanish original of Guevara. But the form is new. Lyly made the discovery that his countrymen liked sermons disguised as prose fiction. In this he was a predecessor of Richardson, as he anticipated him also in his use of letters. Even more important is the fact that, in his second part, he describes his own contemporary England and the life that was lived in his own day. In spite of all its affectations of style, *Euphues* stands closer in some respects to *Pamela* and *Clarissa Harlowe* than any romance written in the sixteenth or seventeenth centuries.

Sidney's *Arcadia* is of a totally different character. Called a pastoral romance, it has none of the insipidity of its class; its stirring incidents redeem it from the charge of too much wool and too little wolf. For Sidney, Arcadia is a land of literary licence, in which he is free from facts and probabilities. Dashing off the sheets for no other eyes but those of his sister, he pours into his prose poem the " many fancies " which crowded his enthusiastic, imaginative mind. In the book is expressed the discontent of a young and ardent man with the existing conditions of actual life. It is a medley of his own imaginings, reminiscences of English, Greek and Spanish romances, hints from Sannazaro's *Arcadia* and Montemayor's *Diana*.

It is a jumble of Christianity and paganism, of fifteenth-century knighthood, of medieval tournaments and Elizabethan masques, of Renaissance palaces and gardens, costumes and furniture. It is a knightly Arcadia, an artificial world peopled with shepherds and shepherdesses, kings and queens, princes and princesses. Plot there is none. In his *Apologie for Poetrie* Sidney took Theagenes as his type of a perfect lover. So in his *Arcadia* the only coherence lies in the threads that are strung to the fidelity of Prince Musidorus to Princess Pamela, and of Prince Pyrocles to Princess Philoclea. The course of love runs by no means smoothly. His lovers meet and are separated, lose and find each other, encounter every variety of perilous adventure. They assume disguises which lead to dangerous complications and even bring Pyrocles to the very foot of the scaffold.

Rambling in structure, unreal in substance, the *Arcadia* owed nothing, except in rare passages, to beauty of style. Though Sidney protests against the mannerisms of Lyly, his own " conceits " and tangled sentences are as affected as those of *Euphues*, and, it must be added, at least as tiresome. Yet the *Arcadia* charmed many successive generations of readers. What is the secret of its spell? It lies partly in the varieties of the passion of love which it describes and analyses. It lies, most of all, in the revelation of the author. Its pages radiate the fascinating personality of the poet and lover of poetry, the statesman, the accomplished knight, the perfect type of Elizabethan gentleman, whose heroic death at Zutphen threw an added halo round his name.

Lyly's influence was more superficial, and therefore more short-lived. For a few years romance writers imitated his style, or invoked the patronage of his name for their productions. But, except in the subsequent pictures of low life, none followed him in describing contemporary England. In substance the love-romances, which were to hold the field for the next half-century, owed little to *Euphues*. Their true creators were Robert Greene and his friend and contemporary, Thomas Lodge. They founded the new school to which belonged such writers as Anthony Munday and Emanuel Ford, whose *Parismus* (1598), seventy years after its publication, was still widely read.

Greene was first with *Mamillia* (1583), closely followed by Lodge with *Forbonius and Prisceria* (1584). In his

" love-pamphlet " Greene copied Lyly's style and moralising tone, and he wrote under the spell of his recent sojourn in Italy. But he and Lodge have one significant point in common. Both are admirers of the Greek romance of *Theagenes and Chariclea* ; both allude to the book ; both, like Heliodorus, make the constancy of their lovers the pivot of their plots. Mamillia's loyalty is rewarded by marriage with Pharicles. " What perilles suffered *Theagines* to keepe his credit with Cariclia ! " reflects Greene as he tells the story of his own hero. For his heroine Lodge claims direct descent from the fair Ethiopian. Prisceria is the granddaughter of " *Theagines* of *Greece*, the co-partner of sorrowe with Caricleala, the straunge borne childe of the *Ægyptian* king." It is on the pattern of Heliodorus that the new romances are modelled. In this respect they make an advance on the chaotic methods of medieval fiction. They have a central interest on which the story hinges. It may be overlaid by other incidents, but it persists. Even in *Parismus* the hero and heroine are at last united, and Parismus marries Laurana.

On these principles Greene frames his " love-pamphlets." He takes a pair of lovers, preferably of royal birth but ignorant of their descent, sets them down in some imaginary country, plunges them into every peril which his inventive faculty can devise, and rewards their constancy with marriage and a kingdom. Written in poetic prose, abounding in classical allusions, embroidered with a profusion of rich description, his romances are interspersed with verse which is often of exquisite quality. Lodge's work shows similar characteristics. A more careful writer, his polish produces a languid prettiness, which in *A Margarite of America* (1596) is not unpleasing. The interest of the stories depends entirely on the bare facts of the varied incidents. It is external only. The actors are puppets, not creatures of flesh and blood. Even their love does not develop in growth. It springs into full stature at first sight. Where all is unreal, one unreality the more is immaterial.

Written by the most successful novelist of the day, Greene's *Pandosto, the Triumph of Time* (1588), under the name of *Dorastus and Fawnia*, was frequently reprinted.

Its popularity lasted into the eighteenth century ; it was
paid the rare compliment of two French translations. But
its greatest honour is that it supplied the plot of *The Winter's
Tale*. The scene is mainly laid in the maritime country of
Bohemia. In that strange kingdom, whose coasts are
reached by sea, reign both Pandosto and Leontes. It is
there that Dorastus and Fawnia play the parts of Florizel
and Perdita. A hundred and fifty years later the book was
still known, but it had descended to the kitchen. In *Clarissa
Harlowe* the fire at Mrs. Sinclair's house was caused by a
cook-maid who, sitting up to read *Dorastus and Fawnia*
by candlelight, set fire to the calico window-curtains. In
1589 Greene chose for the setting of his *Menaphon, Camilla's
Alarum to Slumbering Euphues* the pastoral world of shepherds and shepherdesses. He was again followed by Lodge,
whose *Rosalynde, Euphues' Golden Legacie : found after
his Death in his Cell at Silexedra* appeared in 1590, the
year of the publication of the *Arcadia*. The obvious
artificiality of a pastoral setting suits the unreality of the
new romances.

Menaphon is Greene's best work in the class of love-
romances. It contains the beautiful song of Sephestia to
her child, "Weepe not, my wanton, smile upon my knee,"
which may suggest to the charitable that, in his better
moments, Greene's thoughts turned to his deserted wife
and child. But, as a writer of pastorals, Greene was surpassed by his friend. *Rosalynde* was Lodge's masterpiece.
On the whole, it is the finest work produced by any of the
Tudor writers of prose romance. The story is universally
known, for Shakespeare follows it closely in *As You
Like It*.

Both in manner and in matter, short stories on Italian
models, romances of chivalry, pastorals and love-pamphlets
formed a literature of the Court, and not of the people.
Remote from contemporary realities, moulded by foreign
influences, they represented a spirit that was passing.
Feudal England was being transformed into a commercial
nation. Towns were growing, new classes rising into wealth
and importance. Citizens and traders, as well as courtiers
and scholars, demanded mental occupation and literary

entertainment, and it was in their own actual lives that they were mainly interested. In the last decade of the sixteenth century native writers of prose fiction set themselves to supply the demand. An anti-romantic reaction began, in which were blended democratic sympathies, realistic ambitions, and a revolt against foreign fashions. Many experiments were made in popularising the existing forms of prose fiction; but no known writer except Deloney broke free, both in form and matter, from the traditions of romance.

Writing for his bread, and sensitive to social changes, Greene recognised the new market. He gave the support of his name to the movement towards the presentation of actual facts in the lives of his contemporaries at home. After 1590 he determined to write no more pamphlets of imaginary loves. The one apparent exception is his *Philomela*, published in 1592. But there is no reason to doubt his statement that the book was written at an earlier date. In his amusing *Quip for an Upstart Courtier* (1592) he sided with the home-spun cloth breeches of the citizen against the swaggering velvet breeches of the courtier. It was to a jury of traders that he submitted the question whether native or foreign fashions deserved the greater respect, and their verdict was in favour of home-made goods.

Greene began by turning to his own experiences for his material. His *Never too Late*, though disguised in an Italian form, is, like his *Mourning Garment*, mainly an autobiographical fragment. Both books were published in 1590. His *Farewell to Follie* (1591), his *Groats-Worth of Witte* (1592), and his *Repentance of Robert Greene* were more directly and avowedly founded on his own life. In his vivid transcripts from the underworld of London, Greene was again describing scenes which pass'd under his own eyes. He did not, however, deal with rogues in the manner of Spanish writers. No trace exists of the influence of Mendoza's *Lazarillo de Tormes*, which had reached England in 1568-9, but did not gain its widespread popularity till the following century. Greene's attitude is that of warning. In the passage from feudalism to industrialism, the course had been strewn with social wreckage. The break-up of baronial households, the dissolution of the monasteries, the decay of guilds, the enclosure of commons had multiplied beggars and vagabonds, and swollen the organised community of crime.   In Spain, similar conditions had produced the new class of prose fiction, which took for its hero the *picaro*, or rogue, round whose ingenious rascalities centres a series of adventures.   But, in this country, alarm predominated over the curiosity with which society had received the revelations, made by Awdeley or Harman, of the number and boldness of the " fraternitie of vacabondes."   It was felt to be dangerous to elevate an " Abraham man," or an " upright man," into the hero of a narrative in the *Gusto Picaresco*.

Greene followed popular feeling, and wrote to expose, rather than to applaud, the stratagems of pimps, prostitutes, swindlers and thieves.   So effective was the exposure of their wiles in his *Notable Discovery of Cosenage* (1591) that his life is said to have been attempted.   He continued the attack in his *Disputation between a Hee Conny-Catcher and a Shee Conny-Catcher* (1592), taking his quaint title from the cant name for a rogue derived from the pedlars who, in country districts, exchanged pins and needles for rabbit-skins.   In almost his last book he returned to the campaign. *The Black Bookes Messenger* (1592) told the life and death of Ned Brown, a notorious ruffian, who went to the scaffold.   It is significant that Greene is careful to vindicate morality. In the *Disputation*, his " conny-catching " courtesan is reclaimed ; in the *Messenger*, Ned Brown is not only hanged, but penitent.

Greene's death in 1592 cut short a literary career which had only lasted nine years.   He did not live to prove his mettle as an interpreter of the movement, at once national, realistic and democratic, to which, in his last years, he gave partial expression.   Other writers, moved by similar influences, took up the work in various forms.

Writers of short stories revolted from the Italian supremacy.   Against their dependence on foreign fashions the anonymous author of *The Cobler of Caunterburie* (1590) protests on the national ground that a better model was supplied by English literature.   His short stories follow

Chaucer, not Boccaccio. Their setting is English, and the story-tellers are representative English men and women. He assembles his company at Billingsgate, where they wait in a barge for the tide to serve for Gravesend. One of the party " puld out of his sleeue a little pamphlet and began to reade to himselfe." Asked what the book was, " marry quoth he, a foolish toy called *Tarlton's newes out of Purgatory*." They discuss the book, one praising, another condemning the tales ; " tush quoth an other most of them are stolne out of *Boccace Decameron*." Then " an auncient man that was a Cobler in *Caunterbury*,"who had read the book, says that " tis indifferent, like a cup of bottle ale halfe one and halfe the other. . . . No no what say to old father *Chaucer*, how like you of his *Caunterburie* tales, are they not pleasant to delight and witty to instruct . . . All men commended *Chaucer* as the father of English Poets, and saide, that he shot a shoote which many haue aimed at but neuer reacht to." Then they fall to telling stories, The Cobbler leading off, followed by The Smith, The Gentleman, The Scholar, The Old Wife, and The Somner. The book was several times reprinted. Its success, however, may perhaps be attributed less to the championship of Chaucer than to the Smith's definition of the " Eight Orders of Cuckolds," the seventh of which is " the Cuckold by Act of Parliament "—the husband who obtains damages for his injury by legal proceedings.

Even in short stories, translated or adapted from Boccaccio, methods were adopted which differed widely from the use of Gascoigne, Rich or Greene. In *Westward for Smelts* (1620), by " Kinde Kit of Kingstone," the setting of the tales is a scene from English life, as distinctively national as the framework of *The Canterbury Tales*. In the season of Lent, when " none but fish must be eaten," a waterman of " Queenhive " sits drinking at the " Red Knight." His boy comes running to tell him of a fare. Hurrying to his boat, he finds a company of fishwives, whose heads are as full of wine as their purses of coin. They agree upon a fare to take them up the river to Kingston. The boy sets the cushions in place, and they put off. In the crowded part of the river, the waterman is too busy in

avoiding the traffic to give an eye to his company. Opposite
Lambeth he finds them all nodding. To rouse them he
sings them a song. The fishwives then agree each to tell a
story, the first to land to be the first to begin.

Six stories from the Italian novelists are told, prefaced
by a description of the teller in doggerel verse. Each tale
is given a national turn. Of this English colouring the best
illustration is the second tale, told by " the Fishwife of
Stand on the Greene." It is the story of *Cymbeline,* as told
by Boccaccio. The boastful husband, who bets on his
wife's chastity, is a sumpterman of Waltham, " not farre
from London—in the troublesome reigne of Henry the
sixt." The villain—Shakespeare's Iachimo and Boccaccio's
Ambrogiuolo—hiding under Mistress Dorrill's bed, waits
till she is asleep. Then he steals the crucifix that lay next
to her heart and carries it to her husband as a proof of her
dishonour. The enraged husband sends his trusty servant,
George, to bid his wife come to him at Enfield, but with
secret orders to kill her on the way. George spares her
life. Disguised as a boy, she wanders northward, where
she meets Edward Duke of York, into whose service she
enters as a page. At the battle of Barnet her husband is
taken prisoner by the Yorkists and the villain left on the
field for dead. There Mistress Dorrill finds him, and on
him the crucifix. She nurses the rascal back to life. He
confesses his crime, and her innocence is vindicated.

Even pastoral romance was brought closer to real life
and made the vehicle of a picaresque narrative. In *Piers
Plainnes Seauen Yeres Prentiship* (1595), Piers tells his
adventures in the service of a courtier, a usurer and a miser
to his master, Menalcas, and his friend, Corydon, until
" the Euening Starre is up," while shepherding his sheep
among the pastures of the Vale of Tempe. The promised
continuation never appeared. Probably the attempt to
engraft low life on the knightly pastoral repelled courtly
patrons without attracting the new and respectable public.

In telling the life of a criminal, Lodge followed Greene,
and in making his rascal a popular hero made a bid for
success. His *Life and Death of William Longbeard* (1593)
is the career of a daring ruffian, who so endeared himself

to the people by protecting their interests against those in authority that he defied arrest.   At last, smoked out of his refuge in Bow Church, he was captured and hanged.   Like Greene, Lodge was careful to vindicate morality.   Not only was his villain executed, but he made a most edifying end. The book met the same fate as Greene's *Black Bookes Messenger*.   It seems to have fallen from the press still-born.

In another direction, Lodge had already shown his sympathy with the democratic movement by attempting to adapt an old romance for popular reading.   Abandoning the prose poem and its artificialities of style, he rewrote in bald prose the romance of *Robert, Second Duke of Normandy, surnamed Robin the Diuell* (1591).   Taking the medieval story as his foundation, he professes to correct it " out of the old and ancient antiquaries," and claims to " stand not so much on the termes, as the trueth."   The age was not sufficiently sophisticated to write or enjoy an historical novel.   It paid verbal homage to history by taking real personages as characters ; but it had no feeling for its sanctity, no conception of chronology or geography, no interest in the exact reproduction of the manners and customs of the past.   Lodge does not hesitate to make *Theagenes and Chariclea* as well known at Babylon in the days of Robin the Divell as it was to Elizabeth and her courtiers.   In love with Emine, daughter of the Emperor of Rome, the Soldan of Babylon justifies himself to his princes by a reference to the pages of the Greek romance. " Theagines a Greeke, loued Cariclia a Moore, & your Souldan a Mahometist, his Emine a Christian."

Similar experiments were made by other writers in popularising the older forms of prose fiction.   Thus Nicholas Breton blended with romantic idealism realistic details of contemporary life in *The Miseries of Mavillia* (1599).   The democratic note was successfully struck in Richard Johnson's *Red Rose Knight* (1599), who, though the son of King Arthur, was as truly a man of the people as Robin Hood. But the best known of the writers who attempted to infuse the democratic spirit into romantic fiction was Thomas Nashe, the zealous champion of Robert Greene against the ill-natured Gabriel Harvey.   He was twenty-seven when he wrote *The Unfortunate Traueller, or the Life of Jacke Wilton* (1594).

Five years before its publication he had, in his *Anatomie of Absurditie*, denounced attempts

> " to repaire the ruinous wals of *Venus* Court, to restore to the worlde that forgotten Legendary licence of lying, to imitate afresh the fantasticall dreames of those exiled Abbie-lubbers, from whose idle pens proceeded those worne out impressions of the feyned no where acts, of Arthur of the rounde table, Arthur of litle Brittaine, sir Tristram, Hewon of Burdeaux, the Squire of low degree, the foure sons of Amon, with infinite others."

The protest suggests that, if Nashe himself attempted a work of prose fiction, he would be a searcher after truth to contemporary realities. The opening scene of *Jack Wilton*, in which the hero practises his knavery on the " peere of quart pottes—the greate Lorde of Syder," fulfils the implied promise. It is the most vividly realistic picture of contemporary life which English prose fiction had yet produced. For a parallel it is necessary to return to Petronius. On this ground alone, the forgotten book would deserve to be revived by M. Jusserand and edited by Sir Edmund Gosse.

Had Nashe continued in the same vein, and used his flexible plot to describe contemporary life above and below stairs, his book would have been of enduring interest. But he either made his experiment half-heartedly, or found that the influence of the old romance was still too strong. Jack Wilton tells his " owne tale," and tells it with humorous intention. Starting as a page, he travels as a servant to the Earl of Surrey, changes places with his master, and marries a rich and beautiful Italian, Diamante Castaldo. The scenes are laid in France and Italy, not in England, and in the time, not of Elizabeth, but of Henry VIII. History is used as a cover for melodramatic improbabilities at least as great as the " feyned no where acts" which he condemned in his predecessors. The story bristles with real events like the siege of Leyden, or with real personages like Erasmus and More, Luther, Carlstadt and Cornelius

Agrippa. But chronology goes to the wall. In one instance he falsified history with remarkable success. The episode of Surrey and the fair Geraldine, though it reads like a satire on the idealisms of love, was for many years accepted as authentic fact. Nashe fell, as it were, between two stools. Neither historical novelist, nor realistic painter of contemporary society, he remained, as he said himself, an " outlandish chronicler."

Jack Wilton has a literary interest as the first notable figure in a long line of English adventurers. But the difference between it and the picaresque narratives of Spain is marked. Jack Wilton is not a professional rascal, at war with the world, glorying in his profession, and held up to admiration for the ingenuity of his subterfuges. On the contrary, he is " sweet Jack " to his master, and not his enemy. The choice of a *chevalier d'industrie*, instead of a knight-errant, as a hero is significant of the democratic trend of literature. Yet neither Nashe nor his contemporaries, who tried to pour the new wine into the old bottles, caught the popular taste. With the exception of *The Cobler of Caunterburie* and Richard Johnson, they failed to attract the new public. University wits and literary Bohemians were ill qualified to catch the true significance of the popular movement. Between them and the civic and social life of prosperous citizens, their journeymen and apprentices, a gulf was fixed. They could paint, from their own experiences, the inhabitants of the underworld of the metropolis, who, in rags or tarnished finery, lived by their wits, the nimbleness of their fingers or the sale of their persons. But of the interests, activities or ambitions of the " Worshipfull Companies," craft-guilds and workshops of London and the provinces, they knew little or nothing. Yet it was here that the popular forces were gathering which transformed England. The spirit of the movement needed as its interpreter one who knew from inside the new world of trade and labour.

It found expression in Thomas Deloney, whom Nashe calls " the Balleting Silke Weaver of Norwich," and the prodigious success of his novels proves his intimate knowledge of the needs of an artisan literature. Throughout the seventeenth century, and even later, *Jacke of Newberie* (1596–7), *The Gentle Craft* (part i., 1597 ; part ii., 1599 ?) and *Thomas of Reading* (1600 ?) were, in various forms, repeatedly reprinted. None of Deloney's contemporary rivals had had his experiences among his fellow-craftsmen, in the provinces, as well as in London, or had served his successful apprenticeship in the art of instructing and entertaining popular audiences.

Details of Deloney's life are meagre.[1] The date or place of his birth is uncertain. Of his early years nothing is known. Contemporary allusions to him only begin when his reputation as a ballad-writer was recognised. Circumstances suggest that he may have belonged to the colony of French or Walloon refugees. He was certainly not unlettered. His first literary enterprise (1583) was the translation of a Latin tract, and he had absorbed a miscellaneous mass of reading from romances, jest-books, historical, dramatic and ballad literature. As a novelist, however, his real education lay, not in books, but in men, in his training as a tavern minstrel and in his humorous observation of the realities of everyday life.

In 1586 Deloney published his first collection of ballads, and rapidly established himself as the poet of the people. His themes were as various as the parts that a minstrel was required to fill ; now, a metrical paraphrase of historical episodes from the chroniclers ; now, a versified scene from medieval romance ; now, a sentimental ditty of domestic life ; now, rhymed news-sheets, serving up hot to his public events of the day ; now, fired by patriotic pride or religious feeling, some ringing lines of dignified verse. In these different subjects he exercised and perfected his gift of narrative in simple, forcible English. In 1596 he offended the Government by a lost ballad on the scarcity of bread. When he emerged from hiding, it was as a writer of prose fiction. Thus, in his own literary career, he illustrated the transition from stories told to listeners to stories written for readers.

The known facts of Deloney's career are collected in the admirable edition of his *Works* by Mr. F. O. Mann (1912). More recently, M. Abel Chevalley has published a suggestion study of *Thomas Deloney et le Roman Corporatif*, of which the first chapter appeared in *Le Navire d'Argent* for February 1926.

Deloney's three novels were published between 1596 and his death in 1600. Familiar though he was with romances of the Middle Ages, it was not through them that he approached his task ; and where, as in " the pleasant History of S. Hugh " in *The Gentle Craft*, their influence is strongest, his own work is feeblest. He was rather the true heir of the more plebeian traditions of medieval and Tudor jest-books. As the sixteenth century advanced, these miscellaneous collections of anecdotes changed their form. Grouped round some central figure, they were approximating to picaresque narratives of a hero's adventures. Popular jest-books, imported from Germany and Northern Europe, like *Howleglas*, *The Parson of Kalenborowe*, *Frier Rush* or *Dr. Faustus*, all possessed this unity: Native writers followed the lead. They gathered their " Geystes " or " Merie Tales " round persons who were celebrated, like Scogan, the Court fool of Edward IV, for practical jokes, or for wit like " Master John Skelton, Poet Laureat," or were notorious in their profession like Long Meg of Westminster, or, like Friar Bacon, had names to conjure with. On the lines of this movement Deloney worked. With one distinctive difference, his *Jacke of Newberie* might have been entitled the *Geystes* of John Winchcomb. Deloney gives his hero an individuality with which none of his predecessors had invested their central figures. But nothing shows the source of his inspiration more clearly than his treatment of love. In his novels it is not a romantic passion ; it is, rather, as in jest-books, provocative of laughter and stratagem, the main element in his comic underplots.

Deloney constructs his novels as Elizabethan architects built their humbler homes. As they filled the interstices between their timber uprights and crossbeams with brick or rubble, so Deloney used a framework of history or tradition, and filled in the spaces with material freshly drawn from contemporary life. The two parts of *The Gentle Craft* form a history of the shoemakers' trade ; *Jacke of Newberie*, a real personage, and *Thomas of Reading*, a more legendary figure, are histories of the trade of the Clothiers and Clothworkers. But the interest of the books lies less in history than in the graphic details of Elizabethan realities, drawn from his own humorous observation of his fellow-artisans.

Deloney gathered his material in the provinces, as well as in London. Following his trade in various centres of the textile industry, and especially in Berkshire, he stored his mind with local customs, traditions, dialects, folk-lore, folk-songs, topographical features of roads and the countryside. These he wove into and round the careers of his two Berkshire celebrities. In his hands, for instance, the vague tradition of the murder of Thomas Cole by the " Ost and Ostess " of the Crane at Colnbrook becomes a vivid, powerful scene, in which the forebodings of the old man and the splash of blood on the hand of the woman are almost worthy of Macbeth. Settled in London, and living among his fellow-artisans, he used his humorous, observant eyes to similar purpose. He gathered the material for the pictures in *The Gentle Craft* of aldermen and master-workmen, journeymen and prentices, City dames and serving-wenches, minstrels and swaggering bullies, which he set in the background of familiar streets and of the full-blooded, tavern-haunting life of Elizabethan London.

By freeing himself from romantic traditions, and by painting what he saw around him in the world of labour and of trade, Deloney opened a new field of prose fiction. For his time, also, his humour, his character-sketches and the briskness of his dialogue are remarkable. But among novelists he had few imitators, and none succeeded. Here and there the names of novels suggest imitations of *The Gentle Craft*. Contents, however, sometimes belie titles. Thus *The Honourable Prentice : or, This Taylor is a Man* (1615), by W. Valens, is not a work on Deloney's lines in praise of the tailor's craft. It is, on the contrary, a life of the famous soldier, Sir John Hawkwood, who preferred the sword to the needle. The son of an Essex tanner, and apprenticed to " a Taylor " and " linnen Armorer," he took service in the army, " rather willing to be so imployed then to sit all day on a shoppe boord making trusses, sowing stockins, or fashioning, or shaping of Garments." One avowed follower Deloney found. William Winstanley, in

The Honour of Merchant-Taylors (1668), states that he was fired to write his history by " the general acceptance " of *The Gentle Craft* by " the *Cord-wainers* " and of " the History of the *Six Worthy Yeomen of the West*, and *Jack of Newbery* by the *Weavers*." Four-fifths of a lifeless production are devoted to Hawkwood and the fortunes of two pairs of lovers. The book only deserves mention as evidence of Deloney's prolonged popularity.

On the development of realistic prose fiction Deloney's influence was small. Needy men of letters were forced to consider their livelihood, and if Deloney, as a contemporary says, was " buried honestly," he had " died poorly." Apart from the growing absorption in politics, two other reasons may be suggested for the neglect of a promising line of advance. One is the rivalry of the stage. Dekker, Chettle, Middleton, Heywood, Samuel Rowlands appropriated the field in which Deloney was a pioneer, and novelists avoided competition with the all-conquering playwrights. The other reason is the fascination which religious questions increasingly exercised over the classes to whom Deloney especially appealed. The growing interest in the external realities of contemporary life was diverted into another channel by the vivid realisation of the internal and spiritual conflict of the human heart. A foretaste of the coming movement is given by Richard Johnson's *Seaven Champions of Christendom* (1596), which owed its prolonged triumph mainly to the blend of religion with chivalry. As the seventeenth century advanced, the true rivals of Deloney in popular favour became writers like John Reynolds with *God's Revenge against Murder*, or John Bunyan with *The Pilgrim's Progress*, who appealed more strongly to the same uncourtly audiences.

In an age so rich in imperishable literature it may seem waste of time to ransack the dust-heap of forgotten books. But, apart from their interest as experiments in prose fiction, Tudor romances and novels played a considerable part in the private life of our ancestors. They fascinated and enthralled successive generations. Ardent spirits might make their own romance, scour the Spanish main or singe the beard of the King of Spain. In London, spectators

K A

might crowd the scanty spaces of the Curtain, the Black-
friars or the Globe to see Falstaff, Beatrice and Benedick,
or Malvolio play their parts. But the great mass of the
inhabitants of the country were home-keeping men and
women. They never saw a play or had the opportunity to
stretch their limbs and gaze on wider horizons than those of
their immediate surroundings. To them prose romances
and novels supplied a growing need. During long winter
months it was not Shakespeare or Spenser who varied the
entertainment of cards, dice, chess or shovel-board. It was
the writers of prose fiction, like Robert Greene and his
fellows, who supplied the stories which, as Burton says,
"some delight to hear, some to tell, and all are well
pleased with." Literature can, perhaps, afford to forget
their experiments; but in the history of social life they hold
a definite place.

CHAPTER IX

In the development of English novels, the Stuart period seems, at first sight, to be a period of complete stagnation. Elizabethan experiments were discontinued, promising lines of advance abandoned. National energies seemed to be absorbed in the triumphs of the drama ; English writers of prose fiction made little head against foreign invaders ; French heroic romances swept them from the field. The world was peopled with princes and princesses disguised as shepherds and shepherdesses, with Medes and Egyptians, ancient Romans and Merovingians, moving in surroundings as remote as themselves from history, probability or experience. Yet even beneath the surface of these unpromising masquerades is revealed a growing respect for truth to nature and for imitation of real life, which bore fruit during the first half of the eighteenth century. The almost simultaneous appearance, in France, of Le Sage, Prévost and Marivaux, and, in England, of Defoe, Richardson and Fielding, shows that, in both countries, the novel was awakening to a consciousness of its special place in literature.

Why did *Jack Wilton* (1594) wait a hundred and thirty years for *Moll Flanders* (1721) ? The main reason—and it is common to both France and England—is that prose fiction was still in search of itself. Writers had formed no clear view of their aim, the form which their art should take, the province which it could legitimately claim from epic poets or dramatists. The interest of the century lies in tracing the halting steps by which they advanced towards the organisation of a new species of literature. Gradually they seemed to see that, on the quest for truth, both internal and external, they might establish an independent literary art. By degrees they recognised that life must be, not merely invented or imagined, transcended or degraded, but observed, copied and reproduced as faithfully as their means allowed. They learned that their actors, within as well as without, must be recognisable likenesses of real men and women, and that their methods must be accurate observation, truth to nature, the working-out of character through the action of the narrative. Advance was hesitating ; but, when once writers had definitely turned in the right direction, progress became rapid.

Throughout the greater part of the century, French influences predominated in prose fiction. Both in France and in England the movement towards nature, facts and individuality was favoured by the success of character-sketches, by the multiplication of letters, autobiographies and memoirs ; and, above all, by the triumph of prose comedies of real and contemporary life. In both countries, a reaction against the ideal extravagances of heroic romance provoked an equally exaggerated farce in novels of low or middle-class society. Truth lay between the two extremes. Yet the new writers were protesting, in the name of common sense, against the excessive licence of the imagination. They were appealing from its insincerities to living models and to likenesses that every contemporary could criticise. But, apart from the interest of parallels or contrasts in the literary or social history of the two countries, some detailed reference to the progress of prose fiction in France is necessary. French influence went beyond predominance. During more than half the period, France supplied English readers with the bulk of their romances, and, later, of their short novels. It was in the works of foreign writers that our Stuart ancestors sought their light reading. They adopted as their own the prose fiction of France.

In 1607–10 appeared the first two parts of D'Urfé's *Astrée*. The dust of three centuries lies thick upon the romance. Yet *Astrea* once ruled the fashionable world of France with an absolute sway that few ·oks have ever rivalled. The third part was published in 1618, the fourth and fifth in 1627—two years after the author's death. Both the method of publication and the construction of the romance illustrate a difference between readers of yesterday and of to-day. Only a leisured age could wait twenty years to know whether Celadon and Astrea were made happy, or could tolerate the seventy subordinate histories which impede the march of the story.   At the time, neither drawback checked the immense popularity of *Astrea*. Dramatists took from it the subjects of their plays.   Corneille and Bossuet borrowed its materials.   St. François de Sales, Fénelon, La Fontaine, Racine, Boileau acknowledged its charm.   A century later, the boy Rousseau was reading the book through the night till the swallows twittered under the eaves ; or, a pilgrim to the scenes of the story, was asking his way to Le Forez so eagerly that he was supposed to be seeking work at its forges.

The form of *Astrea* was new in French literature ; but D'Urfé was not its originator.   He owed it to the *Diana Enamorada* of Montemayor, which the curate in *Don Quixote* spared because it was the first book of the kind.   Englishmen have an additional reason to spare it, because the episode of Felismena supplied part of *The Two Gentlemen of Verona*.   The love-scenes between Diana and Sireno, told in prose and verse, are idyllic and pastoral in their setting ; but with them mingles the medley of characters, incidents, subordinate histories, fighting, magic and giants which characterised the prose fiction of the day.

On this union of the pastoral idyll with the romance of chivalry Sidney had framed his *Arcadia*.   On it also D'Urfé moulded *Astrea*.   His choice was suited to the times.   The most artificial form of literary fiction, an Arcadia of shepherds, can never have been accepted as a reality.   But, by contrast with contemporary conditions, visions of the peaceful simplicity of pastoral innocence have sometimes seized the popular imagination.   They did so after the French Revolution.   They did so, also, at the dawn of the seventeenth century.   Weary of fifty years of civil and religious strife, satiated with the cynical licence of the courts of the Valois, France was willing to dream of pastoral peace and honest love.   D'Urfé may have thought that an unrelieved pastoral was too insipid for a martial age.   At any rate, he does not abandon the romance of chivalry. He denounces fighting and tournaments as outrages to humanity. Love, not war, is the occupation of his community. Yet war remains an accident of their lives, and, when the necessity arises, Celadon doffs his female disguise and fights like a Paladin.

In spite of its length, its iterations and insipidities, *Astrea* comes near to being a great book. If social influence is a test, it achieved greatness. In prose fiction, it made three notable advances. For the first time, love is recognised as the sovereign passion of the novel. Early romance writers had acknowledged its power to inspire knightly prowess. Amadis, sure of the love of Oriana, was invincible ; banished from her presence, he was as one dead. But the interest of medieval stories lay rather in perils and adventures than in the course of love. Its onset is irresistible as fate, its inception mechanical, its triumph instantaneous. A dart from Cupid, a magic potion, a vision of surpassing beauty—and hero or heroine is overpowered. The most individual of passions, it is treated impersonally and uniformly. But in *Astrea* its moods are discriminated, analysed and illustrated by episodes subordinated to the main story of Celadon and Astrea.

D'Urfé is not duped by his idealism. He knows that love-making is not always a polite art, or tinged with Italian Platonism. Valentinian and Eudoxia, for instance, impersonate the animal passion which pastoral writers had embodied in satyrs, or Montemayor in giants. So also Hylas, gay and witty, stands for the inconstant lover, the ancestor of Don Juan and Lovelace. He alone refuses the test of the magic pool, which, if love is faithful, reflects both lover and loved, because no mirror could contain the images of all the ladies whom he loved.

In two other respects, D'Urfé improves on previous writers of romance. His scenery is not that of some imaginary kingdom of Nowhere. It is a faithful picture of the district which he knows best, the *bienheureux pays* of Le Forez, which surrounds the home of his childhood and youth. Similarly, his figures are not invented without regard to truth or probability ; they are drawn from insight and observation. Reality is not the goal of *Astrea* ; but it is its starting-point. The book, though it attempts no exact delineations of D'Urfé's contemporaries or of the society of his day, abounds in living touches from his own experience. Thus the note of political disillusionment is a memory of his own championship of a lost cause ; the constancy of Celadon echoes his own youthful passion for Diane de Châteaumorand ; King Euric, who masks his statecraft under a genial joviality, suggests Henri IV ; Galatea, who flatters her own vanity by playing the game of love with the coquetry of a woman and the caprice of a princess, is reminiscent of *la reine Margot*, whose prisoner he is said to have been at Usson, in Auvergne.

As a pastoral writer D'Urfé had few imitators. Of more immediate importance was the social influence of *Astrea*. The romance presents a new conception of the relationship between men and women, founded on the honour of both. It is a challenge to the *Vies des Dames Galantes* of Brantôme. In the preceding period, men had often shown their readiness to die for women ; with rare exceptions, they had not learnt to live in their company. They had treated them with a mocking courtliness which scarcely veiled contempt for the instruments of their pleasure. *Astrea* makes women the centre of society—objects, not merely of desire 'and pursuit, but of respectful homage and devotion. Thus the book became the breviary of a social revolution.

It was the manual of the receptions at the Hôtel de Rambouillet, which opened its doors about 1618. In her *salon bleu*, hung with pastoral scenes in blue-green Flemish tapestry, Catharine de Vivonne, Marquise de Rambouillet, gathered a distinguished company, who came to enjoy the art of brilliant conversation—general, literary, political or psychological. Her object was not only to refine the manners and morals of French society. She sought also to encourage its intellectual tastes and accomplishments. Her example was followed at the receptions of other great ladies. Men and women of letters met men and women of fashion on an equal footing. Before audiences which were critical as well as appreciative were read, for the first time, such works as Corneille's *Cid*, or parts of the *Lettres Provinciales* of Pascal. The *salons* became arbiters of literary as well as of social taste.

On the course of prose fiction the immediate influence of D'Urfé was slight. The stream flowed too strongly in the old channels. Men who were fighting in the Thirty Years' War and the Fronde, or conspiring against Richelieu and Mazarin, might be weary of knights-errant ; but they still hungered for mighty sword-play. Heroic romancers chronicled the exploits of princes, cast in superhuman mould, who led armies and overthrew kingdoms. Surpassing the medieval or Spanish favourites in their interminable length, outdoing them in intricacy of construction, they confounded the confusion of their narratives by imitating the Greek romances and beginning in the middle. Yet, as the century advanced, the prodigious popularity of Gomberville, Calprenède and Madeleine de Scudéri owed much to their success, not only in satisfying the craving for adventure, but in meeting the growing taste for the authentication of inventions by geography, history or contemporary life, and in striking the note of refined gallantry which was required by social changes and the criticism of the *salons*.

The most representative writer of the school is Madeleine de Scudéri. To-day her romances are frankly unreadable. But the skill with which the *Grand Cyrus* (1649–53) and *Clélie* (1656–60) are constructed to gratify a variety of popular tastes is remarkable. The world thirsted for adventure, and perils are multiplied with lavish hand. Its passion for grandeur of sentiment and achievement was gratified by characters who were demi-gods of history. In the street men adored military prowess ; in the *salon* Julie de Rambouillet platonically worshipped Gustavus Adolphus, the Lion of the North. In the *Grand Cyrus* Scudéri painted a heroic warrior who attacked battalions single-handed, and, as Sir Walter Scott calculated, slew with his own hand 100,000 men. The taste for reality was growing. Not only had the Cyrus of history actually conquered kingdoms, but, under the disguise of his exploits, were circumstantially described the recent victories of Condé at Lens, Rocroy or Charenton.

Paris and the provinces were curious to know the features and the habits of their social leaders. Both the *Grand*

Cyrus and *Clélie* were galleries of portraits, highly idealised but recognisable by contemporaries, of the lords and ladies, soldiers, ecclesiastics, academicians and other men and women of literary or social distinction, who frequented aristocratic *salons* or the Saturdays in the *Quartier du Marais*. The tastes and amusements attributed by Scudéri to the Medes, Persians or ancient Romans were really those of contemporary Paris. The promenades of brilliantly dressed women in smart carriages and of well-mounted horsemen enlivened, not only the banks of the Choaspe, but the Cour la Reine which fringed the Seine.

Life at watering-places, excursions on the river, country-house parties, stag-hunts, concerts, musical serenades, surprises (*cadeaux*) are described as the recreations of Sardis centuries before Christ ; they were actually the rage of Parisians in the days of the young *Grand Monarque*. Prince Mexaris, who in the *Grand Cyrus* shows to the Princess Penthea his collections of pictures, statuary, plate and furniture, had many rival collectors in contemporary France, from real personages like Nicolas Fouquet to heroes of fiction like Jean Bedout, the hosier's son, in the *Roman Bourgeois*. Boileau justly condemns Scudéri's travesty of history. But when he blames her for modelling ancient Romans on inhabitants of the *Quartier du Marais*, unintentional praise lurks in reproof. She was at least drawing from the life around her.

Above all, Scudéri satisfied the ideals of the *salon*. Her moral tone is severe ; her sentiments are noble ; her law is duty. In her romances, especially in *Clélie*, are discussed with sound judgment most of the problems which arose out of the position of women in modern civilisation. From her romances, also, may be gathered the social code of refined intercourse which Madame de Rambouillet and her friends established. The *honnête homme* was one who had served his apprenticeship and won his place in polite society by his desire to please rather than to shine, by his consideration for others, his willingness to listen as well as to talk, his tact and sympathy—in one word, by his *galanterie*. In *Clélie*, when the young Mucius Scevola asks Spurius how to acquire these qualities, he is told to become a lover.

It was essential to the education of a member of polite society.

The *Carte du Pays du Tendre* maps out, in jesting mood, the stages by which new acquaintances reach something warmer than ordinary friendship. Tender feelings are founded on respect, gratitude or attraction. To reach *Tendre-sur-Estime*, or *Tendre-sur-Reconnaissance*, the new acquaintance must be constant in his devotion, zealous to serve, skilled in the sonnet, apt at compliments, tolerant of caprice, prompt to defend, generous to forgive. Whether esteem or gratitude ripens into love is immaterial for the training of the *honnête homme*. More is learnt by loving than by being loved, for the one expands the soul, while the other may only flatter the vanity. To win a wife, much less a mistress, is not the necessary goal of the polite lover. It is enough that Sylvander and Clytimène should become intimate friends, meeting, to use D'Urfé's phrase, in *honnête amitié*. But Scudéri does not forget the emotion which springs from attraction. It is the passion of love. Though it is not her province, she recognises its existence on her map. Along the road to *Tendre-sur-Inclination* there are no delays, no stopping-places ; the stream which waters the town is a headlong torrent, pouring itself into the Sea Dangerous, beyond which lies, in misty outlines, the Unknown Land.

Buried in the many thousand pages of Scudéri's two romances are signs of real advances towards the art of prose fiction. Human nature is studied, contemporary life observed. Dramatic situations are developed by the play of natural feelings. Varied characters take individual parts in conversation. But the figures are dead, and the length, the complications and the childish improbability of the incidents render the romances to modern taste insufferable. If Mademoiselle de Scudéri, could have concentrated her gifts on a single episode, she, and not Madame de la Fayette, might have written the first modern novel. In one of her subordinate histories, for instance, she introduces the eternal trilogy of the husband, the wife and the lover. Duty wins a hard victory. Would it win a second time? Scudéri cuts the knots by the death of the husband. Dying of his wounds, he commends his wife to the keeping of her lover. Rewards of virtue and happy endings are dear to novelists as well as to comic dramatists. The lovers marry. With the difference of the ending, Scudéri anticipates the story of Madame de la Fayette's *Princesse de Cléves*.

The *Princesse de Clèves* (1678) appeared eighteen years after the publication of the last of the ten parts of *Clélie*. In construction it makes an immense advance. The book is short, the form compact, the unity of the plot unbroken by subordinate narratives. The manners and customs described are those of the Court of Versailles under Louis XIV, though, without any sense of historical incongruity, the scene is laid in the times of Henri II. The story itself is true to all time, for it is a tragedy of the human heart and of married life. With one great exception, the interest of older romances had ended with the marriage of the hero and heroine. Madame de la Fayette discovered the married woman. The Princesse de Clèves finds that she returns the love which Monsieur de Nemours lays at her feet. She cannot, as a more frivolous woman might do, ignore her growing passion. She examines it, probes it, and realises her weakness and her danger. In vain she struggles. At last, in despair, she tells her adoring husband, and begs his help. If he would suffer her to retire from Court, her self-respect would preserve her worthy of his love. He lets her go, though the sacrifice wounds him to the heart. Struck down by fever, he has neither the will to fight against it nor the wish to live. His death sets her free. But can she enjoy a happiness which her own fault has brought within her reach ? She decides that she cannot, bids her lover farewell, and parts from him for ever.

The bare outline of the story shows how far we have travelled from medieval or heroic romance and advanced towards the modern novel. It is, with one exception, the only work of seventeenth-century fiction which the world still reads. The one exception is Bunyan's *Pilgrim's Progress*, the first part of which appeared in the same year (1678) as the *Princesse de Clèves*. Religious allegory though it is, it is also the first English novel. Wide are the differences in the national and social development of France and England which are suggested by the juxtaposition of the two books.

Even in its most idealistic forms, prose fiction was thus approaching closer to realities. It came still nearer to life in the burlesque. When Madame de la Fayette wrote, a group of writers had already protested, in the name of truth to nature, against the insincerities and affectations of pastoral and heroic romance. Among them stand out Sorel, Scarron and Furetière. Sorel, parodist and satirist, champions the moderns against the ancients. In Scarron the *esprit gaulois* rebels against the *esprit précieux*. Narrower in his purpose, Furetière shows the corruption of citizen virtues by aping the Court. But, different as the three writers are from one another, they resemble each other in the choice and treatment of their subjects. Their heroes and heroines are not of princely rank, cast in heroic mould. They are, as Furetière says of his characters, men and women of the ordinary type, soberly plodding the common highway of life, some handsome, some ugly ; some wise, some—and these the majority—fools. Taken together, the three writers present a comprehensive picture of the Third Estate in the seventeenth century; schoolmasters, lawyers, shopkeepers, strolling players, parish priests, peasants, professional rogues, beggars and vagabonds; all painted from life, not as it might be imagined or invented, but as it was actually lived in contemporary Paris and the provinces.

The chief weapon of attack on heroic romances is contrast in the choice of contemporary subjects and in their realistic presentation. Sorel alone attempted parody. In the *Berger Extravagant* (1639) his Lysis is the Don Quixote of pastoral romance. The hero mistakes *Astrea* for real life, and tries, with ludicrous consequences, to live in the Paris of Louis XIII like a shepherd of ancient Gaul in the wilds of Le Forez. In his *Francion* (1622) he had already used the more indirect weapon of contrast. He never acknowledged the authorship of an amazingly popular book, which is said to have passed through sixty editions. Probably the pungency of the satire, written under the influence of Rabelais, on schoolmasters, lawyers and men of letters, made anonymity the safer course.

Francion is a forerunner of Gil Blas, a poor young gentleman with a short purse and a long sword, who encounters
many adventures in pursuit of his beloved Naïs. Not the
least interesting portion of the book is the study of the
mind of a child—rare in early fiction—tortured by the
Gargantuan education at the *Collège de Lisieux* in the
University of Paris.

Scarron's method of attack in the *Roman Comique* (1651–7)
is that of *Francion*. To the tremendous adventures of
superhuman princes and princesses he opposes the
haphazard fortunes of a band of strolling players. The
unfinished book has no plan. One chapter suggests another,
one adventure a second. Such a method of composition
was not unsuited to the happy-go-lucky lives of people
who knew not in the morning what might be their fate at
nightfall. Scarron has the eye of an artist, or a caricaturist,
for telling details. His scenes, like that of the players'
entry into Le Mans, are vivid, full of life and colour. Their
subsequent adventures, often coarse but never prurient,
are told with an infectious gaiety, which, in a paralysed
cripple, racked with constant pain, is amazing. The book
abounds with sly hits at the fashionable romances.
Mademoiselle de Scudéri introduces into *Clélie* not only
Scarron's famous wife, Françoise d'Aubigné, afterwards
Madame de Maintenon, as Liriane, but Scarron himself as
Scaurus. Was she avenging herself on her critic by the
choice of the somewhat unsavoury name ?

Sorel, and still more Scarron, aim at raising a laugh.
Their equal in wit, but soured and morose, Furetière is more
definite in his purpose than either of his predecessors. In
his *Roman Bourgeois* (1666) he paints a picture of citizen
life which is valuable to social history. The Vollichon
family really live. Even the rascally father is redeemed by
his love for his children. But his daughter Javotte has her
head turned by romances, jilts her betrothed, a well-to-do
youth of her own class, and elopes with a *précieux*. The
second part contains, among disconnected sketches,
the suggestion of a tariff of charges for a place in heroic
romances, the scale proportioned to the valour or beauty of
the character. Deadlier than the example of the fate of

Javotte was the insinuation that the *Grand Cyrus* and *Clélie* were peopled with contemporary heroes and heroines who had paid for their portraits.

When once the heroic romances of France invaded England, they gripped the taste of the nation " like glue." Their hold upon this country long outlasted their credit at home. Proofs of their popularity might be multiplied indefinitely, both from fact and fiction. From them post-restoration dramatists drew many of their plots. Among their readers were Charles I and Jeremy Taylor. In the *Apologie for Romances*, which Sir George Mackenzie, the " Bluidy Advocate " of Covenanting and *Redgauntlet* fame, prefixed to his pedantic romance of *Aretina* (1660), he foretells that henceforth all romances would be cast " in the mould of Scudérie." Dorothy Osborne " wept an hour for Almanzor," and " flew in a rage " with Alcidiana. Mrs. Pepys annoyed her husband by sitting up late over the *Grand Cyrus*, and telling long stories from her favourite romance, " though nothing to the purpose, nor in any good manner." Lady Mary Pierrepoint (afterwards Wortley-Montagu) devoured heroic romances, and treasured the works of D'Urfé, Calprenède and Scudéri enough to leave them by will. On a blank page of her favourite *Astrea*, she has written two columns of the names and characteristics of the principal figures, such as " Celadon the faithful," " the wise Adamas," " Climène the volatile."

The library of Leonora, in the *Spectator*, contained the *Grand Cyrus*, " with a pin stuck in one of the middle leaves," and *Clelia*, "which opened of itself in the place that describes two lovers in a bower." Even as late as 1752 it was thought worth while to satirise those who, like Lady Arabella in Mrs. Lennox's *Female Quixote*, modelled their lives on Calprenède and Scudéri. The evidence of Miss Mulso, afterwards Mrs. Chapone (born 1727), is fact, not fiction. Though she became a pioneer in the moral training of the young, she was herself brought up on French romances. " I have (and I am yet alive)," she writes, " drudged through *Le Grand Cyrus* in twelve huge volumes, *Cleopatra* in eight or ten, *Polyxander*, *Ibrahim*, *Clelia* and some others, whose names, as well as all the rest, I have forgotten."

One further illustration may be quoted, because it brings out the relative poverty of the English output. In 1673, Francis Kirkman prefaced the first part of the Spanish *Honour of Chivalry* with the claim to " have long since read " all the extant prose fiction, and with a list of the tales available. He advises a course of medieval and Spanish romances of chivalry. He also recommends the books of three Elizabethans, one of Sidney, one of Greene, and three of Emanuel Ford. But the only native works of Stuart times which he mentions are *God's Revenge against Murder*, by John Reynolds, and three romances which were not printed till the Protectorate, namely : *The Renowned History of Fragosa, King of Aragon*, parts i. and ii., a worthless but short production (1654), consisting largely of letters ; Broghill's *Parthenissa* (1654) ; and Ingelo's *Bentivoglio and Urania* (1660).

In contrast to this meagre output of four books by contemporary English writers, he enumerates, without claiming " to be exact in this Catalogue," existing translations of the romances of D'Urfé, Gomberville, Calprenède, Scudéri and other writers, including three by Biondi, and the *Grand Scipio* of Vaumorière. He concludes by saying that even these romances, though " not long since in great esteem with the *French* and *English* Nobility and Gentry," are now " thrust out of use by the present slighting and neglect of all Books in general & by particular esteem of our late *English stage Plays*." Kirkman rightly attributed the decadence of prose fiction to the triumph of the drama. But he miscalculated the vitality of the French invaders. Their predominance lasted beyond the close of the century.

CHAPTER X

THE STUARTS : NATIVE WRITERS

By stages, similar to those followed in France, English prose fiction crept towards the novel of real life. For the greater part of the Stuart period it showed few signs of independent growth. Novel readers remained faithful to such Elizabethan favourites as Sidney's *Arcadia*, Greene's *Dorastus and Fawnia* or Ford's *Parismus*, each of which, before 1660, had passed through twelve editions. But, for the most part, they lived on fiction imported, not only from France, but from Greece and Rome, Italy and Spain. Greek and Latin romances, like the *Theagenes and Chariclea* of Heliodorus, the *Clitophon and Leucippe* of Achilles Tatius, or the *Golden Ass* of Apuleius, were republished in their Tudor dresses. Italian influence, so dominant in the last half of the sixteenth century, survived in the first complete version of Boccaccio's *Decameron* (1620), and in translations of romances of Machiavelli, Biondi and Loredano.

The fiction of Spain found more favour. Introduced too late, poorly translated, and published piecemeal, Spanish romances of chivalry never laid any firm hold on the cultured classes. But Cervantes was eagerly welcomed. It is significant that, during the seventeenth century, his short stories eclipsed the fame of his greater work. Shelton's translation of *Don Quixote* (1612–20) was followed by Mabbe's version of the *Exemplary Novels* (1640), which were repeatedly republished in various forms. Still wider was the range of Spanish romances of low life. *Lazarillo de Tormes* in his Elizabethan dress, and *The Rogue, or Guzman de Alfarache* (1622) begot a numerous progeny of English, French, Scottish, Irish and Dutch *chevaliers d'industrie*, who took the place of the older knights-errant.

The triumphs of the drama, the fascination of foreign, and especially French, romances, the uncertain scope and limits of the novelist's art, even the stately magnificence of contemporary prose, discouraged the development of an independent school of native writers of prose fiction. Still more unfavourable was the cloud of theological controversy, religious earnestness and political seriousness, which gathered and darkened till it broke into civil war. Nothing could be more alien to the increasing gravity of the period than the literary fashions which prevailed at its opening. Both in style and substance, fiction could hardly have assumed a more fantastic or artificial form than it did in Sidney's pastoral, Greene's " love-pamphlet " or Ford's romance of adventure. Yet the popularity of the *Arcadia* waxed rather than waned.

Besides being frequently republished, it was continued by several hands, including that indefatigable hack-writer, Gervase Markham (1607). It was imitated by Lady Mary Wroth in *Urania* (1621). It was supplemented, adapted, condensed, dramatised, versified. But, except Ben Jonson in *The Sad Shepherd*, no dramatist or romance writer tried to give the pastoral a realistic texture or to nationalise its traditional machinery. Nor did any English D'Urfé apply it to social or moral purposes. Yet, probably through the influence of *Astrea*, platonic love crept into the Court at Whitehall. " Little news at present," writes James Howell in 1634, " but there is a love call'd Platonick Love which much sways there of late."

In different circumstances the Court, already the centre of art and refinement, might possibly have led a movement in London similar to that in Paris. The country houses of the Duchess of Newcastle and of Mrs. Katharine Phillips were feeble copies of the Hôtel de Rambouillet. Social life in England lost something in grace and refinement, and the loss was reflected in the grossness of its prose fiction. But French ladies were more fortunate in their opportunities than their English contemporaries. Puritans would not have tolerated the social leadership of women. More vividly impressed by her share in the Fall than in the Redemption, they associated woman with Eve rather than with Mary.

It was through politics that the prose fiction of the period
LA

made its first experiment in the realities of life. *Argenis* appeared in 1621. Written in Latin and published at Paris, its author, John Barclay, was born in France, the son of a Scottish father by a French mother, married a Frenchwoman, and lived almost all his life in France. Both a political treatise and a heroic romance, *Argenis* has a definite plot. It also introduces, under classical names, and with strongly drawn characters, such real personages as Philip II of Spain, Henry III and Henry IV of France, Catherine de Medici, Queen Elizabeth, the Guises and Calvin.

Translated by two different hands, it made some stir in courtly circles, and its success probably suggested to James Howell, the letter-writer, a similar venture in English. His *Dodona's Grove* (1640) three times reprinted, owed its popularity to its political interest at an exciting time. " The prime vertue of story (says Howell) is verity." What there is of plot, incident or character is founded on recent events and contemporary careers. The threatening situation in " Cardenia " (Scotland), for instance, is discussed. Never had " Tamisond " (London) flourished more with building and bullion and " Bravery of all things." But " a mist " was rising in " Cardenia," where " obstreperous Sermocinators " swayed consciences against " Druina " (England). The damp climate of Scotland, it may be added, goads Howell to call her the " Urinall of all the Planets."

Political tension urges others to use romantic fiction for the ventilation of their views on Church and State, or for the construction of ideal worlds. In the discussion of the relations between England and Scotland, for instance, lies the chief interest of Mackenzie's *Aretina*. But these and similar experiments, before writers had learnt to tell a story, draw a character or reproduce a conversation, can only be classed with prose fiction by a strain of language.

Political discussion was not the only purpose for which prose fiction was employed. Even more in keeping with the gravity of the times and the moral earnestness of Puritanism was its use for religious instruction in short stories, in serious romance or in allegory. The appeal to the "Christian Reader" gave to the thirty "Tragicall Histories," which John Reynolds wrote or translated to illustrate *The Triumphs of God's Revenge against the . . . Sinne of Murther* (1621–3), a great and prolonged success. It is not uninteresting to note that Henry Fielding occupied some weeks of his closing years and failing health in a work of similar scope. In 1752 he printed his thirty *Examples of the Interposition of Providence in the Detection and Punishment of Murder*. Like Reynolds, he appealed to a popular audience. Fifty years later, William Godwin was writing *Caleb Williams* (1794). Trying to paint the tortured conscience of an undiscovered murderer, he fired his imagination by reading " a tremendous compilation, entitled *God's Revenge against Murder*, where the beam of the Eye of Omniscience was represented as perpetually pursuing the guilty, and laying open his most hidden retreats to the light of day."

In his serious romance of *Bentivolio and Urania* (1660), Nathanael Ingelo addressed a more courtly public. He attacks " the impertinencies of Mankind," including " the Writing and Reading of Romances." His Bentivolio (Good Will) is a worthy champion, who, in pursuit of Urania (Heavenly Wisdom), subdues " several *Bravo's*, which infested the Regions of *Anthropia*." Cold and dull though the book is, it had a considerable success. But it was in religious allegory that the prose fiction of Puritanism gained its greatest triumph. Richard Bernard's *Isle of Man : or, The Legall Proceeding in Manshire against Sinne* (1626) had reached a fifteenth edition before the publication of the first part of *The Pilgrim's Progress*. A less successful effort, Thomas Bayly's *Herba Parietis : or, The Wall-Flower* (1650) deserves mention because it grew " out of the Stone-Chamber " in Newgate Prison. A quarter of a century later, John Bunyan used his imprisonment to better purpose.

The coincidence of the publication of the *Princesse de Clèves* and the first part of *The Pilgrim's Progress* in the same year (1678) has been already noticed. Bunyan holds in our literature the same place which Madame de la Fayette holds in that of France. In spite of his allegorical form he, is the first great English novelist. All the requisite gifts are his. In *The Pilgrim's Progress* there are constructive power, rapid narrative, crisp dialogue, purposeful description, an eye for telling detail, and, above all, vivid characterisation. For its purpose the style is perfect. A man of few books, but saturated with the pure English of the Authorised Version of the Bible, Bunyan also commands a wealth of vernacular expressions, from which he selects, with admirable skill, the picturesque phrases sanctioned by homely use. The intensity with which he sees his imaginary world enables him to reproduce his mental visions with a force that makes Milton's pictures of Heaven and Hell, by comparison, shadowy and dim. His autobiographical fragment, *Grace Abounding*, reveals one source of his power. He writes his own experiences. It was across some quiet Bedfordshire lane that Apollyon straddled in all his terrors, and swore that Bunyan himself should go no farther.

Bunyan's dramatic instinct held his allegory in check. But the religious teaching blinded partisans to his literary genius. For years to come he had no imitator in the art of drawing character. England still hankered after tales of adventure. Political or religious romances, which cannot legitimately be classed as novels, still found a formidable rival in prose fiction of the more ordinary type. It is a mistake to suppose that Puritans banned prose romances as sternly as they did stage plays. Novelists were not, like actors, condemned to be whipped. The Press had never been more busy with prose fiction than it was during the period of Puritan ascendency (1647-60). An escape from the grim actualities of life was needed, and publishers gauged the public taste more accurately than painful preachers. Between those years were published translations of Rabelais, D'Urfé's *Astrea*, Sorel's *Francion* and *Berger Extravagant*, Gomberville, Calprenède, Scudéri, and other novelists, Italian and Spanish, as well as French. To this period also belong a number of native romances, such as *Fragosa, Cloria and Narcissus*, Braithwaite's *Panthalia* and Broghill's *Parthenissa*.

Parthenissa (1654), the best-known imitation of heroic romances by any English writer, was written by Lord

Broghill, one of Cromwell's most trusted counsellors. Dorothy Osborne read it, noted its " handsome language," condemned the flatness of its incidents and the excessive amiability of its ladies. Her criticism is just. The romance is long and dull. Its scenes are laid in unknown countries. Its history is false ; Hannibal and Spartacus are both contemporaries of the hero, Artabenes. Parthenissa herself only appears once, if at all. She, or some lady resembling her, is seen to enter a thicket with a young man. Whether the lady was really Parthenissa, or what happened in the wood, the author, even in six parts and a huge folio, failed to reveal, and the public were content to leave her in the grove.

Other English imitators were even less successful. They reproduced the defects without the merits of their models. They never attained to the real elevation of sentiment which often redeems some of the unrealities of French heroic romances. They added a vice of their own. From Sidney they had inherited the delusion of the prose-poem. The lure was fatal. Their fancy luxuriated in fantastic paraphrases and extravagant conceits which overlaid the simplest meaning. Crushed by the additional burden of absurdities of style, they failed as they deserved. Heroic romances remained exotics. John Crowne's *Pandion and Amphigenia* (1665), in which the " Coy Lady of Thessalia " could not decide to take a lover, found few readers. *Eliana : A new Romance formed by an English hand* (1661) was equally neglected. The book was anonymous. But its probable author, Samuel Pordage, intended, if the first part succeeded, to reveal his name and continue his story. Despising the " Mordacity " of the wits, he relied on the judgment of " those fair and wise ones of the *female sex*, whose delight I chiefly aim'd at." Woman proved as critical as the wits. Like *Parthenissa*, the book was never finished. No Englishman of genius protested against the bombastic, stilted style which was considered appropriate to the prose treatment of heroic subjects. The battle for naturalness was fought, without any conscious literary purpose, by obscure writers who, as a matter of business, burlesqued the artificialities of fashionable romances.

The reaction against romantic insincerities of matter and style showed itself, as in France, in realistic representation of the low life of contemporary England. *The English Rogue* (1666) is not a heroic knight-errant of an obsolete chivalry ; he is a rascally knight-errant of industry, whose exploits are his knaveries and debaucheries among the citizens of the London of the Plague and the Great Fire. Modelled on the picaresque fiction of Spain, as well as on *Francion* and the *Roman Comique*, the first part alone is the work of Richard Head. The rest seems to have been written by Francis Kirkman, whose portrait is the frontispiece to the third part.

In *The English Rogue* a faithless wife explains the consequences of her intrigue with a negro by quoting at length the precedent of the " fair Ethiopian." Except in this burlesque of *Theagenes and Chariclea*, heroic romances are not directly attacked. The challenge rather lies in the choice and treatment of contemporary life and in the rough-and-ready vernacular style. The use of circumstantial detail to authenticate invention is another sign of the times. Even adventures must be made plausible. The ship's log of the voyage of Meriton Latroon from Bantam to Venice anticipates the methods of Defoe. As a whole, the book has so little merit that nothing but its indecency has probably saved it from complete oblivion. Yet, filthy though the book is, it has a literary interest. It connects the *Jack Wilton* of the Elizabethans with the *Jack Singleton* and *Moll Flanders* of Defoe and Hanoverian times. But if a blend of invention with fact constitutes fiction, it is not the first or only link. Already George Fidge, in *The 'English Gusman* (1652), afterwards republished as *The Yorkshire Rogue*, had told the story of James Hind—a notorious highwayman credited with waylaying Cromwell—who was, as a Royalist, hanged, drawn and quartered at Worcester in 1652 on a charge of high treason.

A prose fiction was growing which dealt with realities of contemporary life. The picture which it presented might be exaggerated farce ; but it could not deviate far from truth. Every reader knew someone like the characters, and could compare copies with models. As with actors,

so with surroundings. The action occurred in definite
places, and the most squalid ale-house, or worse, must be
accurately described. In England this literature was, in
the main, imported. Before the end of the period, Sorel,
Scarron and Furetière had been published in English. The
Spanish Rogues were already widely known. Now the
English Rogue had appeared, and, within the next twenty
years, he had been joined by a Frenchman and a Dutchman
of similar character.

Heroic romance was menaced by the contrast with the
growing literature of real life. It was also directly attacked
by burlesques, like the translations of Sorel's *Extravagant
Shepherd* (1653), or Subligny's *Mock-Clelia* (1678), in which
a girl imagines herself to be Scudéri's heroine and flees from
every man as if he was her Roman persecutor, Horace.
Native writers tried their hands on similar burlesques.
Samuel Holland's *Don Zara del Fogo* (1656) is a travesty of
medieval and Spanish romances of chivalry rather than of
heroic romances. The knight invokes all deceased worthies,
especially St. George, who, to win the Soldan's daughter,
slew " a Python (*x* acres in length)," and rides forth in
quest of adventures, more amorous than martial. Falling
under the spell of Lamia, he visits, under her guidance,
the nether world, which he finds in an uproar. " *Ben
Johnson* " (*sic*) vaunts himself " the first and best of English
Poets " ; " Chawcer " resents the claim ; and all the poets
take sides in the dispute.

Zelinda (1676) is a direct and amusing attack on heroic
romances. Professing to be a translation from " Monsieur
de Scudéry," it is founded on a story by Voiture. The
heroine is a paragon of perfection. It is, says the writer,
only when he speaks of her that his book is incredible.
Her love for Alcidalis is returned ; but the usual accidents
intervene. The moment came when Alcidalis mounted
" to his Heaven—the Window," and " prostrated himself
at the Shrine, the Bed of his Saint. Like a gay plum'd
Phœnix, wrapped in perfumes, and languishing in Flames
of Love, she lay and trembled like a new yean'd Lamb upon
a Sheet of Snow."

Ridicule, no doubt, contributed to the decline of heroic

romance. But fashion struck the deadliest blow by decree-
ing a shorter form of prose fiction. *Clelia*, for instance,
with its eight thousand pages, its three hundred and fifty
characters and proportionate number of subordinate
histories, is forty times the length of the *Princess of Cleves*.
Space to sprawl encouraged literary indolence. There was
no compulsion to frame a plot, select significant incidents,
choose purposeful details of description, break up interminable speeches into the give and take of real conversation.
Compression necessitated improvements in the art of story-
telling. They did not follow at once. But the reduction
of length was in itself a great advance. The *Exemplary
Novels* of Cervantes had already popularised a shortened
form of story, which in the last twenty years of the Stuart
period became almost exclusively the fashion.

Even in the new form France still predominated. A
hundred novels, translated from the French of Scarron,
Madame de la Fayette, Gabriel de Brémond, and many
others, flooded the book-market. Native writers were
slow to enter the field. Among the first was Lord Broghill,
with his *English Adventures* (1676), of which Henry VIII is
the hero. Even the bait of indecency failed to catch the
public, and his promise to continue the story with the
experiences of Charles Brandon was never redeemed.
Incomparably better work was done by Aphra Behn, the
first woman who, in England, earned her living by her pen.
Her character has unduly suffered from the malice of Pope.
Next to Bunyan, she is the most arresting figure among
Stuart novelists. A hard-working, warm-hearted, unconven-
tional woman, vivacious and witty, with a true touch of lyric
genius, she has been not inaptly compared to George Sand.

Mrs. Behn's *Love Letters of a Nobleman to his Sister* (1683)
appears to modern readers a worthless production, except
as an early example of a story told by letters. To her
contemporaries the book made a stronger appeal. Published
in the year of the Rye House Plot, it is founded on an
episode in the life of Lord Grey, a prominent adherent of
the party of the Duke of Monmouth. While the Duke was
intriguing with Lady Grey, Grey eloped with her sister,
Lady Henrietta Berkeley. Arrested for complicity in

the plot, he had escaped and was, at the time, a fugitive in Holland. Grey and Lady Henrietta, under the names of Philander and Silvia, are the Nobleman and the Sister —or, rather, Sister-in-law—of the *Love Letters*. Philander urges his love on Silvia, pleading that there could be no treachery to her unfaithful sister. Silvia appeals to her lover not to support the man, by whom he was being wronged, in a plot against a generous father, and warns him not to hope to govern a fool. Mrs. Behn evidently shared Grammont's contempt for Monmouth's intellect. At last Silvia yields, and the lovers meet. Fearing discovery, and escorted by Philander's servant, she takes refuge in Holland. There she is joined by Philander, who by bribing his guard had escaped from arrest. Based on actual facts, the story makes a notable advance towards realistic fiction.

Of her other novels, six, including the three best— *Oroonoko*, *The Fair Jilt* and *Agnes de Castro*—appeared before the Revolution (1686–8). Frequently reprinted in the eighteenth century, they have been republished within the last twenty years. Allegory excluded, *Oroonoko* is the most notable novel of the century. It retains many of the faults of the heroic style. But Mrs. Behn tells her story vigorously, with evident sincerity, and she brings into it her real knowledge and experience of life in Surinam. The element of local colouring, found also in *The Fair Jilt*, might alone have kept the book alive. But it drew vitality from another source. It expressed ideas which later generations put to a destructive use. Her Oroonoko is a noble savage, living in " the first state of innocence, before man knew how to sin." Nature is his law. He practises virtue instinctively; the sanctions of natural religion suffice. His magnanimity and fidelity to his spoken word put civilisation to shame. Mrs. Behn anticipates Rousseau, and *Oroonoko* is an ancestor of *Émile*.

Prose fiction, as Aphra Behn left it—she died in 1689— came nearer to the modern novel than it had stood at the accession of James I. For the most part the period records the failure of an experiment. Heroic romance survived into the next century; but it had never taken root as a native growth, and its strength was plainly already spent.

Other literary fashions had sprung up more congenial to the soil. The way had been prepared, mainly by translation, for a literature of real life. During the next thirty-five years the change seemed to come with surprising suddenness. The influence of literary ancestry upon genius can never be measured. It may be great or nothing. But Addison, Steele, Defoe and Swift were at least the heirs of the obscure and often unfruitful labours of Stuart writers of prose fiction.

CHAPTER XI

A BOOK-BOX OF NOVELS (1689–1724)

IN some country-houses the arrival of the book-box from the circulating library is still something of an event. The interest is not confined to the present generation, though formerly the books were bought, not borrowed. A voluntary exile, Lady Mary Wortley-Montagu, lived in Italy from 1739 to 1762. Alert in mind, keen in her varied interests, her letters show her craving for tidings of her friends and for literary news. She asks her daughter for books, and is impatient for their arrival through the British Consul at Venice. On one occasion the box came in her absence.

" After having rode twenty miles, part of it by moonshine, it was ten at night when I found the box arrived. I could not deny myself the pleasure of opening it ; and, falling upon Fielding's works, was fool enough to sit up all night reading."

Most of the books that Lady Mary ordered are now completely forgotten. Her list for 1757, chosen from advertisements in the newspapers, consisted entirely of novels. " I do not doubt," she says, " at least the greatest part of these are trash, lumber, etc." Her daughter, Lady Bute, was plainly of that opinion. Lady Mary defends her favourite amusement :

" Your youngest son is, perhaps at this very moment riding on a poker with great delight, not at all regretting that it is not a gold one, and much less wishing it an Arabian horse, which he would not know how to manage. I am reading an idle tale, not expecting wit or truth in it, and am very glad it is not metaphysics to puzzle my judgment, or history to mislead my opinion."

For many years after the flight of James II, colonies of English, Scottish and Irish refugees were living on the Continent. After the " Fifteen " their number was swollen by Jacobite exiles. Imagine the members of one of these families, who had found an asylum at Dijon or Avignon, and shared the literary tastes of Lady Mary. What were the novels during the period of 1689–1724 for which they would have asked, or that friends in England would have chosen because they were read or discussed at home ?

Both in quality and in quantity the choice was limited. Few notable novels were produced at home between the appearance of *Oroonoko* (1688) and that of *Robinson Crusoe* (1719). Even in quantity the output was poor. During the reigns of William and Mary and of William III, it was, in fact, extraordinarily small. In this respect history did not repeat itself. Politically, the period was a lull after a storm. When Puritanism seemed established under the firm rule of Cromwell, or when the Royalist reaction was apparently secured at the Restoration, the printing press poured out a stream of prose fiction. It was not so in the fifteen years following the Revolution. Scarcely more than twenty-five novels have survived to tell their tales. These were not huge folios. They were thin duodecimo volumes, so that the whole output might have been packed in a single book-box.

One reason for this poverty of production was the fact that the novel was still in search of itself. The temper of the times was positive, inclined to analysis and criticism. Its growing taste for fact and detail was fed by the multi-plication of biographies and autobiographies, journals and diaries, historical annals, the records of travellers and navigators, character-sketches, which studied individuals, though as yet only as types. On many sides there was a marked tendency towards realism. Ideal romances were out of date. But writers of prose fiction were still undecided in which direction to turn. They had not yet learnt that truth to life was the essence of their art, and that in the representation and interpretation of the contrarieties of human nature they might find fields which they could make their own. For the time, no general advance was possible,

owing to the continued predominance of French fiction
and to the immense popularity of the stage.

The French supremacy had changed its form. Heroic
romances of the school of Calprenède and Scudéri had never
been really naturalised in England. Now they were ceasing
to be even an exotic fashion. Yet, in shortened form, they
still found admirers who sought refuge from the coarseness
of the age in their idealised creations. The most popular
romance of the moment, written by an English hand,
belonged to the heroic type. Published in 1687, *Cynthia :
with the Tragical Account of the Unfortunate Loves of Almerin
and Desdemona* rapidly reached a tenth edition. In an
unreal country, at an unknown date, Orsamus and Cynthia,
the monotonously perfect hero and heroine, pass through
the stock adventures, told in the " handsome " language
appropriate to the prose poem, before they are allowed to
marry. It is in favour of the book that it is a duodecimo
volume, and not a folio. But, even in this shortened
form, fame and fortune were not to be won by English
writers from heroic romance. No progress in the art of
novel-writing was to be expected from this discredited
type.

Nor was advance in truth to life or in character-drawing
promoted by the historical love-stories with which, in the
last quarter of the century, French writers flooded the
English market. The labels on the volumes paid formal
homage to history ; the contents were the wildest inventions.
Few famous men or women of the past escaped the ravages
of writers like Gabriel de Brémond, Madame de Villedieu,
the Comtesse d'Aulnoy or Mademoiselle de la Roche Guilhem.
They had discovered that scandal gains in savour when it
is invented of a Dunois, or an Emperor of Morocco, of a
Duchess of Mazarin, or a " Queen Ann of Bullen." Not
even Solon was spared a mistress, and he interrupts his law-
making to kiss her last note, or, under her inspiration,
indites his maxims of love. English writers seem to have
realised that the market for this special product of historical
love-stories was a monopoly of their French rivals. Few
native novelists tried, by any original work on these lines,
to stem the torrent of translations which deluged the press,

enlarged the circle of novel-readers, and standardised the shortened form of the novel.

The Secret History of the Most Renowned Queen Elizabeth and the Earl of Essex illustrates the effect which these historical love-stories produced on popular conceptions of history. It is one of the few works of the kind written by an English " Person of Quality." Published in 1680, and perhaps founded on a previous work, it was repeatedly reprinted for more than forty years. Untrue to the main facts of history, and in detail purely imaginary, it helped to perpetuate a legend which was long accepted as historical truth. In the first part of the book, Queen Elizabeth confesses to her " intimate confident," the Countess of Nottingham, her love, not for her " sweet Robin," the Earl of Leicester, but for his stepson, Robert Devereux, Earl of Essex. It was this passion, she says, which made her reject the hand of the Duke of Anjou and of the Duke of Alençon. Her joy " to see the Earl of Essex was greater than that for the signal victory attain'd " over the Spanish Armada. When the Earl " fell into Melancholy," she guessed that she was the cause of his sadness, and was " resolv'd to fetch it out of him." Essex admitted that he was sick for love. But when the Queen, expecting a different answer, asked who was the object of his passion, he replied, " The Countess of Rutland."

In the second part, Essex is lying in the Tower under sentence of death. The Countess of Rutland confesses to Lady Nottingham that she was secretly married to Essex, appeals to her to intercede on her husband's behalf, and begs her to hand to the Queen the ring which she had given to Essex with a pledge of pardon if he were in danger from any offence. Lady Nottingham is the villain of the piece. In collusion with Cecil, she holds back the ring, inflames the anger of Elizabeth, and persuades her that Essex thought and spoke of nothing but his love for Lady Rutland. Essex is executed. On her deathbed Lady Nottingham tells the Queen the truth. Elizabeth sickens, and dies of remorse Historians treat the story as apocryphal. It may be pointed out that Essex was four years old when Elizabeth rejected Anjou, was only fourteen when Alençon died, and had been, ten years before his death, publicly married to Frances, daughter of Sir Francis Walsingham, who had borne him five children.

Uncertain of the real scope of their art, smothered by the competition of French rivals, would-be novel-writers were still further discouraged from prose fiction by the immense popularity of the comic theatre. As a native growth, English tragedy was in the last stages of decay. Romantic comedy and pastoral drama were alike extinct. But the comedy of real life was at the height of its triumph. The world flocked to see its manners and morals reflected in the mirror which Congreve, Vanbrugh, Farquhar, Mrs. Centlivre and a swarm of other writers held up to contemporary society.

The playwrights scarcely attempted any drawing of character; but they created types which have been again and again reproduced with such modifications as social changes demanded. In the witty, vivacious dialogue of their prose comedies, in their brisk action, or in their cleverly devised situations, are represented fops and fine gentlemen, with Lord Foppington at their head, braggarts, virtuosos, city aldermen, country boobies, busybodies like Marplot, fine ladies, card-playing wives, English *précieuses* with their affectation of French tastes and French vocables, town misses, country hoydens, Abigails and gentlemen's gentlemen, pimps and procuresses. It was the comic dramatist and not the novelist who painted or daubed, with frankly realistic touches, pictures of men and women in the London of the Stuarts and of William and Mary. Not even Jeremy Collier charged them with exaggeration. The footlights were merciless to unrealities in the representation of contemporary manners; audiences demanded truth and knew when they saw it. If plays were coarse and indecent, so also was the age. Dramatists had no moral standard; but those for whom they wrote had almost as little. Women thronged the theatres, even if they wore masks to save their faces or flocked to first nights lest they should damage their reputations by attending the second performance of a new play.

Prose comedy set the example of the realistic representation of contemporary life. With the model it also helped to supply the means of imitation. Congreve was master of a style which was easy, natural without vulgarity, lively, pointed, epigrammatic. In its flexibility, it was capable of being used for all the purposes of everyday life. The added power and range which the change gave to novelists were immense. Elizabethan and Stuart prose was admirably adapted by its stately magnificence to ceremonial occasions. But it is impossible to imagine a dinner-party described in the style of Bacon, or the fashions discussed in the sonorous periods of Hooker, or some tit-bit of scandal served up in the lofty manner of Milton.

In the hands of inferior writers, the exigencies of such a literary style had much to do with the unrealities of heroic romance. They imposed on story-tellers a pitch of sentiment which was impossible and incredible. Their dignity exacted the wearisome metaphors, periphrases and circumlocutions which deprived writers of directness and simplicity. When a novelist, desirous of saying that night came on, felt constrained to write that " Phœbus, necessitated, yielded place to his sister Cynthia," he was certain to be driven to further absurdities. Lovers confessed their mutual passion, not in the half-strangled incoherences of real life, but in long and high-flown speeches which are wholly unconvincing in their cold elaboration. Now, however, novelists, largely by the help of the comic dramatists, and subsequently of the essayists and letter-writers, were supplied with a prose style which was sufficiently supple to be applied to every use that was required in telling a story in every tone of feeling.

Furnished with a model, and supplied with a style, it was still many years before novelists found themselves. No real advance was made till half way through the reign of Queen Anne, and then the great step forward was made, not by novelists, but by the *Tatler* and the *Spectator* (1709–12). To the representation of real life by the comic dramatists the essayists added the development of character. Novelists hesitated. It was necessary to destroy before it was possible to build. Defoe levelled to the ground the fantastic fabric of the heroic romance. In the barest possible realism were laid the foundations of the new construction. He is the connecting-link between the ideal romance and the novel of real life.

No novel-writer of outstanding merit appeared between the death of Aphra Behn and the advent of Defoe. But the period from the publication of *Oroonoko* (1688) to that of *Robinson Crusoe* (1719) is not barren of interest to students of literary origins. In England, as well as in Spain and France, it was among beggars, or strolling players, or rascally adventurers, that writers served their apprentice-ship in painting from real life. However imaginary the incidents, the setting required observation and accuracy in details. *The English Rogue* of Head and Kirkman (1665) was followed, within a few years after the Revolution, by Scottish, Irish and Welsh Rogues. But the promise implied in the titles of the three books is not fulfilled by the performance. There is scarcely any hint of those national characteristics which afforded such rich material to subsequent novelists. The rogue is the same, whether the scene of his adventures is laid in Ireland or Scotland.

The *Irish Rogue* (1690) has for its sub-title *The Comical History of the Life and Actions of Teague O'Divelly*. Most of the incidents take place in Ireland ; but, like his English model, the hero also takes a voyage, and Spain and France are the scenes of some of the adventures. His name is borrowed from that of the rascally Irish priest who figures in two of Shadwell's comedies. His father was " a Kern or Tory, living by the length of his Sword and the force of his Pistols " on the plunder of the villagers, till he was " hanged in a Wythe," for " an *Irish-man* naturally hates even the scent of Hemp." No other national characteristic is noticed, except that " the Native Irish carry a kind of irreconcilable hatred to the English."

Poor though the book is, it is cleaner and more varied in its incidents than the *Scotch Rogue* (1706). *The Life and Actions of Donald Macdonald, a High-land Scot*, is adorned with a frontispiece of the hero, armed with claymore and target, and clad in tartan jacket and trews. Donald Macdonald is a foundling, who is put to school " to learn the *English* Dialect and . . . the *Latin* Tongue." But he

MA

spends his time at " Cat and Doug, Cappyhole, riding the Hurley Hacket, playing at Kyles and Dams, Spang-Bodle, Wrestling and Foot-Ball." Golf, unless it lurks concealed in some of these unfamiliar sports, does not seem to have been played so far north as " *Skyraffin.*" Eventually the hero robs his foster-father, runs away, and encounters adventures which are monotonously amatory and discreditable.

The series of rogue stories are worthless in themselves. Yet they are not without literary interest. The scenes are laid in countries more or less familiar ; the incidents are possible, and occur in contemporary times. Truth to human nature still lies between the two extremes—between the exaggerated elevation of heroic romances and the exaggerated degradation of the picaresque novelists. But the class of stories to which the series belong illustrate the growing taste for fact and the gathering strength of the reaction against ideal extravagance and unreality. Most of the prose fiction of the day imitates, in shortened form, the model of the older school, and adopts its stilted style. The stories make wearisome reading.

Only here and there does patience meet some slight reward. One illustration will be enough. Readers of novels written in the last fifty years are familiar with the stock device of locking *and double-locking* a door. They know that the extra precaution, and the sense of fancied security which it gives, always prelude a crisis. Expectation is thrilled. Faith in originality is staggered by finding the same expedient in the seventeenth century, when perhaps the mechanism of locks permitted its adoption. In *The Siege of Mentz, or the German Heroin* (1692), Clarinda locks *and double-locks* her lover, Peregrine, into his bedroom in order to prevent his fighting a duel with her unwelcome suitor, Count Mansfelt.

If so trivial a claim justifies the rescue of *The Siege of Mentz* from the dust-bin, other books which have no claim at all may be left in that receptacle. Only three novels of the period 1688-1703 are, for various reasons, deserving of notice. One is *Incognita : or, Love and Duty Reconcil'd* (1692). Another is *The Player's Tragedy : or, Fatal Love, a New Novel* (1693). The third is *The Adventure of Linda-mira, a Lady of Quality* (1702).

The dedication of *Incognita* is signed " Cleophil." Its real author was William Congreve, and the reprint in 1713 bears his name. Apart from the fame of the writer, the book is, in itself, noteworthy for its promise. It is, however, a curious illustration of the strength of literary tradition that so keen an observer of the contemporary life and manners of his own fellow-countrymen should, as a novelist, lay his scene in Florence, and choose an Italian and a Spaniard for his heroes. Yet Congreve, in his Preface, clearly distinguishes between heroic romances and his own novel. The former, he says, are " generally composed of the Constant Loves and invincible Courages of Hero's, Heroins, Kings and Queens, Mortals of the first Rank " . . whose " lofty Language . . . and impossible Performances, elevate and surprize the Reader into a giddy Delight which leaves him flat upon the Ground whenever he gives of." The aim of his own book, produced " in the idler hours of a fortnight's time," is humbler. It is to bring about the happy marriages of two couples who have entangled them-selves in an intricate complication. But he prides himself on being the first novelist to satisfy dramatic laws. His story is completed within three days.

Aurelian, the only son of a wealthy Florentine, has finished his education at Siena. There he has made friends with a young Spaniard, Hippolito. The two young men journey together to Florence. They find the city busied with preparations for the wedding of a kinswoman of the Great Duke. In order to enjoy the amusements, they decide to conceal their arrival. Instead of going to the house of Aurelian's father, they take a lodging and, in borrowed clothes, attend a masked ball. There each falls in love with a lady, and each, when asked his name, gives to his lady that of his friend. Neither knows the state of the other's heart, and each thinks that the other's melancholy and sighs are but the sympathy of friendship. Out of the inter-change of names arise the complications and the conflict between " Love and Duty," which are eventually reconciled. Some vivid details in description, some humour in the situations and some wit in the conversations make the book, even now, readable. Congreve is also the first novelist to adopt the later device of introducing himself to the reader and acting as the showman of his own comedy of errors.

The second of the three books, *The Player's Tragedy*, is noticeable for a different reason. Anonymous, and poorly written, it owes nothing to the reputation of its author or to its own merits. What is remarkable about the novel is that it appears to be founded on a real incident which had horrified London a few months before its publication. It is probably the second instance of such a use of social events by an English novel-writer. On December 9, 1692, William Mountfort, a leading actor of the day, was murdered at his own door in Howard Street, Strand. Jealous of Mrs. Bracegirdle's supposed attachment to Mountfort, Captain Hill, who was himself paying court to the fascinating actress, sought vengeance on his rival. He was helped by Lord Mohun, then a boy of seventeen. While Mohun held Mountfort in conversation, Hill, from behind, struck the actor a heavy blow on the back of the head, and, before he had time to draw, ran him through the body. Mountfort died the following day.

It seems certain that it is on this event that the novel is founded. Bracilla, "the Young, and the Charming," is an actress who had "grown up on the Stage." She had shown a "cold indifference" to all her admirers, till she met Monfredo, who is described as a playwright as well as an actor, and as excelling on the stage in the part of a lover. A young soldier named Montano adored Bracilla. He wrote her letters and verses in which he eloquently pleaded his passion. But she paid him no attention. Gerardo, an experienced man of the world, explains to the ardent young lover that an actress is only moved by money, and that, through one of the convenient ladies who act as go-betweens, he must ascertain and pay Bracilla's price. An aged gentle-woman is accordingly employed, who occupies a consider-able part of the book in narrating her experiences. By a trick she passes off on Montano a female client of her own as Bracilla. When the young man discovers the deception, he kills Monfredo, in whom he imagines a successful rival.

It is scarcely possible to doubt that Bracilla represents Anne Bracegirdle, who, as a child, was brought up by Betterton and his wife. No real value can be attached to the evidence of such a book ; but, for what it is worth, the story confirms the moral reputation which the actress bore in her profession. A few years later, it may be added, Mrs. Manley, in the *New Atalantis*, refers to Mrs. Bracegirdle under the name of Bracilia as " the Usefullest as well as the most agreeable Woman of the Stage." The description of Monfredo is also appropriate to Mountfort, who wrote several plays, and, according to Cibber, was, as an actor, especially excellent in the *rôle* of a lover. There is no special resemblance in Montano to Hill, except his name and his description as a captain in " His Majesty's Gens d'armes." Perhaps from prudence, the writer makes no reference to Mohun, who had been acquitted of the murder.

The third book, *The Adventure of Lindamira*, is, on its merits, the most noteworthy of the three. It is the first novel of English domestic life, and the writer anticipates Richardson by telling his story in the form of letters. The author gives his name as T. Brown. Whether the book is the work of the man of " facetious memory " is uncertain. It is not generally included among his publications. But, whoever he was, he writes easy, colloquial English. In his preface he declares his purpose :

" If the Histories of Foreign Amours and Scenes laid beyond the Seas, where unknown Customs bear the greatest Figure, have met with the Approbation of English Readers, 'tis presumed that Domestick Intrigues, managed according to the Humours of the Town and the natural Temper of the Inhabitants of this our Island, will be at least equally grateful. But, above all, the weight of Truth, and the Importance of real Matter of Fact, ought to overbalance the feign'd Adventures of a fabulous Knight-Errantry."

In the preface to this obscure novel is the manifesto of the new school of prose fiction.

Lindamira tells the story of her life in a series of twenty-four letters to her friend Indamora. In the affectation

of the names and the introduction of the irrelevant episode
of Doralissa, the author, as it were, pays formal homage
to heroic romance. But the story itself, told in simple
style, confines itself to probabilities in the contemporary
life of England. Lindamira, young and apparently good-
looking, has her admirers in London. Rather to her mother's
dismay, she will have nothing to say to the foppish young
gentleman of the Temple who is possessed of a good estate.
She cannot tolerate her next suitor, Sir Formal Trifle, whose
name is borrowed from Shadwell's comedy, *The Virtuoso*,
and, like his prototype, is a pedantic prig. She would rather,
she says, " have been shut up in some horrible vault with
Ghosts and Hobgoblins, Screech-Owls and Bats, than to
have been the Bride of so nautious and disagreeable a
Man." After this episode, she is sent out of London to
stay with her grandmother. With her maid she sets out in
the stage-coach. At Highgate they take up two passengers.
One of them, a young barrister of Lincoln's Inn named
Cleomidon, proves to be all that her heart desires in face,
mind and figure. The attraction is mutual. Lindamira
rejects with scorn the suit of her grandmother's chaplain,
and, when she meets her fellow-passenger by accident in
the country, they become lovers. Cleomidon has the
prospect of succeeding to a good estate belonging to his
uncle. But he must marry to the taste of the old man,
who has already chosen his nephew's wife. Lindamira
discovers this obstacle, and, sooner than injure her lover's
worldly prospects, sacrifices herself. Without telling him
her reason, she sends him about his business. Hurt by her
seeming frivolity of purpose, Cleomidon marries the plain,
disagreeable woman whom his uncle had chosen for him.
Her death sets him free. Meeting Lindamira again, he
finds that she has remained true to her first love. All ends
happily with the marriage of Lindamira " up to her wishes."

   Lindamira, as has been already noted, is the first novel—
for *Euphues* is not an exact parallel—in which a continuous
narrative is told by letters. The novelty lies, not in the
correspondence, but in the use to which it was put. Imaginary letters, which had never been really exchanged, had
become, in the course of the previous half-century, something

of a literary fashion. Occasionally used in the old romances to authenticate the accuracy of the chronicle, they were employed by Lyly in his *Euphues* to expound his views on religion and education. Nicholas Breton, in his *Poste with a Packet of Mad Letters* (1603 ?), extended their use to a great variety of topics. The amazing popularity of *God's Revenge . . . against the Sinne of Murder* (1621–3) owed something to the one hundred and forty letters on miscellaneous subjects which are tabled in the contents as an attractive feature. Margaret Cavendish, Duchess of Newcastle, in her *CCXI Sociable Letters* (1664), used them in an amusing fashion to paint scenes which illustrated " the Humors of Mankind." *Five Love-Letters of a Nun to a Cavalier* (1678), like the translation of the letters of Eloisa to Abelard, bring us closer to the method of Richardson. Lindamira only told the incidents of her life ; she did not, like the Portuguese nun, reveal the heart of a woman betrayed. The *Five Love-Letters* were, in the next thirty years, frequently reprinted, with or without the *Answers of the Chevalier Del.*

It was with an imitation of the letters of the Portuguese nun that Mrs. Manley began her career in prose fiction. *A Letter from a supposed Nun in Portugal* is added to her letters describing *A Stage Coach Journey to Exeter* (1696). In this latter book Mrs. Manley imitates Madame d'Aulnoy, whose *Ingenious and Diverting Letters* (translated 1692), described Spain, its people, scenery and buildings, with some spirit and vivacity. Interspersed with Madame d'Aulnoy's descriptions are stories of adventure told by fellow-passengers, and each letter is dated with the time and place at which it was supposed to be written. Within a few years the book had reached its tenth edition. On this model Mrs. Manley founded her coaching journey, each letter dated from the halting-place of the coach, and mainly consisting of the experiences of the passengers.

If Mrs. Manley can be relied on, the coach halted every night, started in the summer between two and three in the morning, was attended at its departure by all the beggars in the neighbourhood, dined at ten off a heavy joint, and did not travel on Sundays. The thin duodecimo volume is a trumpery production, inferior to the same writer's *Court*

*Intrigues in a Collection of Original Letters from the Island
of the New Atalantis* (1711). Of these forty-one letters, two
or three are not without a faint interest. In the story, for
instance, of the elusive Mrs. Lucas, a sketch of country life
is painted with touches of colour which contrast not un-
pleasantly with the generalities and stock epithets of
conventional descriptions.

In her letters, Mrs. Manley imitated her French
predecessor. In her *Power of Love : in Seven Novels* (1720)
she followed Mrs. Behn, without her sincerity. Unlike her
model, she blends no incidents of real life with her tales of
foreign countries, which, in their ferocity, recall the worst
of the melodramatic horrors of Cinthio. The book failed, as
it deserved, and the promise of further stories was not
fulfilled. Her chronicles of the scandals of society struck
out a newer line. To them she owes her place in the history
of the development of prose fiction. In her portraits of
personages of the day, however exaggerated, she was
obliged to paint recognisable likenesses, to rely on the
interest left in men and women as individuals, and to
be accurate as well as distinctive in some at least of her
details.

Strictly speaking, neither *The Secret History of Queen
Zarah and the Zarasians* (1705), nor *The New Atalantis*
(1709), nor her own life told as *The Adventures of Rivella*
(1714) can be classed as novels. Immensely popular, they
were read, not as works of fiction, but, under the thinnest
veil, as records of fact. To prevent any doubt as to the
persons intended, keys were published with later editions.
In these society chronicles, Mrs. Manley followed the
methods of the French historical love-stories, and, with
remarkable audacity and a larger admixture of truth,
applied them to contemporary life. Her preface to *Queen
Zarah* explains her object. " The Romances in *France*,"
she says, " have for a long Time been the Diversion and
Amusement of the whole World . . . but that Fury is very
much abated. . . . The Little *Histories* of this kind have
taken Place of *Romances*." The writers of these histories
" ought not to chuse too Ancient Accidents, nor unknown
Heroes, which are sought for in a Barbarous Countrey, and

too far distant in Time, for we care little for what was done a Thousand Years ago among the *Tartars* or *Abyssines*." Mrs. Manley makes no such mistake. She took her material from life in her own time and country.

The first part of *Queen Zarah* is a scandalous history of the rise of the Duke of Marlborough, and of the Duchess Sarah, whose mother was " Janisa, a Woman who mov'd in a low Sphere." In *The New Atalantis*, Virtue and her daughter Astrea revisit Angela (London). They arrive at the moment of the death of William III. Moving unseen through the crowds, they observe the consolation which " great Anna " and her " She-favourite " take, not in tea, but " in sparkling Champaign." They watch the statesmen hurrying to pay their court to the new sovereign. The " graceful person that appears upon the high Loll in his Chariot and six Horses," is " Count *Fortunatus* " (Marlborough). In the " Prado " (the Park) all the well-known figures pass before Astrea, under fanciful names, and few of the Whig nobility escape some scandalous charge.

Reference is made to the story of General Talmash, " sent upon a desperate attempt to lose his life upon a distant shore." The private morals of Somers and Halifax are attacked with circumstantial details. In St. John, " all that is eminent is but borrowed from Fontenelle and Rochefoucault." As a popular orator, none is " more vigorous, fuller of Motion, more vehement in Speech and Gesture," than Bishop Burnett ; but his character is " marred by the snares of Beauty, Pride, Faction, and some other Vices." Sir Richard Blackmore is described as " an Æsculapius run mad after Apollo," who " prescribes in Verse, eats, drinks, sleeps, walks, rides in Verse." Addison is " Maro," whom " Politicks and sordid Interest have carried out of the Road to Helicon."

As an aspirant to dramatic fame, Mrs. Manley handles actor-managers tenderly. Betterton, born for everything " that he thinks fit to undertake," would have been " eminent in any Station of Life he had been called to." Rival playwrights receive fewer compliments. Mrs. Centlivre is " a wonderful gay lady," who " either sings well or thinks she does." " That Black Beau (stuck up in a pert Chariot), thick-set, his Eyes lost in his head, hanging Eyebrows, broad Face, and tallow Complexion " is Richard Steele. Against him she bore a grudge. Speaking of herself in *Rivella*, she says that she was " an utter stranger to what is meant by Hatred and Revenge," except " in the case of Mr. S——e," whose " notorious Ingratitude and Breach of Friendship " compel her to expose him.

The interest of *The New Atalantis*, like that of Eliza Haywood's *Memoirs of a Certain Island Adjacent to the Kingdom of Utopia* (1725), or her *Secret History of the Present Intrigues of the Court of Caramania* (1727), depended on the identification of the real personages who masqueraded under fictitious names. Mrs. Manley was, therefore, driven to note superficial features which distinguished her actors as individuals. For the most part she relies on their personal appearance or on facts and incidents in their public careers. No delineation of character is attempted. But the men and women were those of her own day. The scenes in which they played their parts were close at hand. The unsavoury scandals that she rakes together were, if not invented, contemporary gossip of the backstairs of existing palaces and great houses. Thus, crude, and inartistic though her work is, it has the interest of individual life in the reign of Queen Anne.

The immense advance made by Addison and Steele in the art of novel-writing cannot be more strongly illustrated than by the juxtaposition of the coarsely daubed portraits of Mrs. Manley with the exquisitely finished picture of Sir Roger de Coverley. Yet the writers have this in common. Both reject generic descriptions of human beings as types ; both seek for the distinctive touches which give individuality to their literary sketches.

No creations of eighteenth-century novelists are better known than the little group of figures assembled in the *Coverley Papers*. Sir Roger himself is the most definite, as well as the most lovable, character that had yet appeared in prose fiction. Begun by Steele, and tinged with his habitual sentiment, the study of the old knight was developed and perfected by Addison with a keen humour so

mellow as to overpower the faint blend of his characteristically indulgent cynicism. A very human being, whose
faults and virtues are disarming or engaging from their
simplicity, Sir Roger was fortunate in meeting his death
at the hands of his creators. No coarser workmanship
marred the perfection of the picture. Less elaborately
finished than the central figure, the minor actors are effectively individualised. However small their parts, they
are alive. Subordinated to the human interest is a background of London and provincial life, each scene touched
in with a quiet distinctiveness of colouring which is at
once fresh, delicate and true. With the added charms of
the easy grace of style, and of the indescribable art of
mingling grave and gay, the pensive with the whimsical,
the *Coverley Papers* are a masterpiece of prose fiction.

The methods and the materials employed by Steele and
Addison are those of modern novels. But the biographical
portion of the *Tatler* and the *Spectator* has not the unity
and the continuity which can bring it within any sound
definition of a novel, even in serial form. It is rather the
apotheosis of the character-sketch, which was a favourite
form of the seventeenth-century essay. Sir Thomas Over-
bury, for instance, used the sketch to display his disagreeable wit and crisp antithetical style. With considerable
powers of observation, he draws, in hard outline, among
other types, the representative characteristics of a country
gentleman. Steele and Addison seize on similar traits ;
but they handle them in a different spirit. They do not
exaggerate them for purposes of satire and ridicule ; nor
even, as in Fielding's Squire Western, to heighten the
comic effect. The supercilious, dogmatic tone is dropped ;
the harshness of outlines is softened, as in real life ; the
type is humanised into a living man.

As a masterpiece of character-drawing, the *Coverley
Papers* offered a model to novelists. Had they been cast
in the continuous form of a novel instead of that of detached
essays, the significance of the example might have been
sooner appreciated, and its influence on the development of
prose fiction more immediately felt. The lesson was not
learnt. Among contemporary novelists it had no followers.

The realism of Defoe satisfied, by more direct means, the growing taste for facts and the reaction against extravagances of imagination.   In his aims, as well as in his choice and treatment of subjects, he stands in the baldest contrast to the older writers.   His genius for verisimilitude turned his successors in the right direction.   It gave a new starting-point to the novel.   The portrayal of real life required that nature should be accurately observed and faithfully imitated.   It was in the school of Defoe, and not from the model of Sir Roger de Coverley, that novelists learned to extend the principle to the delineation and interpretation of character.

Defoe stumbled on novel-writing as it were by accident. Born a Nonconformist, and bred to the ministry, a rebel in the days of Monmouth, a merchant " beyond seas," a brick and pan-tile manufacturer, a political agent repeatedly employed on secret missions, a pamphleteer, a satirist in doggerel verse, a biographer, economist, " projector," journalist, editor of newspapers, he lived seventy crowded, strenuous years—1659–1731.   The number of his identified publications is prodigious.   Among them his half-dozen novels appear as a by-product, and a late one   He was fifty-nine when he wrote *Robinson Crusoe* (1719).   But, as Richardson all his life wrote letters, so for many years " unabashed Defoe " had practised the art to which his first novel owed its fame.

Seventeen years earlier, his success in palming off his inventions as facts had condemned him to a fine, the prison and the pillory.   He had published an anonymous pamphlet, *The Shortest Way with Dissenters* (1702), in which he suggested that, to rid England of the " poison," a law should be passed to hang the preachers and banish their congregations.   He wrote, so he afterwards stated, to expose to ridicule the extreme opinions of high-flying Tory Churchmen. But the caricature was so life-like that the pamphlet was accepted, read and discussed as a genuine expression of their views.   When the secret of the authorship leaked out, the Government decided to prosecute Defoe for seditious libel. The ferocity of the punishment can only be explained by political rancour and the exasperation of dupes.   Released from Newgate after a year's imprisonment, he found that his business, such as it was, was ruined. Writing became the chief support of himself and his family. In need of bread, he was not fastidious as to the means by which it was obtained. He contrived to sell his pen to both Whigs and Tories, to persuade each party that he served it exclusively, and to impose himself on the public as " The True-Born Englishman" who was its loyal, independent servant.

Such a career necessarily bred enmities. Many hands were against Defoe. Superior to his antagonists in mental power, literary capacity, command of temper, dexterity and audacity, he turned their attacks to his advantage with the public. Assaults on his character were the penalty of his independence, a part of the martyrdom which he endured in the cause of honesty at the hands of partisans and hirelings. The one taunt which wounded him was that of want of scholarship. It is of himself that he is speaking when he remembers " an author in the World, some years ago, who was generally upbraided with Ignorance and called an Illiterate Fellow by some of the ' *Beau Monde*' of the Age." He gives details of the knowledge which his author possessed, each paragraph ending with the refrain : " Yet this Man is no Scholar."

> " This (he continues) put me upon wondering, ever so long ago, what this strange Thing called a Man of Learning *was*, and what is it that constitutes a *Scholar* ? For, *said I*, here's a man speaks five languages and reads the Sixth, is a master of Astronomy, Geography, History, and abundance of other useful Knowledge (which I do not mention, that you may not guess at the Man, who is too Modest to desire it), and yet they say, *This Man is no Scholar*."

Applied to his own working knowledge of a wide range of subjects, the description of his author's learning is not exaggerated.

To the command of a mass of information, both general and special, Defoe added a natural genius for journalism. A master of every known branch of the art, he was ingenious in devising new expedients. He is credited with the invention of the leading article, or, as it was then called, the Introductory

Letter.   He developed the society paragraph, which increased the circulation of the Press from political clubs and coffee-houses to the boudoirs and tea-tables of private houses.

The first interviewer, he gained from Jack Sheppard the particulars of his life.   An artist in puffing his own wares, he used his information in a manner which might have taught a lesson to the recent Congress of Advertisers.   From the cart, on the way to Tyburn, Jack Sheppard handed to a friend his last dying speech and confession, with a request that it should be printed.   The scene was duly reported in the newspaper ; but it had been arranged by Defoe, and the document was his own narrative.   For the event of the moment he had an unerring instinct.   Even from his cell in Newgate he published, within a few days of the occurrence, a minute account of the great storm of 1703, fortified by letters from all parts of the country, some of which may perhaps have been genuine, describing its " casualties and disasters."   First in the field with circumstantial obituary biographies of celebrated men, he was equally prompt with lives of obscurer individuals who caught the public eye, like Dominique Cartouche, " broken on the wheel at Paris," or Captain Avery, " King of the Pirates," or Rob Roy, whose career he compiled from " an authentick Scotch MS."

With inexhaustible energy, Defoe continued his political and journalistic activities for many years after the accession of George I.   *Robinson Crusoe* was not written in leisured seclusion.   At no time was Defoe more deeply immersed in politics, or more closely connected with the Press. Nominally in opposition to the Whig Government, he was secretly in its pay.   His duty was to gain the confidence of the Jacobites and control of the Tory Press.   He earned his salary.   In 1718 he reported to his employers that three newspapers, still passing as Tory organs, were so ' disabled and enervated . . . as to do no mischief or give any offence to the Government."   In such delicate circumstances, the task of managing, or conducting, or contributing to, at least six journals might well have exhausted his energies ; it stimulated him to write the novels which have made his fame.

Modern research has proved that Defoe did not turn novelist in order to occupy his retirement. So great was the licence that he exercised in dealing with real persons and events that he could scarcely hope to enjoy greater freedom in manipulating the puppets of his inventions. A man of business, he wrote for profit, and no writer of the day was a shrewder judge of the mind of the middle-class Englishman. His experience on the Press had been supplemented by secret missions in various parts of the country, undertaken for the purpose of sounding public opinion. When, therefore, Defoe turned to novel-writing, it was because he believed that he would find a market for a new kind of prose fiction.

The commercial instinct of the veteran literary trader was correct. As civilisation and wealth spread downwards, and, with improved communications, extended from London to the country, a reading public was forming, curious about themselves, eager for facts, anxious for documentary records, suspicious of the imagination, looking askance at enjoyment of its products as something between immorality and waste of time. The reaction from imaginative poetry and ideal romance to prosaic realism was violent ; taste had swung completely round.

To supply the wants of this new public, Defoe was, both by nature and by training, admirably fitted. His precise, definite, matter-of-fact, commonplace mind had been disciplined by years of practice to state whatever case he desired to present clearly and forcibly, to preserve an appearance of impartiality, to assume the seeming artlessness of the plain, honest man, to array in support of his statements apparently trivial details and unimportant circumstances, to call to his aid a mass of corroborative evidence.

He applied similar processes to his fictitious biographies. Aiming at something beyond that illusion which makes readers willing to suspend their critical faculties, his object was to give to his narratives so convincing an air of authenticity as to create the delusion of truth. On this end was concentrated his genius for verisimilitude and for circumstantial invention. The methods by which he gave to his fictions so lifelike an appearance of veracity have been analysed by Scott and dissected by Leslie Stephen in their comments on *A True Relation of the Apparition of one Mrs. Veal* (1706). They may have been obvious, not of the highest kind, and even not worth while. But by their exercise, Defoe produced at least one work which the world acclaims as immortal.

Defoe's novels belong to the period 1719–24. They are too well known to require analysis. Most of them are *pièces de circonstance*, founded on recent or contemporary events, such as the shipwreck of Alexander Selkirk, the exploits of Captain Avery, the escapes of Jack Sheppard, or the outbreak of the plague in France in 1721. The interest of the records of *Moll Flanders*, or *Roxana*, is, as he himself said, independent of time, place, profession or class, and he probably utilised recent materials collected for his " Scandal Club " and social paragraphs. Four of the fictitious biographies, *Captain Singleton* (1720), *Moll Flanders* (1722), *Colonel Jack* (1722), and *Roxana* (1724), are in the picaresque style—incidents strung round pirates, pickpockets or prostitutes. Two of his novels purport to be history itself, the *Memoir of a Cavalier* (1720) and the *Journal of the Plague Year*, 1665 (1722.) *The Military Memoirs of Captain George Carleton* (1728) are no longer attributed to Defoe, but are considered to be the genuine work of a real Captain Carleton.

It was Defoe's first novel, *Robinson Crusoe*, which in 1719, as now, completely captured popular imagination. Here his very limitations helped his art. He makes no effort to excite pity for the lonely castaway. He is hard, dry, matter-of-fact. Whether, in avoiding emotional appeals, he followed the bent of his own mind or exercised artistic restraint, there can be no question that he made his picture truer and more life-like. He is inventing the recollections and impressions of a " Mariner of York " thrown on a desert island. In such circumstances, a typical Englishman of the eighteenth century, unimaginative, unemotional, at once practical and religious, would never expatiate on the beauties of the landscape, analyse his own feelings, or sit down to pity himself. He would do as Robinson Crusoe did—thrust away from his mind his passing moments of dejection or of panic, pit his ingenuity and tenacity against his difficulties, and buckle to the task of making his life as comfortable as circumstances allowed. He would have no ideals of noble savages whose primitive instincts are higher than the average standards of civilisation. To him, Friday would be a black man, to be made a useful servant and a Christian. So it is that in *Robinson Crusoe* Defoe has realised a type of the men who, among solitudes, hardships and dangers, have been pioneers and builders of the British Empire.

Defoe claimed that his stories were written, not for frivolous amusement, but with a moral purpose and for the instruction of mankind. Whether the claim is true, whether it was made to increase their circulation or to save his own reputation, it is impossible to decide. *Colonel Jack, Moll Flanders*, and their like illustrate, he says, the miserable end that attends a life of vice and crime ; *Robinson Crusoe* is, so he states, an allegory of his own life. If the last statement is even partially true, it gives significance to a sentence, and to the reflections on it, which he puts in the mouth of his hero. "Necessity makes an honest man a knave." Similarly his thieves and prostitutes protest that, but for the compulsion of circumstances, they would have been virtuous.

Is Defoe thinking of his own career ? Could he plead that he was driven into dishonesty by necessity, and that he did not enjoy, for its own sake, the daring ingenuity of his shifts, stratagems and deceptions ? The questions may be answered in different ways. But literature owes Defoe too great a debt to be uncharitable. He can at least plead that, in his hard, struggling life, he himself practised the lessons, which he professed to teach in *Robinson Crusoe*, of "invincible patience under the worst of misery ; indefatigable application and undaunted resolution under the greatest and most discouraging circumstances."

CHAPTER XII

SAMUEL RICHARDSON

BETWEEN the publication of *Robinson Crusoe* (1719) and that of *Pamela* (1740), prose fiction produced only one work of genius. In 1726 appeared *Travels into Several Remote Nations of the World*, by Lemuel Gulliver, " First a Surgeon, and then a Captain of Several Ships." Strictly speaking, the book may be excluded from the legitimate field of the novel by its primary object, if not by the impossibilities of its incidents. Swift's design is, not to paint, but to satirise " the animal called man." *Gulliver's Travels* therefore belongs to the same class of literature as More's *Utopia* (1516), or Bacon's *New Atlantis* (1626), or *The Description of a New World called the Blazing World*, by the " Thrice Noble, Illustrious and Excellent Princesse, the Duchess of Newcastle " (1668), in which prose fiction is employed for the purpose of expounding the author's view of an ideal polity, or of the advancement of science, or of mechanical progress.

Judging from the contempt with which Swift spoke of Mrs. Haywood as " a stupid, infamous, scribbling woman," he had himself no ambition to be a novelist. Yet, in more than one direction, he helped materially to advance the art. To its resources he added his temperamental humour and irony. He set an example of the charm of narrative. He extended realistic methods to a new sphere. He surrounded his imaginary worlds of Brobdingnag and Lilliput with the same air of veracity which Defoe gave to his narrative of real life. The abundance and familiarity of common-place detail authenticated his unreal creations by their circumstantiality. Yet, with all its minuteness, he preserved its perfect consistency, whether he was working to the scale of pygmy or of giant. At every turn, the effectiveness of his pictures is heightened by the imperturbable gravity and apparently innocent bluntness with which he stated his most whimsical absurdities. To future novelists, also, he bequeathed the model of an admirable English style. Always clear clouded by no literary artifices or mannerisms, it never becomes stagnant, because it ripples and sparkles with the play of ironic humour.

During the twenty years which separated Defoe from Richardson, *Gulliver's Travels* stands out by itself in prose fiction. Yet, within that period, upwards of a hundred novels by native hands were published. The quantity of the output is significant of the growing demand for some form of literary relaxation. As compared with the preceding thirty years, the rate of production was doubled, if not trebled. None of the writers contributed anything to the advance of the novelist's art in their own or kindred fields. Instead of developing on the lines of the *Coverley Papers*, or of *Robinson Crusoe*, or of *Gulliver's Travels*, writers imitated the short " Histories and Novels " of the " late ingenious Mrs. Behn." No name of literary distinction was set to a novel. Novels were still despised by men of letters. Theatrical authorship attracted the best pens. It was the readiest road to literary fame and fortune. Congreve had deserted novel-writing to win wealth and celebrity as a dramatist. Fresh from their triumphs as essayists, Addison and Steele turned to the production, not of novels, but of plays. Unless the Licensing Act had been passed in 1737, Fielding might have continued his theatrical work and never written *Tom Jones*. With an unacted tragedy in his pocket, Smollett crossed the Border to seek his literary fortune in London.

A " Person of Quality," or " of Honour," or " of Distinction " is sexless, and, if men wrote novels, they wrote anonymously. The best work was done by women. By far the most popular novelist of the day—male, female or anonymous—was Eliza Haywood. For her own generation her pale swarm of Clarinas, Cleomelias, Idalias, Lasselias and Placentias had an immense attraction. Her short stories were many times reprinted, both separately and in the collected form of the four volumes of her *Secret Histories* (1725 and 1732). She had an eye for dramatic situations and seems to have instinctively felt that, without sentiment, bald matter-of-fact statements, however plausible, were too dry a soil for the expansion of the novel. Her instinct was justified by her success. She was, however, capable of better things. Her best work, though still imitative, was done twenty years later, when the art of the novelist had been transformed by Richardson and Fielding. The difference between her stories before and after *Clarissa Harlowe* and *Tom Jones* illustrates the change that had been worked both in the structural form of novels and in their truth of representation. Her *History of Miss Betty Thoughtless* (1751) and her *History of Jimmy and Jenny Jessamy* (1753) are on the direct way to becoming modern novels of real life and character.

In the progress of novels, the richness of output at this particular period is more interesting than the poorness of quality. The mass of production implied a felt demand for literary entertainment. Defoe's commercial instinct was not at fault when, towards the close of his career, he employed his journalistic skill and experience on prose fiction. The great circulation reached by the *Spectator* proved that a reading public already existed. To it were now added readers whose literary tastes were perhaps less fastidious. Every day the middle classes were growing richer, better educated, more important than they had ever been before ; they demanded a literature, not merely for their instruction and improvement, but for the amusement of their increasing leisure. For this new public Defoe successfully catered. Of its growth and tastes, the publication of the first collection of novels by various hands affords a slight but significant indication. In 1720–1 Samuel Croxall published in six volumes *A Select Collection of Novels*. Foreign fiction was till the fashion. To the twenty-six novels Cervantes was by far the largest contributor. In the second edition (1729) the title was enlarged to *Novels and Histories*, and ten stories were added, in six of which historical personages like Henry II and Fair Rosamund, Jane Shore, Lady Jane Grey, Mary Queen of Scots, the Earl of Essex and Massaniello play the principal parts. But only two novels by

English hands—*Charon* and *The Black Mountain* are included.

It is evident from the success of Defoe, of Croxall's *Collection*, and, it may be added, of Mrs. Haywood, that, in the second quarter of the eighteenth century, the demand for a representation of life, whether as it was or as it was desired to be, was growing fast. For more than a century after the close of the Elizabethan age the triumphs of the stage had arrested the growth of the novel and starved its production. Plays read at home in private, as well as acted on the stage in public, had given it little room for development. Now, however, society was moving in a direction which was as unpropitious to the old drama as it was favourable to the modern novel. The world had lost its earlier faith in ideal heroes, who fashioned their own fate by energy of will, determined their destiny by their own choice of action, and, whether it led to victory or defeat, asserted their individual freedom. Society was veering towards the view that men, so far from being masters of their fate, were creatures of their environment. Neither Le Sage nor Defoe assigns to his actors any definite characters. Gil Blas is a chameleon who takes his colour from his surroundings. But no contemporary dramatist attempted to weave the web of circumstances in which men are caught and held. They still worked on the old aristocratic conception which no longer expressed any national sentiment. The theme had lost its inspiration. The thrill could not be recaptured by rant and fustian.

The serious drama showed little sign of life ; for some years social comedy had taken its place. Even at its zenith the comic stage had never represented any wide range of national life, and the social world, which once applauded its cynical licence, had changed. Always shallow in its presentation of human nature, it had behind it no permanent solidity of substance. A great genius like Molière might conquer restrictions of space, create characters, and round them off into individual human beings. Inferior artists evaded their difficulties by labelling each figure with some distinctive quality. Congreve might conceal the poverty of his human material by the dazzling wit of his dialogue. But his successors and imitators failed more and more to keep touch with social changes. Their plays were still cast in the post-Restoration mould ; their figures were wrinkled types, who had lost the vivid freshness of colour that they once possessed, and whose familiar parts rang false to realities. Social comedy had become a survival of the past rather than a living organ of the present. Like tragedy, it was in decay.

Freed from the rivalry of the stage, novelists had their opportunity to create a new form of imaginative literature. They were also favoured by the direction in which public curiosity was turning. Intellectual and social tendencies, which accompanied the rise of the middle classes, converged on the study of human nature and the problems of human existence. Here was a field to which the novel might be so adapted as to develop to the full the advantages which it possessed over every other form of representative art. for the dissection of the heart and the analysis of springs of conduct. Philosophical speculations or controversies on free will and predestination may not have greatly exercised the conscious mind of society ; but they filled the air and quickened the growing interest in character and personality. Social changes contributed to similar results. Increased leisure, the spread of education, improved communications, new facilities for travel, combined to stimulate a desire to know how other people lived, what they thought and felt as well as what they did. For the moment the public was only curious as to the present ; but, as the century advanced, the interest extended to the past. Even if the stage had still represented contemporary society, something wider and deeper would have been required to satisfy the new curiosity. A demand had been created for a representation of life which was true, not only to its external features, but to the mental and moral phenomena of the human heart and brain. If the novel could meet this need—if, that is, it could treat life subjectively as well as objectively—its welcome and its position in literature were assured. The opportunity for novelists of real life and character had come, and with it came the men.

For centuries before the reign of George II, fictitious narratives in prose had fascinated their listeners or their readers. Yet, though Richardson and Fielding had hundreds of predecessors, they were, in a true if limited sense, the founders of the modern novel. The heroes and heroines of the older romances were shadowy figures, paragons of beauty or courage, moving through a panorama of disconnected adventures at the caprice of their creator, in surroundings as vague and indistinct as themselves. Richardson and Fielding completed the picture of real life which Defoe had left unfinished. To the faithful presentation of external facts, they added the revelation of the inner workings of mind and character, which interpret action and intensify the interest of incident. They also, for the first time in long works of fiction, recognised that stories must have a beginning and an end. They brought together groups of human beings in plots which were unravelled by the play of character in the grip of circumstance. The actors live because the parts which they enact follow from their own individualities. Both writers believed, and were justified in believing, that they were creating a new species of literature. When the novel left their hands, it was still in the experimental stage ; but it had become a novel, just as a play is a play or a poem a poem. Novelists had found themselves. The search was over ; the goal and the means of reaching it were ascertained. Henceforward the interest of the history lies in the perfection of the instrument and its application to new fields.

Those who, familiar with the triumphs of modern novelists, read for the first time the work of Richardson are so struck with his imperfections that they think him hopelessly obsolete. Those who come to him, as his own generation came, conversant only with the prose fiction of his predecessors and contemporaries, are impressed with his freshness and novelty. To read *Pamela*, the first of his three novels (1740), is to enter a new world of literature. He had created " a new species of writing," and was conscious that he had done so. Eight years later he produced his masterpiece. *Clarissa Harlowe* is an intimate portrait of a true woman, painted by a man. How came it that, in the prosiest of periods, this new tragic ideal was created by a plodding, humdrum printer when he was nearly sixty ?

Nothing that is known of the domestic and literary life of the elderly citizen fully answers the question. But something is explained.

The external facts of his prosperous career are few and simple. Born (1689) and bred in a Derbyshire village, he was intended to take Orders; but his father, by trade a joiner, became too impoverished to afford him the necessary education. In 1706 he was " bound apprentice to Mr. John Wilde of Stationers' Hall." Hard-working and conscientious in his master's service, he used his scanty leisure in self-education, taking care, as he himself notes, " that even my candle was of my own purchasing." His seven years ended, he worked in a printing office, took up his freedom, and finally set up for himself as a printer. He married, as his first wife, his master's daughter, Allington Wilde, prospered in Salisbury Court, printed (among other works) the *Journals of the House of Commons*, and eventually (1754) became Master of the Stationers' Company. His commercial career was as uneventful as it was successful. He bore its burdens alone. Even when drinking the waters at Tunbridge Wells, he conducted his affairs by coach-borne correspondence. His constitutional bashfulness did not prevent him from building up a considerable business. Yet his shyness grew upon him to such an extent that, latterly, he gave all his orders in written notes. He died in 1761 at the age of seventy-two.

In most of his opinions, Richardson was little in advance of his own day. But, both as a boy and as a man, he stood apart from his male contemporaries in something of the mental and moral isolation which often characterises genius. Never "fond of play," the child was nicknamed by his schoolfellows "Serious" and "Gravity." But as a teller of stories he was popular. Some of his tales were taken from books, others were his own invention. Fifty years later, he remembered that he had had the power to move his audiences, and that all his stories "carried with them a useful moral." Shy with boys, he was, like Cowper, more at his ease with the opposite sex. The girls of the neighbourhood gave him their confidences, asked him to write their love-letters, and liked him to read aloud to them over their needlework, and to comment on what he read. Male society was uncongenial to him. Even in mature years, he remained, in habits, tastes or interests, as unlike other men as he had been unlike his schoolfellows in boy-hood. Abstemious in food and drink, he abstained for many years from wine, meat and fish. He never swore ; his most lurid oath was : " What ! the duce is in it." He was never, to his knowledge, in the company of a loose woman. He never gambled, and enjoyed no form of sport. He never rode anything more exciting than a wooden " chamber-horse," which he used for exercise. He dis-approved of duelling, though Clarissa is avenged in a duel which he describes with plenty of spirit.

Throughout his life he preferred the society of women to that of men. From women he learned to know human nature and to regard it with a feminine eye. At his country home at North End, Hammersmith, or, later, at Parson's Green, he spent his week-ends in a " flower-garden of ladies " of all ages. Among his elder guests was a sprinkling of younger women, more vivacious than his own four daughters, whom he describes as " shy little fools," and who alone survived out of a family of six sons and six daughters. Surrounded by a company of female worshippers, he breathed an atmosphere of incense, which for most men, however elderly, must have been unwholesome. To his natural temperament the peculiar training was congenial, and under it he expanded. Contact with female delicacy of perception sharpened his own acute observation of subtle gradations of feeling. His inventive faculty was stimulated by finding that his own interest in minute details was shared by his audience, and that he gratified their wishes as well as his own inclinations by " telling us all about it." To the party of ladies as they sat round a table, drawing, flowering muslin or making ruffles and borders, Richardson read aloud, between tea and supper, the last pages which he had finished of *Clarissa Harlowe* or of *Sir Charles Grandison*. They applauded, discussed, commented ; more rarely they criticised. In this feminine school, he learned to accomplish a feat which no man has attempted with greater success. With rare insight into her nature, he painted a true woman, and his picture is none the less valuable because it is drawn with that genuine admiration which female novelists rarely display towards their own sex.

Richardson's correspondence gives little indication of the studies that he pursued, and of the books that he read, at the formative period of his life, when he was educating himself. He learnt no language but his own. He could not have read *Marianne* in the original French, though he might have read the translation which began to appear four years before the publication of *Pamela*. Of Latin or Greek he was equally ignorant. The scholarship of the pedant Brand in *Clarissa Harlowe* seems to have been supplied to him by a friend of Brasenose College, Oxford. On the other hand, his taste in poetry is significant of literary independence. "Who now reads Cowley?" asked Pope, and of Spenser, Addison had written the lines:

> But now the mystic vale, that pleased of yore,
> Can charm an understanding age no more.

Yet Cowley, and more especially Spenser, were Richardson's favourite poets. Just as he revolted from the unemotional coldness of his contemporaries, so he rebelled against their narrow standard of classical correctness. Fond of "sentimentising," to use his own word, and warming his imagination in the glow and colour of the *Faerie Queene*, he seems, on one side of his nature, a pioneer of the romantic reaction; on the other and larger side, he belonged essentially to his own generation. It was on the everyday life of his contemporaries that his short-sighted, observant eyes were fixed, and he described it with the realism that Defoe had made the fashion of his early manhood. His writings show no trace of the love of scenery or of the enthusiasm for the past which characterised later movements. For him, neither the Gothic revival nor the aspiration and mystery of romance had any attraction. Pious, he resisted infidelity. Sentimentalist though he was, he had no sympathy with the return to nature. He chafed at none of the existing conventions which repressed emotion; a supporter of Church and State as by law established, he desired no reversion to a simpler social order. In his first novel he married a waiting-maid to a gentleman ; but, so far from preaching any gospel of equality, he disparages his heroine by insisting on her abject sense of the inferiority of her condition. His morality was utilitarian ; if *Pamela* taught a lesson, it was that virtue is materially rewarded in this life, and that propriety pays.

Richardson has left two sketches of himself in letters written in 1748–9. The first was sent to one of his liveliest correspondents, Lady Bradshaigh, the childless wife of a Lancashire country gentleman. For some months they had corresponded without meeting. But, on one of her visits to London, they arranged to meet in the Mall on a Saturday when Richardson was walking through it on his way to North End, and, in order that she might recognise him, he described his personal appearance. So life-like was the portrait, that the lady knew him at a distance of three hundred yards :

" Short, rather plump than emaciated, notwithstanding his complaints ; fair wig ; lightish cloth coat, all black besides ; one hand generally in his bosom ; the other a cane in it, which he leans upon under the skirts of his coat usually, that it may imperceptibly serve him as a support, when attacked by sudden tremors, or startings, or dizziness, which too frequently attack him, but, thank God, not so often as formerly ; looking directly foreright, as passers-by would imagine, but observing all that stirs on either hand of him without moving his short neck ; hardly ever turning back ; at some times looking to be about sixty-five, at other times much younger ; a regular even pace, stealing away ground, rather than seeming to rid it ; a grey eye, too often overclouded by mistinesses from the head ; by chance lively, very lively it will be, if he have hopes of seeing a lady whom he loves and honours ; his eye always ' on the ladies.' "

Another less well-known sketch, written at Tunbridge Wells, catches him in characteristic attitudes. After watching the gay octogenarian, Cibber, carry off the beautiful Elizabeth Chudleigh from a crowd of young adorers, he promises to show Miss Highmore

" . . . a still more grotesque figure. A sly sinner, creeping along the very edges of the walks, getting behind benches, one hand in his bosom, the other held up to his chin, as if to keep it in its place ; afraid of being seen, as a thief of detection. The people of fashion, if he happens to cross a walk (which he always does with precipitation), *unsmiling* their faces, as if they thought him in the way."

" You cannot see him," he adds, " unless I show him to you."

The shy, elderly citizen, who, in places of public resort, scurried across the paths or hid behind the benches in order to see without being seen, used his near-sighted eyes to some purpose in his three novels, *Pamela* (1740), *Clarissa Harlowe* (1747–8), and *Sir Charles Grandison* (1753–4). They dealt respectively with humble, middle-class and high life. In all three the story is told by means of letters. Richardson was not the discoverer of this method. Brown, in *Lindamira* (1702), had already told the events of the domestic life of his heroine in a series of letters. For the last half-century the letters of the Portuguese Nun and those of Eloïsa to Abelard had been immensely popular for their revelation of the passionate hearts of women. When Richardson wrote, he was living in the letter-writing age, to which belonged Swift, Horace Walpole and Lady Mary Wortley-Montagu. From his childhood he had himself practised the art. Before he was eleven, he had written a letter of moral reproof to an elderly lady old enough to be his grandmother ; at thirteen, he became not only the recipient of the secrets of the hearts of the young women in the neighbourhood of his Derbyshire home, but the writer of their love-letters.

In maturer years, his weak eyesight tolerated writing better than reading. Instead of a book, his little tablet was his constant companion, and, in his small, beautifully formed handwriting, he carried on voluminous correspondences on a variety of subjects. He probably, therefore, chose to tell his story in letters because long practice had familiarised him with this form of composition. But other considerations had their influence. For one who had been bred in the school of Defoe, the choice of method was limited. If fiction was to be plausibly represented as fact, it must be told in the first person by the principal actor, in the form either of autobiography, of personal memoirs or of letters. Anxious to give an air of veracity to his story and to authenticate its minutest details, Richardson naturally chose the method with which he was most familiar. In their peculiar intimacy, intended only for the eye of the recipient, letters were also specially adapted for his purpose of revealing character. They are heart-to-heart talks ; they reflect every shade of feeling as it comes and goes ; they catch the most fleeting impression while its outline is still clear ; they offer endless opportunity for those agitations of sentiment in which Richardson delighted. Finally, letters passing between intimate friends are the nearest approach to oral communication, and approximate most closely to the give and take of talk between actors on the stage.

The dramatic capabilities of letters appealed the more strongly to Richardson because his original conception of a novel seems to have been that of a play adapted to private reading. The idea chimed in with the fashion of the day. There was truth, as well as point, in Pope's line : " Our wives read Milton and our daughters plays." Standard plays formed a staple part in domestic reading. Both Richardson and Fielding allude to the practice. Harriet Byron excuses her report of conversations in dramatic form by saying to Miss Selby : " I know, my dear, that you love to read plays." A play of Farquhar is one of the few literary occupations that Fielding allows to Amelia. But it is difficult to read a play intelligently without the interpretation of acting. Richardson aimed at making it easy by filling up the gaps and omissions and supplying a continuous narrative. Where the dramatist condensed, he expanded. He chronicled the circumstances, dissected the emotions which they aroused, analysed their effects on the minds of his characters, added the criticisms of their correspondents on those impressions, and so explained and led up to the successive stages in the development of the plot to its conclusion. It was in this untrodden field that, with the greater space at their command, novelists asserted the superiority of their instrument over that of playwrights. One restriction on his liberty of expansion Richardson imposed upon himself. Congreve was proud of being the first author to bring a novel within the dramatic unity of time. Richardson seems to have thought that, for novelists, a year was a reasonable limitation, and he completes the tragedy of Clarissa within twelve months. It is significant that he calls *Clarissa Harlowe* a dramatic history, and prefixes to *Sir Charles Grandison* a list of his *dramatis personæ*, quaintly arranged under the three heads of Men, Women and Italians.

Richardson was himself a student of the dramatic literature of his day. Without detracting from the independence of his genius he was, as is suggested by his *Correspondence* (edited by Mrs. Barbauld ; 6 vols., 1804), especially indebted to three plays for hints and suggestions. One was Otway's *Orphan*. The plot turns on a similar outrage to that perpetrated on Clarissa Harlowe ; the true and even tragic pathos of Monimia struck his imagination. Richardson believed that the distresses of ordinary men and women in everyday life appealed more strongly to the general public than the heroic woes of princes and princesses, because they " come nearer to us." In his opinion, the play owed " its success more to this consideration than to any other, its characters being all of a private family." It was one of his principal reasons for trying the same experiment in his ,*History of Clarissa*. Another play was Rowe's *Fair Penitent*. His Lovelace is an elaboration of the " gay Lothario," who for a similar crime meets the same fate at the hand of the avenger of his victim. The third play is Steele's *Conscious Lovers*. When Richardson discussed with Mrs. Donellan his project of painting the portrait of a perfect hero as a counterpoise to Lovelace, she at once laid her finger on his model. " Generous Bevil " is the prototype of Sir Charles Grandison.

Richardson's first novel, in which, at the age of fifty-one, he discovered a " new species of writing," was independent of any dramatic suggestion. In a letter to Aaron Hill he has recorded how *Pamela* came to be written. He had been commissioned, in 1739, by the publishing firm of Messrs. Rivington & Osborne, to write " a little book of familiar letters on the useful concerns in common life." Turning over various subjects in his mind, he " thought of giving one or two as cautions " to young girls in domestic service. Then he remembered a story told him some twenty years before by a friend, who had been making a summer tour in England. At one of his stopping-places, his friend asked who was the owner of a fine place in the neighbourhood. The innkeeper told him that the place belonged to a Mr. B., who had married a maidservant, who, he said, was " one of the greatest beauties in England and in the qualities of her mind had no equal." As a young girl of twelve she had been taken into the service of Mr. B.'s mother, to wait upon her person. At the age of fifteen, her beauty attracted the notice of her mistress's son, who, after his mother's death, tried to seduce her. She resisted all his attempts, though at one time she was in her despair almost driven to drown herself. Won by the charm of her character, as well as of her face and figure, he offered her marriage. As his wife, she " made herself beloved of everybody, and even of his relations, and now had the blessings both of rich and poor," who, at first, despised her. The story gave Richardson the hint :

" When I began to recollect what had, so many years before, been told me by a friend, I thought the story, if written in an easy and natural manner, suitably to the simplicity of it, might possibly introduce a new species of writing, and might possibly turn young people into a course of reading different from the pomp and parade of romance-writing, and dismissing the improbable and marvellous with which novels generally abound might tend to promote the cause of religion and virtue."

Urged on by the interest of his " worthy-hearted " wife, and a girl who was staying in the house, to whom he read the successive portions as they came from his pen, he finished the manuscript within three months. With business-like care, he dockets his copy with the dates when the book was begun and finished—November 10, 1739—January 10, 1739–40.

How closely Richardson followed the lines of his friend's story is shown by one of the outstanding passages in the novel. Like her prototype, Pamela, by the side of the Lincolnshire pond, contemplates drowning herself in order to escape from her persecutor. She indulges in all the luxury of imagining the feelings which would be aroused by the discovery of her dead body; the remorse of Mr. B.; the pity of the neighbours; the vindication of her character. Saved by her piety, she turns away, and determines to live and resist. But her morality is not of the highest order. Her virtue, though never a spiritual inspiration, safeguards her against the brutality of Mr. B. She was safe, so long as there was no treason in her own garrison. She began to suspect that a traitor existed, when she heard that her master had narrowly escaped accidental death by drowning. She cannot help rejoicing at his safety. "What is the matter," she asks herself, "that, with all his ill usage of me, I cannot hate him." Later, she discovers that she has given him her heart. In a passage, in which Richardson shows his delicacy of insight, she takes herself to task:

"Therefore will I not acquit thee yet, oh credulous, fluttering, throbbing mischief! that art so ready to believe what thou wishest! And I charge thee to keep better guard than thou hast lately done, and lead me not to follow too implicitly thy flattering and desirable impulses. Thus foolishly dialogued I with my own heart; and yet, all this time, this heart was Pamela."

She was not put to the test of a change from violence to tenderness. Her prudence reinforced her virtue, and, despairing of winning her by other means, Mr. B. offers her marriage. Without exacting any penitence from her would-be seducer, she accepts him with obsequious gratitude and a humility which is almost servile. At the wedding, when the bridegroom had finished the sentences "With this ring I thee wed," etc., she drops a curtsey and says: "Thank you, sir."

London went mad over *Pamela*. Not to have read the book was at least as great a want of good breeding as " not to have seen the French and Italian dancers." Society paid its tribute to the novelty of the experiment. Yet, if Richardson had written nothing more, prudent Pamela's most enduring monument might have been Fielding's parody. The continuation of the story, in which Pamela reclaims her libertine husband, scarcely deserves mention. But, in 1748, Richardson produced his masterpiece.

In all the circumstances, *Clarissa Harlowe* is one of the marvels of our literature. The advance which Richardson had made in knowledge of human nature is striking. The publication of his book proceeded in the same leisurely fashion as the story itself progressed. Four volumes appeared in 1747, and the remaining four before the end of 1748. The plot is simple. To avoid a hateful marriage, Clarissa escapes from home and trusts to the honourable protection of Lovelace to convey her to a place of safety. He takes her to a house of ill fame, where he eventually drugs and violates her. She rejects his subsequent offer of marriage, pines away and dies. As the story developed, Richardson was implored by his friends to give it a happy ending. To the same effect, appeals reached him from strangers in different parts of the country. To all entreaties he turned a deaf ear. On the conclusion of his tragic story he was rightly inexorable. He knew that marriage with her betrayer could never restore Clarissa's self-respect, and that the only cure for her sense of the shame of her humiliation was death. The central feature of the book is disgusting : the detail is meticulous ; the progress of the story leisurely to the point of exasperation. Perhaps also, at first sight, the figure of Clarissa, in her pale-coloured paduasoy, her Brussels lace cap, her flowered cuffs and apron, may seem to modern eyes faded and old-fashioned. Yet, as the patient, deliberate touches gradually throw upon the canvas the picture of the tender, maidenly girl, whose heart had hardly begun to unfold with the spring-like warmth of an unacknowledged fancy before it was numbed, withered and frozen to death, the conviction slowly grows that Clarissa is no conventional heroine but a high imaginative effort.

The pathos of the final scene in its elaboration misses the effectiveness of bare simplicity. But it is true. It even survives the shock of Clarissa's purchase of her coffin and her use of it as a writing-table ; it remains tragic to the close.

The extreme length of the story disguises the massiveness of its construction. No detail is omitted, but nothing is irrelevant : everything fits into its place in the development of the climax. Intensity of purpose is one secret of Richardson's power. The deliberation of his advance heightens the impression of unrelenting fate. Clarissa's weakness and irresolution play into its hands. All the circumstances converge on the same end. As the clouds gather, mass and concentrate, the cumulative effect is striking. It is strengthened by contrast with the restraint, again against the advice of his critics, which Richardson exercised in dealing with the death of Lovelace. He elaborates no agonies of remorse, no tortures of awakened conscience. Challenged to a duel by Clarissa's cousin, Lovelace dies by the hand of her avenger.

In the character of Lovelace, Richardson attempted a harder task than that of painting paragons like Clarissa or Sir Charles Grandison. He had to draw the portrait of a man who is half angel, half devil. He succeeds in making Lovelace clever, witty, audacious, full of vitality, a charming companion, likely to attract a young girl's fancy. But the vicious side is exaggerated. Lovelace is such a villain as a woman might imagine who is ignorant of men and inexperienced in vice. Here is a man who has thought over marriage only to reject the idea. He is not swept off his feet by passion, for in Richardson's scheme of morality, passion found no place. He has not even the zest of the hunter for the pursuit and capture. He deliberately plans the ruin of the girl for a cold-blooded motive, and, to strain belief to the utmost, he discloses his scheme, discusses its progress, and announces its success in a series of letters to another man. Psychologically possible, he is certainly incredible.

Whether Thomas Carlyle ever read *Sir Charles Grandison* may be doubted. But when he called Lafayette a " Grandison-Cromwell," he knew that the name of Sir Charles

Grandison was proverbial for the typical fine gentleman of the eighteenth century. The novel was published in seven volumes between November 1753 and March 1754. Some of his lady friends reproached Richardson with painting men only as profligates ; he, and only he, could give them an ideal hero. Others among the younger women acknowledged their liking for Lovelace, and doubted whether they could love a " tame man," or one to whom they had nothing to forgive. Worse than all, rumours reached him that " Tom Jones " was the hero of many girls, and that young men had their " Sophias," and had even given the name to a " Dutch mastiff puppy." Piqued in his vanity as a moralist, and in his jealousy as an author, he wrote *Sir Charles Grandison* to give the world " the example of a man acting uniformly well through a variety of trying scenes, because all his actions are regulated by one steady principle."

Sir Charles Grandison possesses every gift of fortune, as well as the love of three beautiful and wealthy ladies, whose rhapsodies are supplemented by a chorus of praise from a variety of sources. Even Sir Charles himself swells the triumphal music by reporting, with becoming indifference, the compliments which he receives. Young, rich, well-born, perfect in figure, dress, deportment and accomplishments, a consummate master of the small-sword, he is honourable and courageous. He does the right thing with a self-conscious air, and says it, not without a touch of pomposity. He portions his sisters handsomely, buries his father with dignity, behaves generously to the dead man's mistress and her children, reclaims a reprobate uncle by providing him a wife, refuses to fight duels or dock the tails of his horses. Prig though he is, he is likeable rather than insufferable. Naturally, he does no wooing ; he has only to toss his handkerchief to one or other of his adorers. His royal progress is made so smooth that his true character is never tested by misfortune.

Sir Charles is brought on the stage with an appropriate flourish of trumpets. In an excellent scene he rescues Harriet Byron from her abductor. Harriet at once loses her heart to her rescuer. Sir Charles, though attracted, is more reserved. It turns out that he is conditionally engaged to a noble Italian lady, Clementina della Porretta. He is quite willing to marry either lady, or even a third—his lovely ward, Emily Jervois, whose shy discovery that her filial regard for her guardian is really a much warmer feeling is treated by Richardson in his best manner. Sir Charles moves serenely through the tempests of emotion that he has aroused. But Harriet Byron, whom Richardson intended to be a compound of Pamela and of what, in happier circumstances, Clarissa would have been, never has a chance of sympathy. In fiction, as in real life, young women who are madly in love and unreserved in its expression exact too much from readers or friends. In the end, Clementina, torn by the conflict between her love and her duty, as an Italian and a Catholic, to her country, her family and her faith, decides against marriage with an English Protestant. The sacrifice costs her her reason, and Sir Charles and Harriet are married.

In literary finish *Sir Charles Grandison* is superior to *Pamela* or *Clarissa Harlowe* ; in human interest it is inferior to both. It suffers most from the epistolary form of narrative, and gains from it fewest advantages. But the most damaging criticism is that the novel is untrue to the manner and habits of contemporary society. Of this charge the present generation can scarcely judge. The scenes are laid partly in Italy, of which Richardson knew nothing ; partly in the fashionable world of London, which he never entered. His ignorance of Bologna is excusable ; less pardonable would be mistakes in what he professes to be a picture of English social life. He himself recognised his danger. In one of his letters he asked :

" How shall a man, obscurely situated, never delighting in public entertainments, nor in his youth able to frequent them, from narrowness of fortune, had he had a taste for them ; one of the most attentive of men to the calls of his business ; his situation for many years producing little but prospects of a numerous family ; . . . naturally shy and sheepish, and wanting more encouragement by smiles to draw him out than anybody thought it worth their while to give him ; . . . how, I say, shall such a man pretend to describe and enter into characters in upper life ? How shall such a one draw scenes of busy and yet elegant trifling ? "

His blunders struck those of his contemporaries who themselves knew the fashionable world. Walpole spoke contemptuously of his pictures of high life " as conceived by a bookseller." Chesterfield said that " whenever he goes, *ultra crepidam*, into high life, he grossly mistakes the modes, but," he adds, " to do him justice he never mistakes nature." Lady Mary Wortley-Montagu was more violent in her belief that Richardson should confine his pen to " the *amours* of housemaids and the conversation at the steward's table." Yet, like Chesterfield, she felt his power. " This Richardson is a strange fellow. I heartily despise him and eagerly read him, nay, sob over his works in a most scandalous manner."

In England, *The Sentimental Journey, The Man of Feeling*, and a host of inferior works were more or less descended from Richardson, and his analysis of emotion set in progress a literary movement which still inspires novelists who, perhaps, have never read a line of his works. It was as the first sentimentalist that Richardson exercised his widest influence. He knew that England was, in this respect, less susceptible than the continent. In *Sir Charles Grandison* he says : " The French only are proud of sentiments at this day ; the English cannot bear them ; story, story, story is what they hunt after, whether sense or nonsense, probable or improbable." Continental nations were not concerned whether his pictures of English society were true or false. They were profoundly impressed by his transcripts of the inner life, and deeply stirred by his emotional appeals. Free from national colour, his characters attracted the peoples of every country. For the first time in the history of prose fiction, an English writer was acclaimed by Europe as a master.

Translated into French by Prévost, Richardson's novels were prodigiously popular in France. Walpole grudgingly admits several times in his correspondence that his " tedious lamentations " were the talk of Paris. Diderot founded

La Religieuse upon Clarissa Harlowe, and in an almost dithyrambic " Eloge " ranked Richardson with Moses, Homer, Euripides and Sophocles. Still more striking is the extent to which his influence affected Rousseau's *Nouvelle Héloïse.* And that influence endured. Balzac, George Sand and Alfred de Musset did homage to a man whose life was singularly contrasted with that of any of the three admirers. Nor would it be wholly fanciful to suggest that, in the twentieth century, *Marie-Claire* is in the direct line of descent from *Pamela.* In Germany, Goethe himself studied Richardson's art and the secret of his power over German hearts, and though *Werther* is inspired by Rousseau, it is from Richardson that the inspiration was indirectly derived. Few writers have left a literary offspring which departed so widely from the original type. Luxuriating in sentiment, Richardson played with fire. Experience shows that sentiments cannot always be " curbed by virtue," or regulated by moral maxims, when the sanctions of both restrictions are doubted or denied. Richardson's propriety would have been outraged if Julie and Lotte had taken their places by the side of Pamela and Clarissa at the table of his surburban garden at North End. He would have been still more horrified by the swarm of wild doctrines, subversive of much that he cherished, which might, by the application of sentiment to theory, have traced to him their parentage.

CHAPTER XIII

HENRY FIELDING

A KIND-HEARTED, generous man, Samuel Richardson's nature was warped by literary vanity and jealousy of rival authors. He never forgave Henry Fielding for laughing at *Pamela*; believed that he had taught the younger man " how to write to please "; persistently depreciated his writings, while professing never to have opened *Tom Jones* or more than begun *Amelia*. In the latter book, he found the characters and the situations " so wretchedly low and dirty," that he could not read beyond the first volume. His criticisms are cattish. After stating that Parson Adams was copied from the Rev. William Young, he goes on to deny to Fielding the power of invention.

" In his *Tom Jones* his hero is made a natural child, because his own first wife was such. Tom Jones is Fielding himself, hardened in some places, softened in others. His Lady Bellaston is an infamous woman of his former acquaintance. His Sophia is, again, his first wife. Booth, in his last piece, again himself. Amelia, even to her noselessness, again his first wife. His brawls, his jars, his gaols, his spunging houses, are all drawn from what he has seen and known."

When Fielding attempted to draw a good woman, said Richardson, he " knew not how, and lost his genius—low humour—in the attempt." Similar criticisms he felt bound to repeat to Sarah Fielding, and to protest to the sister against the " continued lowness " of her brother's writing. To these attacks Fielding made no reply. He had given the first provocation by wounding the literary vanity of his rival. There was in him nothing of the spiteful littleness of Richardson. In his tribute to *Clarissa Harlowe* he made his public *amende* with the characteristic bigness of nature which has endeared him to generations of readers.

In character, temperament, education, experience, outlook, no two men could have differed more widely than Richardson and Fielding. The differences are naturally reflected in their novels. In one man, shy and retiring, a vegetarian and a water-drinker, the pulse of life trickled sluggishly ; in the other, buoyant in spirits, sanguine of temper, made for enjoyment, it raced like a torrent. Both had from the first their own way to make. Placed in a printer's office, Richardson followed the prosperous but narrowing career of the industrious apprentice. When he began to write, he had a comfortable income at his back. Thrown on his wits in London at twenty-one, Fielding had the choice (as he says himself) of becoming either a hackney coachman or a hackney writer. He chose the latter trade. He wrote for bread, with duns at his door, generally in poverty, often in want ; and, in later years, in physical suffering.

As there is a traditional Rabelais, so there is a legendary Fielding. Scant justice was done by their own generation to the serious earnestness of either. A hard hitter, Fielding had made many enemies among party journalists. Personal abuse was showered upon him. " Several writers (he said in 1748) attempted to blacken my Name with every kind of Reproach ; pursued me into private Life, even to my boyish Years ; where they have given me almost every Vice in Human Nature." Partly on these reports, which he was not unwilling to believe, partly on the assumption that, in Tom Jones and Captain Booth, Fielding was painting his own character and career, Richardson founded his view that his rival was a low blackguard, who had degraded his birth and education. On the same grounds, Dr. Johnson reached a similar conclusion. Novels are dangerous quarries for autobiographical material, and little is certain about Fielding's personal history. Tantalising gaps still defy research. His letters are few, and contemporary allusions rare. The notes of Lady Louisa Stuart, which embody the recollections of her grandmother, Lady Mary Wortley-Montagu, and of her mother, Lady Bute, are valuable.

But Murphy, the only biographer who wrote when the facts
were fresh, was intentionally sparing of details. Even
Fielding's portrait was drawn from memory, and not from
life.

Born in 1707, at the home of his maternal grandfather,
Sharpham Park, near Glastonbury, Henry Fielding died at
Lisbon, October 8, 1754.   His father, Edward, was a
soldier who served under Marlborough " with much Bravery
and Reputation."   His mother, Sarah, was the daughter
of Sir Henry Gould, one of the Judges of the King's Bench.
In his paternal descent the most interesting point is his
relationship to Lady Mary Wortley-Montagu ;   on the
maternal side, it is the legal connection, which probably
decided his ultimate choice of the Bar as his profession.
The marriage was not to " the good liking " of the Goulds.
They distrusted the prudence of their son-in-law.   The
judge left a sum of money to be invested in the purchase
of an estate for his daughter's sole use, " her husband having
nothing to doe with it."   If she died without a will, the
property was to be divided among her children.   The
estate, which was bought, was East Stour, in Dorsetshire.
There Henry Fielding's brother and four sisters were born ;
and there, in 1718, Mrs. Fielding died, intestate.

Two years later, Colonel Fielding married again.   This
second marriage caused a family quarrel, which ended in a
Chancery suit brought by Lady Gould on behalf of her
grandchildren.   In 1721 she filed an affidavit, in which
she alleged that Colonel Fielding had married, as his second
wife, an Italian woman, who was a Roman Catholic, and
had kept an eating-house in London ;   that the Colonel
threatened to bring up his children in the religion of their
stepmother ;   and that he was receiving the rents of East
Stour.   Edward Fielding, in reply, denied the eating-house,
admitted the receipt of the rents, but pleaded that he spent
more than the amount on the education of the children,
and that his son Henry had been, for more than a year,
maintained by him " at Eton Schoolc, the yearly expence
whereof costs upwards of £60."   The case was decided in
Lady Gould's favour.   She obtained the custody of the
children that they " may not be under the influence of the

Defendant's Wife, who appeared to be a Papist." So the
boy remained at Eton, spending his holidays with Lady
Gould at Salisbury.

Fielding carried away with him from Eton some life-long
friendships and a lasting love of the classics. He read
widely all his life. To Cervantes and Molière he owed much,
and something to Le Sage, Scarron and Marivaux. But it
was in the literature of Greece and Rome that he especially
delighted. In the dregs of poverty he found consolation
in reading a moral treatise by Cicero ; Plato accompanied
him on his voyage to Lisbon ; he projected translations of
Aristophanes and his favourite Lucian ; and in the library
which he left behind him at his death were more than 130
volumes of Greek and Latin authors.

In February 1728 his first play, the comedy of *Love in
Several Masks*, was produced at Drury Lane. A month
later, he entered his name as a student at the University of
Leyden. Returning to London eighteen months afterwards,
he began his struggle to earn a living by his pen. Tall,
handsome, well born, well educated, overflowing with mirth
and wit, he grasped with both hands such pleasures as he
could find. In his Lucianic *Journey from this World to
the Next* (1743) he makes a statement which may be autobiographical. When the departed spirits are brought
before Minos for judgment, the turn of the author himself
comes. He confesses that he had in his youth indulged
himself very freely with wine and women, " but (he adds)
he had never done an injury to any man living, nor avoided
an opportunity of doing good." Minos curtly bids him
enter through the gate and not waste time in trumpeting
his virtues.

More often in debt than in funds, his laced coat and hat
were so seldom out of pawn that they were less familiar
to his associates than his tattered grey cloak. Whatever
money he earned slipped through his fingers. He wooed
fortune with many subjects and forms of literature. In the
first nine years of his comparatively short life he was a
playwright, trying his hand on comedy, burlesque and
political farce. During the middle period, he was mainly
a journalist, the founder of four newspapers on the lines

of the *Spectator*, an essayist, a versifier, a literary critic, a political writer. In his closing years, he was a social reformer and pamphleteer. His four novels, published between 1742 and 1752, were all written in the nobler part of his career.

Between 1728 and 1737 Fielding produced some twenty plays, which were acted on the stage. If his social comedies were not by the author of *Tom Jones*, they would be unread. Hastily produced to meet pressing needs, scribbled on the paper-wrappings of his beloved tobacco, many of them would have gone into the fire if his dinner had not gone with them. The artificial form into which social comedy was cast cramped his powers. He had neither the light manner which was needed for an echo of Congreve, nor the dramatic genius to break the mould and create a new model which would give scope for his commonsense view of society, his genuine scorn for its hypocrisies, his hearty laughter at its follies. The cynical tone of jaded worldlings was uncongenial to him; he could hit hard, but he could not be playful nor quizzical. In burlesque, he could be more natural and sincere. The cudgel fitted his hand better than the rapier, and he used the weapon with effect against the rant of tragedians. His *Life and Death of Tom Thumb the Great* takes off, with broad rather than subtle humour, the bombastic extravagances of tragic dramatists. Much of the fun is now lost, because the text of the writers satirised is forgotten. But the play has at least one claim to be rememberd. Swift told Mrs. Pilkington that he " had not laugh'd above twice in his life," and that one of the occasions was the scene in the original version of the play, where Lord Grizel kills the ghost of Tom Thumb. The other occasion, characteristically added the Dean, was at the antics of a Merry-Andrew.

The social comedies are a hastily-gathered, loosely-bound sheaf of a young man's wild oats. They show little of the real Fielding. His marriage was the turning-point of his life. On November 28, 1734, at Charlcombe, near Bath, he married Charlotte Cradock. Their courtship had begun at least four years earlier. She was the passion of his life; the Celia of his youthful love-verses; in her maiden beauty his Sophia Western; as wife and mother his Amelia. Mrs.

Fielding may have had much to forgive her husband. But in two important points he was not the original of his own Captain Booth. At no time of his life is there any evidence that he gambled, and Murphy testifies to " his tenderness and constancy to his wife." Lady Bute, who knew them both, sums up the gist of the matter when she says " he loved her passionately and she returned his affection."

Charlotte Fielding had nothing beyond what she might inherit from her mother, who was still living. With a wife to support, Fielding staked much on the success of *The Universal Gallant*, produced at Drury Lane in February 1735. The total failure of his play was a disaster. Relief came at the nick of time. Mrs. Cradock died at the end of the month, and by her will, with the exception of one shilling bequeathed to her daughter Catherine, left her whole fortune to her " dearly beloved daughter," Charlotte Fielding. On this legacy of £1,500 the young couple retired to the country, probably to the home of his childhood, East Stour.

In Murphy's well-known account of Fielding's extravagance as a country squire, his yellow liveries, and his coach and four, there are obvious inaccuracies. Probably the whole story is greatly exaggerated. Enough of the money was left to enable Fielding, in 1736, to take the New Theatre in the Haymarket. Financially his venture as a manager succeeded. In politics, first as a dramatist, then as a journalist, he revealed the seriousness of his character, and his genuine detestation of hypocrisy and meanness. His *Pasquin*, produced at the New Theatre in April 1736, satirised theatrical, social and political conditions, and vigorously attacked the corrupt methods of Walpole's Government. The play equalled the run of *The Beggar's Opera*, and it filled Fielding's purse. In the following year, he renewed the attack with his *Historical Register for 1736*, in which, under the name of Mr. Quidam, he brought Walpole on the stage, leading a chorus of false patriots, and filling their pockets with gold. His political farces were a menace to the Government, which Walpole could not afford to ignore. In June 1737 the Licensing Act imposed a censorship on plays. Fielding's career as a political dramatist was closed. He wrote no more for the stage.

In the following November, he entered the Middle Temple as a student for the Bar, and was called in June 1740. Where and how he and his family lived during these and the following years is uncertain. Probably it was at this period that he was helped by George Lyttelton and Ralph Allen, of Bath. He made little or nothing at his profession. Money was scarce, for in 1738 he sold his share in East Stour for £250. *Joseph Andrews* (1742) brought him in £183 11s. 0d. His *Miscellanies* (1743), in which appeared his second novel, *Jonathan Wild*, were published by subscription, and paid him better. But he wrote in the midst of troubles, laid up with the gout, " with a favourite Child dying in one Bed, and my Wife in a condition very little better on another, attended with other circumstances which served as very proper Decorations to such a Scene." To his credit, he did not find party journalism lucrative. As Captain Hercules Vinegar in *The Champion*, he was in the forefront of the Opposition. But in 1741, when he bade farewell to party politics, he describes the Opposition waggon, drawn by a team of ill-matched asses, with a driver who had lost his way and restive passengers. One protested that he would drive through no more dirt ; another got out ; a third observed that the asses were the worst-fed animals he had ever seen. " That long-sided Ass they call ' Vinegar,' which the Drivers call upon so often to ' gee up ' and ' pull lustily,' I never saw an Ass with a worse Mane or a more shagged Coat." Had Fielding been a mere hireling, his powerful pen would have commanded a price.

For months he was absent from London in attendance on his sick wife at Bath. Himself in failing health, tortured with anxiety, he was overwhelmed by the shock of her death (November 1744). His grief was so intense that " his friends feared for his reason." But he could not be idle. His pen was his only means of support. When he reappeared in journalism, the note of his political writing had deepened. Beneath the personal feeling of the political partisan, there had always burned an honest indignation at the degradation of national life, the exclusion of all nobler sentiments from politics, the unhealthy acquiescence of public opinion in the sordid scramble for place, power and profits. He

ceased to be a party politician and became a patriot.   In his
newspapers, *The True Patriot* (1745–6) and *The Jacobite's
Journal* (1747–8), he strove earnestly to shame the nation
out of its indifference, and denounced his brother journalists
as lost to public honour.

" Whatever he desired," says Murphy, " he desired
ardently."   He threw the same ardour which he had shown
in politics into his advocacy of social reforms.   An official
appointment gave him the opportunity.   At the close of
1748, on the eve of his greatest literary triumph, when
Tom Jones was passing through the press, he accepted the
post of police magistrate at Bow Street, and, a few weeks
later, was elected Chairman of Middlesex Quarter Sessions.
The appointment was not then regarded as honourable ;
nor, if honestly administered, was it lucrative.   Determined
to make his office respected, he would be no " trading
justice," swelling his income by fees indirectly derived
from connivance at crime.   On the contrary, he reduced
his official salary from £500 to £300 a year by assistance to
poor suitors.   But the regular income, for the first time in
his life, relieved him from the struggle to earn his daily
bread with his pen.   In broken health and physical pain,
he discharged his duties with extraordinary vigour.   By
breaking up the organised gangs of criminals he made life
more secure for orderly citizens.   During the last six weeks
of 1753 he could say with pardonable pride, though the
effort probably cost him his life, that there was not one
single murder or robbery in the streets of London under his
charge.

Not satisfied with the suppression of crime, he aimed also
at its prevention.   No man of his own generation, or of many
future generations (Wesley only excepted), saw more clearly
the social evils which created rogues and criminals, or
worked with more earnest zeal for their removal.   His
remedies were practical : firmer administration of the
criminal law ; fresh legislation against the sale of gin ; against
pawnbrokers or indiscriminate charity ; restrictions on
gambling houses and places of entertainment ; the improvement of the vile rookeries in which masses of the people
were herded ; the revision of the Poor Law ; the erection

of county workhouses ; the reform of prisons ; the substitution of private executions for the Tyburn holidays, which demoralised the crowd by the spectacle of " Cartloads of your Fellow-creatures carried once in six weeks to Slaughter." In pamphlets, in charges to Grand Juries, in Draft Bills for Parliament, in his fourth newspaper, *The Covent Garden Journal* (January–June 1752), even in the last of his novels, *Amelia* (December 1751), he illustrated by examples the evils that he combated, or elaborated the details of his plans ; or, with passionate zeal, endeavoured to rouse the mass of citizens to abandon the " cursed Maxim that Everybody's business is Nobody's."

Fielding's untiring labours, no less than his buoyant spirits, might conceal from his acquaintance his shattered health. But his friends would not be deceived " by the Cheerfulness which was always natural to me, and which, I thank God, my Conscience doth not reprove me for," into thinking that " I am not sensible of my declining Constitution." So he wrote at the close of 1753, suffering from asthma, jaundice, gout and dropsy. He struggled on till the spring of 1754, when he resigned his office. It was hoped that a sunny winter might prolong his life. In June, " a spectacle of the highest horror," he was carried on board the *Queen of Portugal* at Rotherhithe, and sailed for Lisbon. With him went his second wife. He had married, in November 1748, Mary Daniel, who had been the first Mrs. Fielding's maid, " an excellent creature," says Lady Louisa Stuart, " devotedly attached to her mistress and almost broken-hearted at her loss." Their first child had been born in February 1749. In the *Journal* of his voyage are many grateful references to her care of him and his children. Four months after landing at Lisbon he died.

His *Journal of the Voyage to Lisbon*, published after his death (1755), throws light on the real man. Of his own sufferings he said little and made no complaint. His long struggle had not abated his courage or soured his temper. His invincible gaiety still responded to any favourable circumstances. Lady Mary Wortley-Montagu has noted her cousin's " happy constitution," which forgot troubles " in a venison pasty or a flask of champagne." There was a trace of the old Fielding in his pleasure at the clouted cream, the John Dory, or the " Southam Cyder," of which, with a touch of his improvident generosity, he ordered two hogsheads as presents to friends. He was still amused by the scenes around him ; still delighted in the beauties of nature ; still sought and found the good qualities in bullying captains and dissolute seamen. He had lost nothing of his shrewd insight into human nature, his keen powers of observation, the vigour and liveliness of his character sketches. To the end, he preserved his warm interest in humanity, his tenderness of heart, his gratitude for every kindness.

Fielding said that he left off writing plays when he ought to have begun. His novels, on the other hand, are the finest products of his character and genius, written from ripe experience, in the full maturity of his powers. They were carefully and deliberately composed. Especially is this true of his masterpiece. To *Tom Jones* he gave, as he said himself, the work of " some Thousands of Hours," in the hope that its pages would be " read with Honour by those who never knew nor saw me, and whom I shall neither know nor see." Here, at least, he wrote, not for daily bread, but for immortality. That so high an aim should have been conceived, in all the known circumstances of his life, increases respect for Fielding. His novels were produced under a burden of anxieties which would have crushed men of less resolute courage. Yet his spirits never flag. His view of human nature remains generous and just. Keenly alive to the vast prevalence of vice and misery, he never accepts the cynic's view that selfishness poisons all the springs of conduct, never grows pessimistic, or takes refuge, like Swift, in savage misanthropy. It is as natural to him to find goodness in a rogue, or to conclude that most men err rather from folly than from vice, as it is to praise with genuine enthusiasm the virtues of his friends.

The dates at which his four acknowledged novels were published were : *The History of the Adventures of Joseph Andrews and of his Friend Mr. Abraham Adams* (1742) ; *The Life of Mr. Jonathan Wild the Great* (1743) ; *History of Tom Jones, a Foundling* (1749) ; *Amelia* (1751). There is no reasonable doubt that the anonymous *Mrs. Shamela Andrews* was also his work.

Jonathan Wild stands so far apart from his other novels as to suggest that, though second in date of publication, it was first in order of composition. It is the choice and treatment of subject, and not immaturity of power, that make the suggestion plausible. In originality, in workmanship, in sustained and effective irony, the book is excelled by none of the other novels. It purports to record the life of an historical personage who was hanged at Tyburn in 1725. An unmitigated scoundrel, a blend of the thief and the thief-taker, Wild attained eminence in crime by qualities which lead others to honour. Fielding does not say that Newgate is human nature unmasked. But he does say that courts and palaces are " Newgate with the Mask on." By gravely appropriating to Wild's achievements the eulogistic language which biographers employ in lives of more secure and illustrious criminals, Fielding creates the impression that the spurious or " bombast " greatness of those whose undetected villainies are similarly redeemed by no genuine worth is substantially the same, whether it is rewarded with the gallows or a title. Only those are truly great, says Fielding, who possess the virtues of a good man : " Benevolence, Honour, Honesty and Charity."

Jonathan Wild is an unpleasant book. It has the gloom, the chill, the rank atmosphere of the prison. Even the humour is grim. The callous gaol-birds mock at unselfish motives, and, except in the company of the Heartfrees, every kindly feeling is banished. In 1742, Fielding had made a popular hit with his comic epic of the Road, its coaches, its taverns, its wayfarers, full of fresh air, high spirits and boisterous laughter. He studied the tastes of his public, and it therefore seems unlikely that, a year later, he should have followed *Joseph Andrews* with a book conceived in so different a spirit as *Jonathan Wild*. Nor is it likely that he would have failed to apply to the disconnected episodes in *Jonathan Wild* the experience in plot-building which he had gained from *Joseph Andrews*. But if he had the manuscript by him, partly or wholly finished, he might well have used it to add to his subscriptions by a third

PA

volume of his *Miscellanies*. The facts of his career hint another reason for thinking that *Jonathan Wild* was the first novel to be written. The Licensing Act of 1737 had deprived him of an income and forced him to adopt a new profession. Even his happy disposition might well have been embittered. It would chime with his passing mood of bitterness to compose a book on the text that, outside Newgate and honoured by their fellows, were men of worse characters than those within its walls, and that they, not excluding the whole body of Ministers, might justly change places with the inhabitants of the prison.

In his other novels, Fielding adopts an attitude which is the converse of that assumed in *Jonathan Wild*. Instead of exposing the undetected basenesses of men of high repute, he reveals the good qualities in those who might be called rascals. On many sides of national life, Fielding, as has been shown, rose high above the morality of his contemporaries. But where the animal appetites come into play, he belonged to his generation. In the reign of George II, the moral sensibilities of the nation were blunted. Fielding's own capacities for enjoyment, which amazed his cousin, Lady Mary Wortley-Montagu, presented him to a French critic as an " amiable buffalo." Possibly his youthful experiences may have deepened an inborn vein of coarseness. The effect is seen, not in his Hogarthian pictures of vice, but in his apparent unconsciousness of the brutality of some of his scenes, and his seeming tolerance of a low standard of conduct in his heroes which alienates sympathy. But this insensitiveness, if admitted, is compensated by the characteristic qualities of his moral teaching, which keep the general atmosphere of his novels sane and wholesome. Had they been more refined and elevated in their estimate of moral beauty, they would not have represented with such unrivalled truth the features of contemporary life in Hanoverian England.

In all his novels, Fielding was so emphatically a moralist that critics might reproach him with preaching too much rather than too little. His moral teaching owed little to abstract thought, for it was not in his nature to withdraw from his fellows into the solitude of mountain-tops in order to speculate on the problems of existence. Voracious reader and sturdy Protestant though he was, his ethics were independent of philosophical systems or of religion. The maxims of philosophy could not prevent Square from being a hypocrite, or console the distress of Parson Adams when he thought that his child was drowned. Religion he respected as a useful handmaid to good conduct, and to that practical sphere he limited its province. He distrusted its enthusiasms, suspected its emotions, denied its authority to override reason. No clearer illustration of his utilitarian attitude towards the doctrines and institutions of the Church can be given than the exposition of the Eucharist which he puts into the mouth of Parson Adams.

His own experience of life was the foundation of his moral teaching. But his varied knowledge of the world was moulded by a great intellect, a keen observation, a deep insight, a large and generous nature, into ripe, kindly and humorous wisdom. He was no Mr. Worldly Wiseman. His morality, compared with that of Chesterfield's *Letters*, is like rough homespun, which stands hard usage, beside some subtly-woven silken fabric designed for show and not for wear. He could never have given Chesterfield's infamous advice, " *il faut décrotter cette femme-là.*" The conventions of society were to him insincerities. He knew the fatal objection to Richardson's prudential morality ; it was not true. In this world vice is neither punished nor virtue rewarded. But if men would remember that there are frailties in the best of their fellows, and good impulses even in rogues, they might make what it was intended to be, a pleasant place. He refused to paint perfect heroes, because he had never found perfection. Yet, within the limits of his shrewd common sense, he was an earnest champion of all the homely virtues which, as he thought, could be reasonably demanded from ordinary men ; generous in his warm appreciation of practical goodness ; a hearty enemy of all forms of affectation, meanness or hypocrisy ; a worshipper, with manly devotion, of the type of womanhood which satisfied his generation—not idealised, nor highly educated, but incarnate in flesh and blood, pure, tender, forbearing, true.

In their general atmosphere his three great novels change with the stages of his literary life at which they were respectively written. They represent the morning, the high noon, and the evening of his career. Each has its appropriate charm. *Joseph Andrews* has the freshness, the joyousness, the inexperience of a not very distant youth. In *Tom Jones* the spirits still soar high ; but they are tempered by the considered thought and ripened wisdom of mature manhood. Over *Amelia* hangs the pathos of sunset ; and the tender glow which irradiates the figure of the heroine reflects the sobered outlook of a man who, still young in mind and memories, is conscious that he is old in body.

That a man's writings should thus represent his age at the time of their composition is neither unnatural nor unusual. Such indications of mental and physical change are involuntary, if not unconscious. But no novelist has put more of himself into his work than Fielding. His novels reveal the man, not only indirectly, but directly. The pages are pervaded by his bigness of nature, his humorous philosophy of life, his kindly tolerance of the follies, frailties and foibles of human nature. In the confidential talks with his readers, which he prefixes to his chapters, he drops all disguises, comes into the open as the author, and discusses men and things, his own work, characters, aims and ambitions. In thus avowing the fictitious nature of his narrative, he asserted the rights of its author to omniscience and omnipresence. He offered to his public a re-creation of contemporary life, in which his imagination, working on the materials of his observation and experience, embodied in human form his own conceptions of humanity, grouped his personages artistically, and left them to play the parts in speech and action which were natural to their individualities.

This was a novelty in prose fiction. Defoe had endeavoured to conceal the fictitious character of his inventions, and to pass them off as actual occurrences. Richardson was hampered by the same object. He sailed near the wind in asserting the genuineness of Pamela's correspondence, and he never grows more tiresome than when he labours to authenticate every detail of the information, which he alone possessed, by tracking it to an invented source. Fielding swept aside the convention of the delusion of actual fact ; he aimed openly at the illusion of truth. He claimed for the novel a distinct place in literature as a creative effort of imaginative art.

His contemporaries were puzzled. The presentation of life was so vivid and true that they could not divest themselves of the belief that Fielding was describing himself in his characters, or describing scenes in which he was the principal actor. Richardson expressed this view, with an added touch of venom, when he denied to his rival the power of invention. It is probably true, as he asserts, that Parson Adams was partly modelled on the Reverend William Young, who was curate of Easy Stour from 1731 to 1741, and witnessed Fielding's assignment to the publisher of his copyright in *Joseph Andrews*. But that great character was built up from many sources. It owed, for instance, something both to Young and to Cervantes. Don Quixote and Parson Adams are alike in their guileless simplicity and natural dignity, and a scholar's enthusiasm plays a part in the brain of the English parson similar to that played by romances of chivalry in the mind of the Spanish knight. But it owed most of all to the vivifying power of Fielding's imagination.

Nor need it be assumed, as Richardson assumes, that Tom Jones is the author himself, or that the adventures are reminiscent of his own youth. Fielding was a close observer, and he had a keen insight into human nature, especially of the rather commonplace type. His presentation of what he observed makes a vivid impression of accuracy, sincerity and, perhaps above all, of courage. Tom Jones, therefore, is not necessarily his own likeness. It is rather a closely observed imaginary portrait of an ordinary young man, good-looking, good-natured and good-tempered, whose better instincts are repeatedly swept aside by the hot impulses of youth. The boldness of the picture robbed the novel of its hero, but it replaced him with a real man.

Amelia affords another example of similar misunderstandings. The book, published more than seven years after the death of his first wife, contains her portrait in that of the heroine. Richardson at once assumed that in her husband, Booth, Fielding was painting himself in a background of scenes from his own career. The public followed him by reading into the book the author's contrition for the wrongs which, as they inferred, he had himself inflicted on the dead woman whom he had passionately loved. The inference is unnecessary ; it is also, to a certain extent, contradicted by facts. Few men, looking back on their married life, have nothing to regret in things said or done, and in things left unsaid or undone. Poverty and its shifts were the inevitable lot of the wife of a struggling man of letters ; but, in Fielding's case, the privations were aggravated by the extravagances into which he was betrayed by his generous and sanguine temperament. Here lay abundant material for the haze of remorseful tenderness in which the figure of Amelia is undoubtedly wrapped. But Mrs. Fielding never suffered the worst wrongs that Booth inflicted on Amelia. As has already been pointed out, Murphy, his only contemporary biographer, bears witness to Fielding's constancy to his wife. Nor is there any evidence that Fielding was ever addicted to gambling ; as a magistrate, he had abundant experience of the domestic miseries which were its consequences. That he and his wife were often very poor is true ; but, however great their straits, he seems never to have parted with his library, or Mrs. Fielding with her faithful servant, Mary Daniel, who remained with her mistress till her death.

One curious episode is connected with the portrait of Mrs. Fielding in the character of Amelia. As a girl, she had been in a carriage accident which had permanently scarred her nose. That the injury did not materially mar her beauty is proved by the evidence of Lady Bute. The novel referred to the accident, and to the mask that Amelia was obliged to wear while in the hands of the surgeon. "In a Hurry" Fielding forgot to describe the cure. The book suffered from his omission. Dr. Johnson, who read it through at a sitting, and found Mrs. Booth "the most pleasing heroine of all the romances," attributed the slow sale of the second edition to the public's abhorrence of a noseless heroine. Fielding did his best to remedy the defect. He introduced several passages into the book referring to the cure of the injury. Thus Mrs. James, in cataloguing her rival's charms, says that " her nose, well proportioned as it is, has a visible scar on one side." He even inserted a paragraph in his *Covent Garden Journal* stating that the surgeon who had attended Amelia threatened to bring an action against those people who asserted that she had no nose. Richardson would have been involved in the threatened proceedings, for, according to him, Amelia was Fielding's first wife " even to her noselessness." The story might well have been the text of Sterne's chapter on Noses. It at least warns novelists to be careful of tampering with so important a feature in the faces of their heroines.

Fielding's vindication of the true position of the novel as a distinct and independent branch of imaginative art was an important step in advance. It freed novelists from restrictions which hampered their choice of the form of presentation. It was not his only service to the development of the novel. As a constructor of plots, he has perhaps received exaggerated praise. In this respect, in spite of his rival's long-windedness, he was inferior to Richardson.

The scenes in *Joseph Andrews*, loosely strung to the fortunes of an insipid pair of lovers, are not more firmly compacted than the disconnected episodes in Scarron's *Roman Comique*, or a score of similar works. It is the straggling nature of the narrative, which explains the view of French critics, that Fielding stood in the direct line of descent from the Spanish Rogues, and was, therefore, less original and independent than Richardson. The book suffered from a changed purpose. It began as a parody of *Pamela* ; it ended, to use Fielding's phrase, as a " comic Epic Poem in prose."

Joseph Andrews, the brother of Pamela, is in service to a member of the same Booby family. He opposes the same virtuous resistance to the temptations of Lady Booby which his sister offered to " Mr. B." Carried away by the joy and zest of creation, Fielding forgets the parody, though he returns to it at a later stage, when Parson Adams rebukes Pamela and her husband for laughing in church. When Fielding lost interest in his original intention, the reality of the relationship between Joseph and Pamela ceased to be important, and he begins to play with the mystery of the footman's birth, as a means of strengthening his plot. The final discovery of Joseph's parentage, clinched by his strawberry mark, burlesques those romantic writers, whose heroes and heroines were in the end revealed as princes and princesses.

In *Joseph Andrews*, Fielding served his apprenticeship as a builder. In his two subsequent novels, there was no divided purpose. An afterthought became a guiding principle. His conception of the form of a novel had cleared. Remembering Aristotle's statement that, in drama, Attic comedy and Attic tragedy were related in the same way, as, in epic poetry, the *Iliad* was related to the fragmentary *Margites, or the Booby,* he set himself to write an epic in prose—comic in *Tom Jones,* in *Amelia* tinged with tragedy. In construction *Tom Jones* was his masterpiece. He put his plot to a severe test. In *Joseph Andrews,* that glorious interloper, Parson Adams, who, from the moment of his appearance, held the stage, masks the weakness of the construction. In *Amelia* the interest is so centred in the heroine that, even if the plot were inadequate, the story would retain its unity. But in *Tom Jones* there is neither a dominating personality nor a central figure. Yet the plot holds the story together. Its plan is deliberately laid, closely followed, and leads up to a definite conclusion. The mystery of the foundling's birth, suggested in the title, is the pivot of the whole, and the discovery of his parentage not only unmasks the villainy of Blifil, but removes the last obstacle to the union of Tom Jones and Sophia Western. It is, however, exaggerated praise to claim perfection for the construction. Here, as in *Amelia,* episodical narratives, not entirely irrelevant to the theme, but told at disproportionate length, interrupt the progress of the story. No lover of Fielding would willingly lose the " initial essays " ; but it is difficult, on any artistic grounds, to defend their occurrence. Nor is the conduct of the story flawless. But whatever may be the minor faults in the construction of *Tom Jones,* its ordered march of concerted events towards a preconceived end was an advance on the form of *Don Quixote,* and a new departure, except for the example of Richardson, in English prose fiction.

Fielding brought to bear on his work other gifts besides the power of constructing a plot. His humour is abundant ; his satire and irony, as well as grave, are pervasive. Pathos, as scenes in *Amelia* show, is at his command. But he does not, like Richardson, luxuriate in emotion. He leaves the situations to make their own appeal, and it is not the less effectively made because of its restraint and simplicity. He is the master of an admirable style, which, in its strength and suppleness, gives adequate expression to all that he desires to say. Here, at any rate, his contemporary falls far below him. Richardson writes with the fluent, slipshod ease of a letter-writer. Yet, if any of his readers ask themselves whether he had any style, they must inevitably reply that he had none at all.

But, of all Fielding's gifts, his greatest is his power of creating characters, combined, as it is, with delight in its exercise. His joy in creation is communicated to the figures whom he creates. They act, speak, laugh, quarrel, fight, with a zest and heartiness which reflect something of his own vitality. They are alive with almost superabundant life, not merely as human beings, but as individuals. It is only in those instances, where his natural ardour overcomes his impartiality, that they become types. He adored benevolence; he detested hypocrisy. Where he deals with an Allworthy or a Blifil, he loses his impartiality, and compounds them so exclusively of the qualities which they represent, that each ceases to be an individual and becomes a type of his respective virtue or vice.

Fielding's portraits of women lacked Richardson's delicacy of perception. Yet, if less familiar than his rival with the bypaths of the female heart, he knew at least as well its broad highways. It was Fielding, not Richardson, who discovered for English readers the romance of the married woman. Amelia, the wife who not only forgave but forgot, claims her right to a place by or above Clarissa Harlowe. His men are infinitely superior to those of Richardson. In drawing many of their characters, one feature in his methods recurs so often as to be almost a principle of his art, as well as of his ethics. It is the search for some vein of precious ore in the most unpromising materials. Where he finds it, he tests its genuineness with almost merciless severity. Whether, in Tom Jones, enough of the metal to be worthy of Sophia survives the crowning ordeal of his relations with Lady Bellaston may be doubted. Fielding evidently shared the doubt, for he adopts a clumsy expedient to rehabilitate his character. In order to show that Tom still retains some power of resisting temptation, he makes him reject the hand of a Mrs. Arabella Hunt, who, for the purpose of the proposal, makes her first, last and only appearance in the story. But Parson Adams is proof against every test. The heart of gold, which Fielding found in that brawny Christian, under the shabby coat, torn cassock, rusty wig and battered hat, beats strongly through all its trials, and triumphs serenely over the ordeals of the swill-tub and the scene in Fanny's bed-chamber.

The habitual search for ore in the midst of apparent dross restricted the range of Fielding's observation. He did not look for the refinements of human nature, listen for its aspirations, or contemplate the potentialities of its rise. Consequently, there is little that is elevating or inspiring in his characters. But, within his own allotted scope, he built on the sure foundation of insight into the essentials of human nature, and his work is as solid and substantial as on the day when it was done. His search for homely virtues, under the rough exteriors of commonplace men and sorry rascals, was much more than a literary device. Nor was it merely the instinct of a kind-hearted man. It had a deeper origin and meaning. It was a protest against the formalism of the day, an insistence on the difference between being and seeming, an assertion of his belief that what a man *is* is at least as important as what he does ; perhaps, also, an unconscious appeal to posterity to judge him, not by his manifest faults and frailties, but by the tenor of his life as a whole.

CHAPTER XIV

THE FIRST GREAT PERIOD OF THE MODERN NOVEL, 1740–66

THE world wept with Richardson, and laughed with Fielding. Their success undoubtedly stimulated the development of prose fiction. But the output was so large that it cannot be attributed to their influence alone. It was evident that there was a felt demand for the imaginative presentations of the realities of life. Every change in social conditions has tended to increase the need. The hustle and anxiety of modern competition make the desire of men and women to be taken out of themselves almost universal. Through a story they escape from their own circumstances. Without bodily fatigue or disturbance of domestic habits, they can read a novel. To-day imaginative prose fiction has become rather a necessity than a luxury of social life.

If the influence of Richardson and Fielding did not create the demand for prose fiction, it helped to guide its course. Their life-like pictures of contemporary realities eclipsed romances, and, as heroes and heroines, substituted for princes and princesses ordinary men and women. As an illustration of the trend of literary fashions the *Adventures of David Simple* gains historical importance from its date (1744). Its scenes were laid in the London of the day, and it derives its interest rather from analysis of character than from accumulation of incidents. It marks the direction in which the taste of the public was veering, and it was along this road that Sarah Fielding travelled.

The authorship of *David Simple* lends it a further interest. The sister of Henry Fielding, and one of the " adopted daughters " of Richardson, she follows *Pamela* rather than *Joseph Andrews*. Her hero is a sentimental, vapid youth, who, in search of a real friend, sees different phases of life from his lodgings in various parts of the " Cities of London and Westminster," and hovers, like Sir Charles Grandison, between the loves of two rival ladies. In spite of the words on the title-page, "By a Lady," the public so persistently attributed the book to Henry Fielding that, in a preface to the second edition, he was obliged to deny its authorship.

For some years to come, the demand for pictures of real and contemporary life gathered strength. Francis Coventry, in his *History of Pompey the Little* (1751), with an obvious reference to Fielding, calls his novel an "*Epic Poem in Prose,*" describes the period as a "*Life-writing Age,*" and illustrates the subjects of its biographies: "The lowest and most contemptible Vagrants, Parish-Girls, Chamber-Maids, Pick-Pockets, and Highwaymen, find historians to record their Praises, and Readers to wonder at their Exploits." As a general description of the character of novels of the day the passage is true.

Ten years later the stream of novels of contemporary life had become a deluge. In 1760, George Coleman's play *Polly Honeycombe* was acted at Drury Lane. It was also published with the sub-title of "A Dramatick Novel." Polly, misled by much novel-reading, rejects Mr. Ledger, a prosperous City man, who woos her in the terms of an accountant, for a rascally adventurer, Mr. Scribble, who is a master of the art of writing love-letters. In the Preface, Coleman gives a list of 180 recently published books recounting the "History," the "Adventures" or the "Life" of all sorts and conditions of men and women, generally in the lower sections of society. A Prologue, contributed by Garrick, describes the spell of Romance and the "Toledo blade" of Cervantes, and sings how:

> Her Talismans and Magick Wand He broke—
> Knights, Genii, Castles—vanish'd into smoke.
> But now, the dear delight of later years,
> The younger Sister of ROMANCE appears:
> Less solemn is her air, her drift the same,
> And NOVEL her enchanting, charming, Name.
> ROMANCE might strike our grave Forefathers' pomp,
> But NOVEL for our Buck and lively Romp!
> Cassandra's Folios now no longer read,
> See, Two Neat Pocket Volumes in their stead
> And then so *sentimental* is the Stile,

So chaste, yet so bewitching all the while !
Plot, and elopement, passion, rape, and rapture,
The total sum of ev'ry dear—dear—Chapter.

In this mass of production, continued throughout the century, there were a hundred volumes to one book, a hundred echoes to one voice. Yet the twenty-five years which followed the publication of *Pamela* and *Joseph Andrews* were one of the great periods in the history of the modern novel during its experimental stage. It was remarkably rich in great names. Smollett, Johnson, Sterne, Horace Walpole and Goldsmith may all be considered as literary contemporaries of Richardson and Fielding. Smollett's first novel, *Roderick Random* (1748), followed *Clarissa Harlowe* by a few months, and preceded the publication of *Tom Jones*. *Rasselas* and the first volumes of *Tristram Shandy* were published in the life-time of Richardson. Walpole and Goldsmith alone belong to a slightly later date, for *The Castle of Otranto* (1764) and *The Vicar of Wakefield* (1766) appeared within five years after Richardson's death.

Tobias Smollett (1721–71) was a younger man than either of his two great contemporaries, and found the true outlet of his genius in novel-writing at an earlier age. Averse from sentiment, painting with a full brush, and splashing on his colour, he worked by methods sharply contrasted with those of Richardson. His manner more resembles that of Fielding. Both men, in order to emphasise the effectiveness of contrasts, incline to exaggeration. But 'in Fielding the tendency is restrained by his artistic sense and his desire for accuracy. In this respect, Smollett is to his rival as Rowlandson is to Hogarth. In their delineations of character, Richardson dwells on the principles ; Smollett insists on the practical results ; Fielding, knowing the principles and observing the results, not only notes eccentricities, but treats character as a living whole. Richardson draws men from within, Smollett from without, Fielding from both. Hence, while Richardson's creations are mechanical and Smollett's typical, Fielding's are individual and universal.

It is the fashion to compare Fielding with Thackeray, and Smollett with Dickens. The parallelism seems somewhat unprofitable. Between Smollett and Dickens there are superficial resemblances. Each is a caricaturist, with an eye for oddities, eccentricities and professional idiosyncrasies. But there the real likeness seems to end. On the surface, again, Thackeray resembles Fielding ; but between the work of the two men there is little similarity in substance. What attracted Thackeray to " Handsome Harry Fielding " was his buoyant nature and his frank abandonment to the joy of creation ; but there is little affinity between these gifts and the anxious temperament of his nineteenth-century successor.

A juster view of the two men might be obtained by comparing them respectively with Cervantes and Le Sage. Fielding, like Cervantes, makes the conduct of his actors follow from their dispositions ; his creations are at once individualities and living illustrations of universal principles of human nature. Smollett, like his model, Le Sage, takes men as they have been moulded by circumstances, and insists less on their internal dispositions than on the visible effect of their external conditions. The one is a painter of the deeper elements of character of which manners are the disguise or expression ; the other, of the manners which are the superficial products of surrounding circumstances. Yet between Le Sage and Smollett there are instructive differences. Smollett travels, like Sterne's Smelfungus, with a jaundiced eye, and the testiness as well as the independence of a Scotsman ; Le Sage carries with him the gaiety of a Frenchman who regards the world as a theatre which offers him diversion. Both paint life, but Smollett is most dependent on his reminiscences. With two or three exceptions, Le Sage makes few personal allusions, while Smollett's figures are almost all caricatures of living persons. Le Sage's *Gil Blas* is a comedy ; Smollett's novels are farces. So far as both are moralists, Le Sage preaches virtue by laughing at Vice, Smollett by painting Vice, with crude brutality, in all her naked coarseness.

Between Fielding and Smollett differences of nature and of constitution fixed a gulf which necessarily separates their writings. The broad and kindly humanity of Fielding is sharply contrasted with the ill-tempered inhumanity of Smollett. The one attracts, the other repels. It is as impossible to resist a liking for Tom Jones as it is to feel

anything but repugnance for swaggering, selfish bullies like
Roderick Random and Peregrine Pickle, whom their creator
regards with approving complacency. In graphic force of
style, Smollett is Fielding's equal ; in broad farcical humour
and fertility of comic resource, he may even be regarded as
his superior. But in insight into characters and in their
artistic grouping he is inferior. He is also inferior in the
construction of a plot. Here he is reactionary where
Fielding is progressive. He does not write a real history,
based on fictitious facts, keeping his actors well in view from
the first and conducting them towards a preconceived end.
He falls back on older methods of narrative. Like the
Spanish school of Rogue fiction, he starts his hero on his
career, gathers round him as he goes a group of actors,
reports their haphazard adventures, and concludes with the
mechanical device of marriage. Both writers enriched the
resources of their art. Their vigorous pictures of contemporary life are strongly contrasted by their broad, effective touches with Defoe's minute circumstantiality of fact
or Richardson's meticulous detail of character. Fielding's
gifts to the treasury of the novelist are of greater permanent
value than Smollett's peculiar and more temporary contributions. Yet, if the immediate influence of the two men on
the course of prose fiction were measured, that of Smollett
would probably be found to be greater than that of Fielding.

The grandson of Sir James Smollett of Bonhill, but the
younger son of a younger son, Smollett had his living to
make. The medical profession was chosen for him, and
he studied at Glasgow University. In 1739 the young
medical student arrived in London, his heart in literature,
in his pocket a tragedy and little else. When the theatres
rejected *The Regicide*, he sailed as a surgeon on board H.M.S.
Cumberland to take part in the Carthagena expedition.
Four years later he was back in London. Failing to succeed
as a doctor, he turned definitely to literature for his livelihood. His labours were immense. His first two novels,
Roderick Random (1748) and *Peregrine Pickle* (1751), were
followed by *The Adventures of Ferdinand, Count Fathom*
(1753), *The Adventures of Sir Launcelot Greaves* (1761),
The History and Adventures of an Atom (1768), and in 1771,

the year of his death at Leghorn, *The Expedition of Humphrey Clinker*. In the interval between his first and last novels he produced a vast number of miscellaneous works, and, feared rather than venerated, made himself a position in the literary world which was second only to that of Dr. Johnson.

In the art of the novelist, Smollett represented decline rather than advance. He stepped backwards instead of forwards. His novels are straggling narratives which hurry towards no particular end. They are collections of comic episodes, the sequence of which might be transposed at will—medleys of disconnected adventures encountered by the hero and the actors whom he picks up on his travels. In such a form it was easy to write a novel, and imitators wrote them by the score. But none could imitate the irresistible force of his broad humour, his endless inventions of burlesque incidents, his fertility of resource, the variety of forms of life which he depicts, and the rapidity with which his events succeed one another. The world, as he described it, resembled the close of a pantomime. No such hurly-burly of horseplay and boisterous roar of laughter could have arisen from any other society except that of the days of George II. Even at that period the accumulation of comic disasters seems exaggerated.

To the materials of the novelist, on the other hand, Smollett made valuable contributions. His experiences in the Navy enabled him to paint vivid pictures of the real sea and of seafaring life as it was actually lived. He was the father of the sea novel. His keen eye for anything abnormal detected, not only oddities of feature and figure, but professional eccentricities, national idiosyncrasies, racial peculiarities. He drew from the life sailors like Commodore Trunnion, Hatchaway, Bowling and Pipes, or doctors like Morgan and Macshane, or Welshmen, Irishmen, Jews and, above all, Scotsmen. His Lismahago is, as Scott acknowledged, a lineal ancestor of Dugald Dalgetty. The points on which he seized were superficial. Incarnating, so to speak, external features or particular traits, he missed the living whole of composite human beings. But his portraits are so vigorous that they are unforgettable. They stand out as clearly as do the men whom we habitually meet in our daily avocations without knowing anything of their inner lives and characters.

In his professional and national pictures, Smollett struck a new vein, from which many of his successors, and notably Dickens, quarried some of their most characteristic material. One other novelty in Smollett's work may be noted. It was his boast that he appealed to nature in every particular, and he certainly spared his readers few of its physical details. He therefore represented the extreme recoil alike from idealism and from Richardson's sentiment. Yet he was the first of modern novelists to dwell on the emotion of terror and of awe of the supernatural. Such scenes as that of Roderick Random chained to the deck of the *Thunder* under the fire of the French battleship, or that of Count Fathom in the robbers' cave, or that of the appearance of Monimia to her lover Renaldo, illustrate the sombre power of his imagination, and suggest that, if he had been born twenty years later, he might have been a leader of the Romantics.

Roderick Random follows so closely the course of Smollett's early career that something of its vividness and spirit is derived from fresh recollections of his own experiences. In certain passages *Peregrine Pickle* is finer than its predecessor ; but, as a whole, it is inferior. In its original form it is marred by two serious blots. One is the irrelevant and nasty " Memoirs of a Lady of Quality," which occupy considerably more than half of the third volume of the first edition ; the other is the ferocity and venom of the satire with which, under the thinnest of veils, and in the worst style of Mrs. Manley, he bespattered his contemporaries At the close of his life, Smollett's irritability of temper seems to have mellowed. It does not appear in *Humphrey Clinker*, written a few months before his death, the book by which his genius may be most truly measured. The nominal hero plays little part in the story. He is a Methodist postilion, picked up, on their travels, by the Bramble family. The narrative still has no plot. It is told in the form of letters written by Matthew Bramble himself, or by those who accompany him from one watering-place to another in search of his health. Each letter expresses the point of view of the writer, and the comedy lies in the description of the same scenes by the various members of the party.

QA

Except for one unpardonable passage, the book is free from that coarseness which characterises his other novels, and in fun and humour it is his masterpiece. Bramble himself, his sister Tabitha, an unwilling spinster, her maid Winifred Jenkins, and the niece Lydia are real creations, on which Smollett's fame rests secure. Not, perhaps, in the first rank of novelists, he stands high in the second, and his influence on his contemporaries, on his immediate successors, and on Dickens and Marryat, will always give his work an interest in the history of English prose fiction.

In his novels Smollett, like Richardson and Fielding, found the best expression for his genius, and on them rests his fame. To Samuel Johnson, on the other hand, the literary form was uncongenial, and it is not by *The Prince of Abyssinia* (1759), later known as *Rasselas*, that he is best remembered. Needing money to pay the expenses of his mother's funeral, he chose imaginative prose fiction as the best means for his purpose. The choice is significant of the value of the novel in the literary market. But his conservatism, and perhaps mistrust of his powers, revolted from any picture of contemporary society. Like a seventeenth-century romancer, he chose for his hero a prince, and for his scenes a distant country, to which he may have been attracted by his early translation of Father Lobo's *Voyage to Abyssinia*, adapting his model to modern tastes, not by characters or adventures, but by his own melancholy reflections on the vanity of human wishes.

The plot is well constructed to lead up to the climax of the mad astronomer. Rasselas and his sister, Nekayeh, with the wise old Imlac as their guide, leave their Happy Valley in search of occupations to give dignity and meaning to their existence. They return to their Eden, disillusioned. One after another, human aims and pursuits have been tested and proved to be futile. The book is a fine moral fable rather than a novel. Written in Johnson's happiest manner, the narrative flows easily, distinguished in its reflections and disquisitions by original turns of phrase, often memorable for their force and nobility of expression. Apart from its admirable style, *Rasselas* will always appeal to lovers of Johnson by its personal note. It brings out his sturdy rejection of a facile optimism, his haunting dread of loss of reason, the courage with which he faced the gloom of his outlook ; it reveals, also, a character moulded by rebuffs of fortune into sternness, and a resignation bought at the pain of sacrificed hopes.

Johnson's sermon illustrates the didactic tendency of modern novels of the day. Nine months after the publication of *Rasselas*, appeared a book which bears no trace of the moralist or the preacher. The author, Laurence Sterne (1713–68), has always puzzled critics, and *Tristram Shandy* defies classification. The book stands by itself in literature. Genius toiling in harness to conventionality is a common spectacle. Sterne offers the rarer sight of genius enjoying a roll. The pleasure which he gave himself is scarcely lessened by the reader's suspicion that many of the jerks are not so much spasmodic as studied for effect.

Born at Clonmel, where his father, Ensign Roger Sterne, was quartered, the child was dragged up to boyhood at the heels of a marching regiment. Left by his father's death " without a shilling in the world," he entered Jesus College, Cambridge, as a sizar, in 1773, took his degree, and was ordained. In after-life, Sterne said of *Tristram Shandy* that, if he thought any reader could tell what was coming next, he would tear out the page. His most sudden changes of mood or subject, and all his mechanical surprises of pages covered with asterisks, blank, blackened or marbled, do not create a greater effect of unexpectedness than his choice of a profession. He had no personal fitness for the vocation ; but he had family influence which promised, and secured him, several small preferments. Married, and a father, he lived from 1738 to 1759 at the vicarage of Sutton-in-the-Forest, within a few miles of York. In his parish, he shot, skated, farmed, preached, married, baptised and buried ; at home, " as the fly stung," he read, painted and fiddled ; abroad, without much regard to his cassock, he jested and flirted. But such occupations could not satisfy his hunger for all the light and warmth and colour of life. For twenty years of silence, he stood, as he describes himself, at the window of his parsonage, " in my dusty black coat, and looking through the glass to see the world in

yellow, blue, and green, running at the ring of pleasure."
Then at last he turned to writing.

He was forty-six when, in the early months of 1759, he
began *The Life and Opinions of Tristram Shandy*. The first
two volumes, published in 1759–60, gained him an instant
triumph in London society, which no previous or subsequent
writer has excelled. The last of the nine volumes of the
incomplete work appeared in 1767. On the Continent his
book was as eagerly welcomed as it had been in England.
Paris, like London, made Sterne a lion. He lived his last few
years in a blaze of celebrity. But failing health compelled
him to spend many months in France and Italy. Two books
only of *A Sentimental Journey* (February 1768) had been
published before his death in London, March 18th, 1768.

To the chorus of applause with which *Tristram Shandy*
was received there were discordant notes, especially from
the professional critics. Jealousy may have played some
part. The doors of great houses, at whose area-bells needy
men of letters had vainly striven to tinkle, were thrown
open to the unknown parson from the depths of Yorkshire.
But, in many points, the book was fairly open to criticism.
Both Johnson and Goldsmith objected to its indecency.
Richardson took similar ground. Writing to Bishop
Hildesley, on September 24th, 1761, he says : " Who is this
Yorick ? you are pleased to ask me. You cannot, I imagine,
have looked into his books : execrable I cannot but call
them ; for I am told that the third and fourth volumes are
worse, if possible, than the two first ; which, only, I have
had the patience to run through. One extenuating circumstance attends his works, that they are too gross to be
inflaming." Grossness is a less appropriate word for Sterne's
indecency than impudence. Yet he worked in an atmosphere so charged with innuendo, suggestion, double meaning
and dashes that, even in idyllic scenes, the reader often
catches a glimpse of the leer of the satyr among the vine-
leaves. Another well-founded charge is that of plagiarism.
Sterne borrowed freely. We are prepared to bow to old
acquaintances at every turn ; yet some are so transformed
that we hesitate. What he took from others he often made
his own, and stamped his debts with his own individuality

Out of his wide range of reading, he helped himself from many sources. But probably he owed most to Rabelais, Burton, John Arbuthnot, and, above all, to Cervantes, whose influence is the foundation of his work.

Whatever objections might be reasonably urged against *Tristram Shandy*, the public were right in recognising it as a work of genius. The eccentricity might have repelled, had not the substance attracted. The book had the novelty both in feeling and in manner for which many people were vaguely seeking. The wave of sentiment which Richardson had set in motion was rising. Sterne caught the tide as it turned, and helped to swell it into a flood. His sentimentalism was not, like that of Rousseau, militant and a solvent of society ; rather it was, if used in moderation, a valuable cement to social life. So also his emotional outbursts over a fly, a captive starling or a dead ass were, when less artificial and more restrained, humanising influences. No movement triumphs without exaggeration. His lachrymose sensibility was no greater an excess than the matter-of-fact callousness which it opposed.

Within the century, no just balance between the two was struck ; and to Sterne's influence must be mainly attributed the mawkish unreality which characterised much of the prose fiction of the next forty years. If he is blamed for some of the immediate evil, he must be credited with some of the ultimate good. His protest against inhuman prejudices was probably as unconscious as the appeal which his book made by force of constrast against the literary brutality of the day. Through Smollett's early work, and that of his many imitators, ran a note of violence. They represented life as a pandemonium of horseplay. Their colours shouted ; their actors bawled their boisterous jokes. Deafened and dizzied, their audiences had welcomed *Rasselas*, and now turned with relief to *Tristram Shandy*. Here were pathos, sentiment, sly humour, and, if there were indecency, it was draped. Here, too, were character-pictures, painted with an artist's eye for light and shade and colour—living figures, grouped in effective contrast, each revealing himself by personal traits in natural, vivid talk. Both in feeling and in manner, the public found in *Tristram*

Shandy, with all its many faults, something that they had dimly desired.

Considering the social conditions of the times, the one thing that is not surprising in the book is its success. Surprise is its essence. The surprises begin with the contrast between the profession and the performance of the title. Tristram Shandy was barely breeched when the ninth volume of his life and opinions ended. Without plot, plan or order, the book has little unity except the continual advertisement of the author's whimsical nature. He works by the irony of cross purposes, by the opposition of incongruities, by rapid transitions of mood, even by sudden changes of style. His principal characters are artistically grouped for humorous effect—the two Shandy brothers ; Uncle Toby and his comrade-in-arms and satellite, Corporal Trim ; or Uncle Toby, sitting in his sentry-box, pipe in hand, and searching the left eye of Widow Wadman for a mote, unconscious of its " lambent delicious fire " ; or Walter Shandy, the acute reasoner, and his placid wife, Mrs. Shandy, who never could be induced to ask a question or to remember whether the world stood still or went round. When the actors talk, neither understands the other, and each goes his or her way.

Between these creative efforts of the imagination Sterne deliberately interposes masses of irrelevant digressions. As the beauty of a mountain lake, with its green margin of fertility, is enhanced by the barren bleakness of its surroundings, so the scattered gems gain lustre from the dreary wastes of Slawkenbergius and his kindred in which they are embedded. So, also, his rapid transitions of feeling are calculated to heighten the effect of contrast. His moods seem as capricious as those of April ; sun, rain and mud do not alternate more rapidly than do Sterne's laughter, tears and dirt ; he outrages the sympathy which he has just elicited by an indecent gesture ; he shoots his irrelevant rubbish on the spot which, a moment before, he has consecrated. Even his style varies with his whims. At times he is clearness itself ; at others, he invites his reader to play hide-and-seek with his meanings. Now he shows himself a master of easy idiomatic English, of melody of words, of felicity of phrasing ; now, as the occasion offers, he is at pains to entertain his company in the dressing-gown and slippers of intimacy, his sentences in disarray, his constructions down at heel.

Where so little is artless, doubt arises whether anything is sincere. The conclusion is often drawn that all is unreal —the pathos, the sentiment, the humour, even the indecency. Yet it may be suggested that Sterne's moods are emotionally true to his sensitive, shallow nature. On its soft, receptive surface play all that he sees, hears, fancies or feels. Each object, tone or thought, however evanescent, leaves a mark. None penetrate far enough to stir emotion, still less to tug at his heart-strings or gain any permanent hold on his volatile temperament. He reflects each as they pass in quick succession. Men of harder and deeper nature not only miss much that Sterne noted ; they are also absorbed in such impressions as they do receive to the exclusion of inconsistent feelings. They mourn or laugh whole-heartedly, and repel the intrusion of comedy into grief or of pathos into laughter. But Sterne has no sense of the dignity of emotion. He courts its incongruities, and chokes a laugh with a sob, or smiles slyly through his tears. In this field he finds the clash of contrasts which for him creates much of the humour of life.

It is also to the mingled softness and shallowness of his nature that he owed the delicacy of his perceptions as well as his directness of presentation. However minute the detail on which he fastens, he transcribes it exactly as it is in itself, and not, like other men, through the medium of its emotional effect. His descriptive powers are shown at their best in the idyllic scenes of *The Sentimental Journey*. In their grace and delicacy they resemble the vignettes of groups and landscapes painted by a master's hand on the exquisite paste of old Sèvres.

Firm ground is difficult to find either in Sterne or in his work. Built up from the early recollections of a child who, with open eyes and ears, had haunted the mess-room and the barrack yard, Uncle Toby is not only his greatest creative achievement, but a proof that he could appreciate sterling goodness of character. For his father he seems to have cherished a real affection, and his devotion to his daughter, Lydia, is the one pleasing feature in his private life. Little else is solid. The philosophy which he puts into the mouth of Mr. Shandy throws but faint light on his own mind.

It is wiser to imitate Uncle Toby and whistle " Lillibullero" than to search it for any more serious purpose than that of bantering pedantry. But the insistence on the importance of apparent trivialities and the view that every man is a potential oddity are characteristic of the working of Sterne's mind. He traces the relation of peculiarities to the universal principles from which they have diverged, follows them to the border-line, where they imperceptibly shade off into common humanity, and shows how accident distorts natural types into abnormal exceptions. Working on these theories, the half-crazed brain of Mr. Shandy converts them into paradoxes, on which he builds his so-called science. The destiny of nations or of individuals is governed by freaks of human folly or accidents of nature. This man might have achieved greatness if he had not been " Nicodemused into nothing " by his name ; had Cleopatra's nose been shorter, the fate of the world had been altered.

By its characters *Tristram Shandy* lives ; on them also rests its title to be in substance a novel. Structurally, the book is inartistic from its incoherency ; in detail, true art is often outraged by its ostentatious use. Yet it is as a literary artist that Sterne contributed most to the resources of the novelist. His eccentricities, wilful though they sometimes are, are the eccentricities of genius, and they give to the book the lasting charm of strangeness. Sterne offered the ass, not a bundle of hay or a thistle, but a macaroon. So he offered the reading public something which they have never tasted either before or since.

In 1762 Goldsmith wrote of Sterne and *Tristram Shandy* : " In England, if a bawdy blockhead breaks in on the community, he sets his whole fraternity " of men of letters "in a roar, nor can he escape, even though he should fly to the nobility for shelter." The justice of the charge against Sterne's indecency is, to some extent, discounted by jealousy of an amateur's triumph. But Goldsmith's own practice made good his claim to offer the criticism. *The Vicar of*

Wakefield (1766) contains nothing that can offend the most fastidious purity. In this respect the book stands almost alone in the prose fiction of his day.

There is no pleasanter feature in Goldsmith's short literary career than Johnson's affection for him and keen appreciation of his genius. The doctor treated him with protective tenderness. They were, as was said at the time, the Great Bear and the Little Bear of the world of men of letters. If Goldsmith sometimes received a cuff from Johnson's heavy paw, it was more in play than in anger. It was to Johnson's influence that he owed his election as one of the nine original members of " The Club," which then met at the Turk's Head in Soho. In 1757, at the age of thirty, he had come to London, unknown and destitute. Most of his writing was at first hackwork. But the value of his " Chinese Letters," collected and reprinted as *The Citizen of the World* (1562), was at once recognised by Johnson. When others considered Goldsmith to be only a literary drudge, he was, in the doctor's opinion, " one of the first men we now have as an author."

Jealousy may have occasionally induced Boswell to exaggerate Goldsmith's follies ; but enough evidence exists to show that he was often foolish, both in speech and in conduct. While his literary faculty was exceptionally developed, Goldsmith had never grown up in character. He remained a child in his innocent vanity, his simplicity, his credulity, his ignorance of money matters, his improvident generosity, his inclination to fly off at a tangent from the direction he was pursuing. Like a child, also, he was easily hurt by neglect, acutely sensitive to unfavourable criticism. His genius seemed to be something apart from the man. Hampered by no obstructions from his character and disposition, his literary faculty found that natural, spontaneous expression which is one of the secrets of his art, to use Johnson's words, " of saying anything he has to say in a pleasing manner."

The same detachment, aided by his Irish birth, enabled him to turn his own foibles to a literary use. In practical life he was the most inconsequent of men. Yet, as a man of letters, he repeatedly uses the drollery of inconsequence as an ingredient in his humour. One instance will suffice. The Vicar sells his horse, old Blackberry, to a rogue at a fair, and accepts in payment, not cash, but a draft on his neighbour, Solomon Flamborough, payable at sight. Dr. Primrose cannot resist the final proof of the swindler's financial stability : " Honest Solomon and I have been acquainted for many years together. I remember I always beat him at three jumps ; but he could hop upon one leg farther than I." The argument clinched the bargain, as, in real life, it would probably have satisfied Goldsmith. The gift, so rare in Englishmen, of seeing and laughing at himself as others saw and laughed, may support the view of those who think that in Dr. Primrose the man of letters was partly painting his own character.

As an essayist, verse-writer and dramatist, Goldsmith did the best work of his own time. His one novel, *The Vicar of Wakefield*, stands out clearly from the mass of the prose fiction of the period. With *Robinson Crusoe*, *Tom Jones* and *Tristram Shandy*, it is one of the four novels of the century that even the present generation cannot afford to lose. On the Continent the book was at once welcomed as a masterpiece. In this country its triumph was more slowly gained. Probably contemporaries missed in it the coarser flavours to which they were accustomed. Whether it ever received Goldsmith's final polish is uncertain. There is no reason to doubt the substantial truth of the story that Johnson found Goldsmith arrested for arrears of rent, discovered the manuscript in a drawer, sold it at once to a bookseller for sixty pounds or guineas, and cleared the debt. On the other hand, it is proved that in 1762 Goldsmith had already sold a third share in the book to a Salisbury printer.

At the time of the sale, Goldsmith had not established his reputation by the publication of *The Traveller*. Johnson thought the price adequate. He set no high value on the novel. He told Mrs. Thrale, if her recollection is correct, and if Madame D'Arblay reports her accurately, that it was a " fanciful thing," without much resemblance to real life or nature. The meaning of the criticism is obvious. Johnson's robust sense revolted against the haze of sentiment which pervades the story, smoothing the rough edges of character, toning down the harshness and cruelty of facts, providing for all a happy ending, which contradicts experience. The book has, in fact, something of the softness and unreality of an Elizabethan pastoral.

Goldsmith's own " Advertisement " to *The Vicar of Wakefield* begins with the words, " There are an hundred faults in this Thing." If the book is criticised only as a novel, the depreciation might possibly be justified. But a sentence which follows is as true, and more applicable : " A book may be amusing with numerous errors." Critics may reasonably find fault with the looseness of the plot, its conventional improbabilities, its huddled conclusion ; or condemn as ineffective the wholesale restoration of the family to prosperity ; or regard the Squire as a stage villain, and the incognito of Burchell as a theatrical mystery. Yet the book pleases and amuses. The defects are forgotten in its pure humanity, its humour, its gentle yet penetrating ridicule of human absurdities, its hopeful philosophy of life, or the elevated moral tone which rises high above the utilitarian ethics of the day. No ordinary book could have so soothed the mind of Goethe at a crisis in his mental history, and inspired him with a new ideal of life.

The Vicar of Wakefield is more like the work of Addison and Steele than like that of Goldsmith's own contemporaries. The strong resemblance in manner to the *Coverley Papers*, and the looseness of the plot, almost raise a doubt whether the novel itself was not an afterthought ; whether, in fact, Goldsmith did not begin with a character-sketch, of a Country Parson in the manner of " Sir Roger de Coverley " or his own " Beau Tibbs," and, as the portrait grew under his hand, tacked on the accessory characters and incidents. By whatever steps he advanced, he drew one of the great figures in prose fiction. Though Dr. Primrose does not reach the full stature of Parson Adams or " my Uncle Toby," he does not fall far below his two predecessors. Each of the three is distinct and individual ; yet all in one respect bear a family likeness to Don Quixote.

The continual intrusion of rough realities on the imaginary world of their simplicity surrounds them with a humour which is at once ludicrous and pathetic. Upon the Vicar crowd misfortunes which are not of his own making, though they are rather encouraged than averted by his innocent vanity and his ignorance of the world. He knows that neither his happiness was the reward of virtue, nor his misery the punishment of vice. If prosperity, then, was won and kept by worldly prudence, temporal ills and joys must be trivialities which Heaven disdains to distribute. In this spirit, he endures misfortunes with dignity and a cheerfulness more active than resignation. On one point he had sinned against his own light. Knowing the influence of a name upon human fortunes, he wished to call his eldest daughter Grissel. Overborne by his wife, he christened her Olivia, and her romantic name destined her to be the victim of romance. Had Mr. Shandy lived in the same part of Yorkshire, he would have observed with delight the confirmation of his theory.

On the character of Dr. Primrose rests the fame of the book. But to the interest of the central figure must be added the charm of the constant ripple of quiet humour, the flashes of a satire which is none the less poignant because it is never fierce, and, perhaps above all, the fascination of the style. Goldsmith's narrative English is so easy and spontaneous that the words seem to fall instinctively into their natural sequence, and it wraps the reader round in a sense of confidence and contentment which is often quickened into lively pleasure by those unexpected turns of phrase and epigrammatic sayings that make *The Vicar of Wakefield* a storehouse of familiar quotations.

Goldsmith was an Irishman. So also, by the place of his birth and on his mother's side, was Sterne. Richardson and Fielding were English; Smollett was a Scotsman. Thus, in the first of the great periods of the modern novel, each part of the then United Kingdom contributed to its development. Amateurs, as well as professionals, assisted in its growth. Richardson's business was printing, not writing. Sterne, for twenty years before he wrote, had discharged the duties of a country parson, his brain seething with miscellaneous reading, crochets, whims and fantasies.

A third amateur who wrote during the period demands

notice from the influence which his book exercised on the course of prose fiction. No one could be more remote, in all outward circumstances, from the professional circle of men of letters who frequented the purlieus of the Temple than Horace Walpole. A Member of Parliament and a sinecure placeman, he lived in the very heart of the social and political world. Now at a ball masquerading as Aurungzebe or disguised as an old woman, now sitting out a debate in the House of Commons, now treading on princes at Ranelagh or picknicking at Vauxhall, now at the faro table winning a *milleleva*, now hurrying in his slippers to see a fire—he was indefatigable in collecting, to use his own words, "the follies of the age for the information of posterity." It was in brilliant letters, and not in the form of a novel of contemporary society, that he gave his material to the public. A "virtuoso," a "dilettante," and also a real connoisseur, his other tastes and pursuits directed him to a different field. His *Castle of Otranto* (1764), published two years before *The Vicar of Wakefield,* may have borne as little resemblance to life in the times of the Crusades as his castellated Gothic villa at Strawberry Hill bore to a feudal keep. But the book was epoch-making. It showed that, at the very moment when novels of contemporary life were at the height of their triumph, the romantic reaction was already at work. It turned writers of prose fiction towards the historical novel, and, for this reason, it belongs to a subsequent chapter.

With Goldsmith closes the first great period of the modern novel. Within those twenty-five years it had become the most important product of eighteenth-century literature. Its triumph coincided with the rise of the middle classes to social influence. Despising ideals, absorbed in realities, strongly leavened with Puritanism, concerned in practical morality and interested in social reform, they found in the new novel an expression of themselves which they had missed in older literary forms. With a sure instinct Richardson met their needs. He used fiction, not only to paint real life, but to teach moral lessons, and his appeal to sentiment was designed to set in motion principles of right conduct. On similar lines Fielding followed. Himself a moralist, he rather protested against Richardson's narrow view of morality than against his didactic purpose. With a wider experience of life, a larger humanity, more virile sympathies, and with unrivalled truth, he represented the national characteristics of his audience.

Goldsmith filled the gaps which his predecessors had left with his fireside pictures. His domestic scenes illustrated the family life which was dear to his public, as well as the homely virtues of simplicity, kindness and unselfishness which the average man, whatever his own practice may be, prizes highly in others. The middle-class movement influenced the other four masters less strongly, or not at all. In spite of his realistic methods, and of the section of society from which his characters are drawn, Smollett stood somewhat aloof from its course. By Johnson and Horace Walpole it was opposed, the one from literary conservatism, the other from aristocratic prejudices. It did not supply Sterne with his audience, and if, as Goldsmith suggests, he found shelter with "the nobility," it was because they recognised that his appeal to sentiment had neither the Puritan austerity of Richardson nor the humane simplicity of Goldsmith, but was the indulgence of an artistic nature in a romantic luxury.

It is evident that, within the great period 1740–66, masters of prose fiction had experimented in many of the directions in which it ultimately advanced. During the succeeding half century the experimental stage continued. But two broad streams of fiction may be distinguished which met in the swirl of the French Revolution, only to part again and pursue their separate courses. One stream was that of the novel of contemporary life, manners and character, which touched its highest point in the work of Jane Austen, and in her found a feminine rival to the universality of Fielding. The other, more remote in its origin, and fed by many tributaries, reached its highest mark in the work of Walter Scott, and in him, with all the differences produced by the lapse of three eventful centuries, found a link with Sir Thomas Malory. In the two following chapters each current will be, as far as possible, separately followed.

CHAPTER XV

NOVELS OF CONTEMPORARY LIFE AND JANE AUSTEN

NEARLY half a century separated *The Vicar of Wakefield* (1766) from *Sense and Sensibility* (1811) and *Waverley* (1814). The prose fiction of that interval moved in two directions : it strengthened that independence which the great masters had won from the drama, and it attempted fresh conquests from the realm of poetry. It is, therefore, marked by two literary trends, each overlapping the other so often that neither can be distinguished by an exclusive label. One trend is the revival of the romantic temperament, which had never accepted the classical supremacy and was now in full revolt. It expressed the love of warmth and colour ; the sense of incompleteness, mystery, and aspiration ; the craving for novelty and adventure ; the eager pursuit of knowledge of the life and thought of the past ; the search for the local colour of an age, a nation, or a scene ; the desire of emotional thrills, whether of awe or suspense.

The other trend represents the recent tendencies of prose fiction. More prosaic and practical, less completely at variance with the principles of Pope and Johnson, it turned its back on the Middle Ages and concentrated its attention mainly on social conditions in England under George III. It is with novels of contemporary life that the present chapter deals.

In the forty-five years which preceded the advent of Jane Austen no novelist appeared, with the exception of Frances Burney and Maria Edgeworth, who is alive to-day in the sense of being read. Misled by the apparent ease of the task, a crowd of inferior writers attempted to write novels. Mediocre though their work is, it has a modest place in literary history. Collectively, it expressed many of the changes in social life ; it kept alive, and even stimulated, the taste for prose fiction; it made experiments

which helped forward the development of the novel—
where they succeeded, by enlarging its legitimate scope ;
where they failed, by defining its manageable limits.

The most characteristic products were novels of sentiment,
of purpose, or of domestic life and manners.   Outside
these three main groups a large number of miscellaneous
works followed older lines.   None of them are of first-rate
importance ; no great character was created.   Yet some of
these books are still interesting, either from their authorship,
their popularity, their subject, or their treatment.   To
this class belong Thomas Amory's *Life of John Buncle,
Esquire* (1756–66) ;   James Boswell's *Dorando, a Spanish
Tale* (1767) ; *The Spiritual Quixote*, by the Reverend Richard
Graves (1772) ; Dr. John Moore's *Zeluco* (1786) ; and Richard
Cumberland's *Henry* (1795).

First in interest and importance, as well as in date,
is *John Buncle*.   The book is pervaded by a zest for life,
so fresh, hearty, and spontaneous that it suggested to
Hazlitt a comparison with the gusto of Rabelais.   Often
discussed, but seldom read, it is a strange experiment in
the possible contents of a novel, with a human being as
the hero and a whimsical plan of construction.   Hovering,
as it sometimes does, on the border-line between eccentricity and genius, and lying out of the beaten track, it
has perhaps excited that exaggerated admiration which
explorers of the bypaths of literature are prone to feel for
their discoveries.   Yet, whether we laugh at or with the
author, John Buncle is so humorous a fellow that he deserves
much of the praise bestowed on him by Hazlitt, Charles
Lamb, and Leigh Hunt.

Amory seems to be serious in his religious opinions and
in his desire to combine information with entertainment.
His hero has a huge enjoyment of food and drink, a love
of picturesque scenery, a critical appreciation of literature,
an interest in many subjects, from medicine to Roman
antiquities, a devotion, mingled with an odd strain of
virtue, to young and beautiful ladies.   An ardent Unitarian,
John Buncle is as arrogantly intolerant of the views of
others as the most fanatical champion of the Athanasian
Creed.   Turned out of doors by his father on account of

his opinions, he sets out to seek his fortunes, " not like the Chevalier La Mancha, in hopes of conquering a Kingdom, or marrying a great Princess ; but to see if I could find another good country girl for a wife and get a little more money."

An eighteenth-century Bluebeard, he marries and buries, within the space of twelve years, seven wives, each of whom satisfies his standard of Christian Deism, health, wealth, beauty, and learning. With admirable gravity he demonstrates the futility of mourning, and on each bereavement immediately instals a successor. His courtships provide pegs for the interchange of opinions on abstruse subjects. The collective learning of the young ladies covers a wide range. With one, he discusses the Hebrew language ; with another, Greek literature and the paulo-post-future ; with a third, science ; with a fourth, mathematics ; and so on. In the end the father, before his death, becomes a convert to John Buncle's Unitarian opinions, and the hero himself, seven times widowed, turns mariner.

As an experiment in the legitimate contents of the novel, *John Buncle* failed. In *Dorando, a Spanish Tale* (1767) James Boswell, the biographer of Samuel Johnson, tested the uses to which the novel might be put as a publicity agency. In his short story of fifty pages he endeavoured to excite sympathy with the claimant in the famous " Douglas case," which occupied the law-courts for seven years (1762–9), and eventually caused riots in Scotland that were only suppressed by military force. *Dorando* follows closely the facts alleged in support of Archibald Douglas. The Duke of Douglas, who in the " Spanish Tale " is the Prince Dorando, had no children and no brother. His only sister, Lady Jane Douglas, was secretly married in 1746 to Colonel James Stewart. They lived together abroad, and, at Paris in 1748, Lady Jane gave birth to twin sons. On the other side it was alleged that the birth was counterfeited and that the children were procured from a Frenchwoman. The Duke refused to see his sister, disbelieved in her children, and cut off her allowance.

Lady Jane died in 1753, as *Dorando* states, from grief

RA

at the death of one of the twins. Eight years later the Duke
died childless, and the estates were claimed on behalf of
Lady Jane's surviving son, Archibald.   The Duke of Hamilton, the heir male, disputed the claim and the legitimacy
of the claimant.   The case came before the Scottish Court
of Session, where, after a hearing of five years, it was decided
against Archibald Douglas by the casting vote of the Lord
President.   On appeal to the English House of Lords the
decision was, in 1769, reversed, and the claim of Archibald
Douglas admitted.   All the principal actors appear in the
story.   Lady Jane is the Princess Dorando who secretly
marries Don Spiritoso, leaves Spain with him, and at Paris
gives birth to twin sons.   Archibald Douglas is Don
Ferdinando, and the Duke of Hamilton is the Prince of
Arvidoso.

Boswell's experiment deservedly failed to arouse public
interest.   A more popular book, in which a great movement
was handled with satiric and humorous intention, and many
interesting details of rural and wayfaring life were preserved,
was *The Spiritual Quixote*, by the Reverend Richard Graves
(1772).   Graves borrowed only the machinery of Cervantes.
The " bee in the bonnet " of *The Spiritual Quixote* is
Methodism.   Geoffrey Wildgoose, after leaving Oxford,
turns Methodist, and roams the country as a preacher,
accompanied by Jeremiah Tugwell, the cobbler, as his
Sancho Panza.   George Whitefield—who had already been
savagely handled by Charles Johnstone, in *Chrysal* (1761)—
is the chief object of attack.   For their first interview with
the famous preacher Wildgoose had prepared himself by
fasting, and, on the way, reproves his companion for the
" ungodly savour " of his pipe.

They are surprised to find the " holy man " in a handsome
room, sitting in an elbow chair, " dressed in a purple night-
gown and velvet cap," and before him, " instead of a Bible
or Prayer-book . . . a good bason of chocolate, and a
plate of muffins well buttered."   Self-indulgence is only one
of many charges.   One episode sounds as if it were founded
on some fact, and it seems the more probable as Graves
was an intimate friend of the victim.   On his travels Wildgoose visits the poet Shenstone at the Leasowes, and is

shown the famous garden, with its vistas, groves, rills, and cascades. In the night the fanatical guest, convinced that his host idolised " Pan and Sylvanus " rather than " Paul and Silas," wrecked the watercourses, and, " called by the Spirit," fled before morning.

A novel on a popular movement might be expected to attract attention. It is more difficult to understand the extravagant praise bestowed on Dr. John Moore's *Zeluco* (1786). Possibly the book owed its favourable reception to the contrast—both in subject and authorship—which it afforded with contemporary prose fiction. Novels were, at this time, as Robert Bage states, " pretty generally considered as the lowest of all human productions." Lifeless though *Zeluco* was, it was not sugar and water, and its author was a writer whose literary reputation was assured. John Moore is now only remembered as the father of the distinguished soldier who died at Corunna. In his own day, however, he was well known as a traveller, a modern linguist, and an authority on " Society and Manners " in continental countries. He was probably the original of Dr. X. in Miss Edgeworth's *Belinda*.

Zeluco's chief merit is that it is well written. Yet it contains three features which still have a faint interest. Most of the chapters are headed with a quotation. Thus the book is an early, if not the earliest, example of a practice which subsequently became almost universal in prose fiction. The fellow-traveller of Smollett, Moore not only follows his picaresque method of narrative, but develops the romantic vein which cropped up among the crudely realistic details of his master. From infancy Zeluco is a Satanic monster of cruelty and depravity, a prototype of Mrs. Radcliffe's Montoni and Schedoni, an ancestor of the Byronic villains of a later date. By making Zeluco a Sicilian and resident at Naples, Moore follows the English convention of embodying monsters, not in compatriots, but in Italians. Lastly, Zeluco's cruelties as the master of a slave-plantation illustrate the scope and limits of public opinion on the subject of slavery.

Abolition was still far off. Labour was needed ; slavery was sanctioned by law, and the moral argument against it

came from the suspected source of natural rights. A
century earlier, Aphra Behn, in *Oroonoko*, had painted the
noble savage who instinctively practised all the virtues of
a primitive state of innocence. In *Lydia, or Filial Piety*
(1755) John Shebbeare had developed the same theme.
Obedience to natural impulses raised Cannassatego, the
Indian chieftain, to a level of conduct higher than that
which satisfied the conventions of European law and religion.
No English Rousseau forged the theory of the State of Nature
into a weapon of revolution, and the practical effects of the
doctrine were rather humanitarian than subversive.

In the imaginary kingdom of the flying people *Peter
Wilkins* (1751) had abolished slavery as inconsistent with
civilisation. But Robert Paltock, the author of that
strange work, was in advance of his age. His fellow-
countrymen were not stirred to abolish property in slaves,
but they were stimulated to a more humane interest in their
condition. Henry Mackenzie, in *Julia de Roubigné* (1777),
pleaded that kindly treatment was more effective than the
whip of the overseer; Yambu responds at once to the
generosity of Savillon. Moore, in *Zeluco*, makes a different
point in the same direction. He shows that existing laws
were an ineffective protection against barbarity. Zeluco
orders the negro slave Hanno to be flogged at such frequent
intervals that the man dies from the cumulative effects of
his legal punishment. Aphra Behn lays the scene of the
barbarities towards slaves in Surinam, Mackenzie in
Martinique, Moore in Cuba. Were English planters more
humane than Dutch, French, and Spanish slave-owners?

As *Zeluco* is reminiscent of Smollett, so *Henry* (1795)
is a careful imitation of Fielding. The author, Richard
Cumberland, was, like Moore, distinguished in the literary
world. Few men of letters in the eighteenth century wrote
on a greater variety of subjects. Dramatist, poet, essayist,
classical scholar and translator, writer of memoirs and
books of devotion, a critic of art as well as of literature, he
was also a novelist. Yet to-day his chief title to fame perhaps is that he was the original of Sheridan's Sir Fretful
Plagiary. Beginning his literary career as a playwright, he
had produced at least thirty-five acted plays before, at the

age of fifty-seven, he published *Arundel* (1789), the first of his three novels.

Cumberland himself thought that his second novel, *Henry* (1795), was his best work. It is closely modelled on Fielding, for whom he had the greatest admiration, and with whom, in his early youth, he had some acquaintance. Masterpiece though he knew it to be, Cumberland thought that *Tom Jones* was " out of date," and he seems to have conceived the ambition of remodelling the book to suit the new social conditions. Beauty, he says, is no longer worshipped with respect. The modern fine gentleman studies only his ease. " Love in him is not an active passion ; he expresses no rapture at the sight of beauty." Henry is as insensitive to female charms as Tom Jones is susceptible. Susan May woos him with a warmth that would have melted an iceberg, but he remains cold.

Mechanically Cumberland's copy is faithful. He emphasises the time which he has spent on his book, takes credit for the construction of his plot, reproduces the confidential talks with his readers, involves the birth of his hero in the same mystery which hangs over that of Tom Jones, lays his chief scenes in the country among squires, parsons, magistrates, doctors, and rustics. He even attempts to modernise Parson Adams by replacing him with Ezekiel Daw, the Methodist preacher, in whom the boldness and assurance of religious enthusiasm are combined with simple-minded ignorance of worldly affairs. But Cumberland has none of Fielding's vitalising power, his humour, or his insight into human nature, and *Henry* is lifeless.

Both Moore and Cumberland were elderly men when they began to write novels. Born before the publication of *Pamela*, both grew to manhood in the great period of prose fiction. Each had fallen under the personal spell of the masters—the one as the travelling companion of Smollett, the other as the disciple of Fielding. More representative of the second half of the eighteenth century were novelists of sentiment, of purpose, and of domestic life and manners. The threefold division is convenient rather than accurate. Zeal for instruction and deliberate cultivation of feeling

were so characteristic of the period that nearly all forms
of fiction were pervaded by both. But novels both of
sentiment and of purpose were passing phases. The one
permanent addition to literature—the one new field that
was opened to prose fiction—was the novel of domestic
life and manners. Mainly in the hands of women, it was a
native growth and independent of foreign inspiration.

Both the other groups are pervaded by French influences.
The *Nouvelle Héloïse* (1761) and *Émile* (1762) had already
appeared. In England the tears which flowed so freely in
novels of sentiment might well up from the elaborate pathos
of Richardson and the lachrymose sensibility of Sterne ;
but they found fresh springs in the emotionalism of Rousseau.
Propagandist novels—moral, educational, or revolutionary
—might be directly descended from Richardson, but they
derived impulse and inspiration from Rousseau's burning
hatred of oppression, his humanitarian enthusiasms, his
power of embodying abstract theories in concrete examples.

The triumph of *Clarissa Harlowe* had been the first sign
of the recoil from unemotional, matter-of-fact realism.
Now, swollen from other sources, foreign as well as native,
the rising tide of sentimentalism flooded the country. It
carried Henry Mackenzie to a short-lived fame. His best
known work, *The Man of Feeling* (1771), was included in the
illicit library of Lydia Languish. But to the present generation it seems incredible that such tearful appeals should
have found response. Harley is a bashful, sentimental,
sensitive hero, such as Richardson might have painted and
Fielding would have parodied. He dies in the swoon into
which he was thrown by the discovery that Miss Walton
returned his love. A purposely disjointed story, the author,
who professes to be the editor, explains its fragmentary
chapters by the fact that the curate who was first entrusted
with the manuscript had found it " excellent wadding "
for his gun.

In the next quarter of a century the gush of sentiment
rose to a torrent. These were days when people flocked
to the play to weep over *The Stranger*, when ladies were
painted leaning on columns bearing the inscription " Sacred
to Friendship," and when the severest poetry tolerated

in Mayfair was that of Hayley. The ingredients of the novels which expressed this cultivated enjoyment of exaggerated feeling were simple. Authors had only to

> Take some Miss of Christian name inviting,
> And plunge her deep in love and letter-writing,
> Perplex her well with jealous parents' cares,
> Expose her virtues to a lover's snares,
>
> .   .   .   .   .
>
> Make her lament her fate with " ahs " and " ohs,"
> And tell some dear Miss Willis all her woes.

In fiction of this class all the players tread the stage in sock and buskin. The morality is beyond the reach of poor humanity, or below its average standard ; the circumstances are strained ; the heroines are hairdresser's dummies of impossible beauty, sweetness, and sensibility ; the heroes out-Grandison Sir Charles, and overpower their mistresses with chaste aphorisms till they no longer resist their criminal advances.

The general effect of such novels was that of vague, sickly, languishing prose poetry, without truth to nature, individuality of character, or locality of scenery. The language was as precious as the feeling was mawkish. Both were burlesqued by Beckford in *The Elegant Enthusiast* (1796), written under the pseudonym of The Right Honourable Lady Harriet Marlow. Even if the parody had been more telling than it is, it came too late. The habit of indulgence in excessive sentimentalism had grown too strong to be satisfied with its own self-expression. It modelled—and for many years to come—the heroines who wept, swooned, rhymed, harped, and tottered through the wild tales of terror. Borrowing many of the properties of Mrs. Radcliffe, it had created its own form of sentimental romance which was at the very height of its absurdity at the time when *The Elegant Enthusiast* appeared. From one danger England escaped. In the application of sentiment to abstract theories lay the chief peril of the subversive doctrines of the day. No English writer of novels of revolutionary purpose succeeded in striking the emotional note of Rousseau.

Novels of purpose are born in periods of mental ferment,

like the French Revolution or the third quarter of the nineteenth century. Instead of presenting life and character in their completeness, propagandist writers exaggerate sections of both, and sacrifice artistic effects, as well as truth, to the delivery of their message. Their novels, however interesting the phase of thought that they illustrate, cannot reach the highest standard of literature, and their power passes with the conditions which gave them birth. But they may be so charged with passionate intensity of feeling that they become great books. Notably is this true of *Uncle Tom's Cabin*, where the scorching heat of deep emotion blinds even critics to its flaws.

The first English novel of purpose is *The Fool of Quality: or, The Adventures of Henry, Earl of Morland* (1766–70), by Henry Brooke. Desultory and chaotic, it is, as his candid friend tells the author, " a fortuitous concourse of atoms." Such interest as it has lies, not in its novel-substance, but in its fine thoughts, admirably expressed, on the ideal education of a Christian gentleman and on a variety of subjects, moral, social, political, and religious, illustrated by tales and the incidents of the story. Glowing with the enthusiasm of a reformer, it is a striking interpretation of the teaching of Rousseau. It despised social conventions and believed in the simple goodness of the humble ; it opposed the wisdom of Nature's teaching to the educational folly of pedagogues ; it set the virtues of Nature's gentleman against the vices of those to whom society restricted the title. Its reforming zeal, its studied pathos, its mystical vein, its acceptance of the doctrine of " conversion," so attracted John Wesley that he republished the book, with his own omissions, in the lifetime of the author.

Less than a century later (1859) the original work was republished as a whole, with a preface by Charles Kingsley, who was perhaps fascinated by the physical training and muscular Christianity of its hero, as well as by the similarity of its social teaching to that of his own novels of purpose, *Yeast* and *Alton Locke*.

The Fool of Quality exercised little influence on contemporaries. But it opened the floodgates for didactic fiction. In the stream were represented almost every phase of the mental upheaval which preceded and accompanied the course of the French Revolution. The most sincere work was done in novels of educational and moral purpose. Revolutionary novelists were more half-hearted in their advocacy of their political and social doctrines. Holcroft alone accepted the whole programme, and even he was opposed to force. In the portions of the revolutionary creed which others adopted they showed little unanimity. Even on such a subject as the relations between the sexes they were divided. A similar hesitation marks the treatment of other doctrines. The foundations of institutions, laws, and customs are indeed called in question. Harrowing instances of the cruel operation of social laws are arrayed to prove that whatever is is wrong, that sympathy is never at fault, that hard cases cannot be right. In exaggerated contrast with the products of civilisation, primitive virtues and brotherly love are personified in heroes and heroines whose fortunes exemplify the superiority of Nature over Art.

But the new ideas excited little enthusiasm, or only enough to extinguish humour. The ring of Blake's lyric anarchism was wholly absent from the prose fiction of revolutionary purpose. No writers were true rebels against the existing social order, or prepared to sacrifice their own traditions and conventionalities to the realisation of their day-dreams. All except Holcroft were content to imagine their ideal State among the mountains of Switzerland or the forests of North America. Their novels, therefore, suffer from all the artistic defects of their class without attaining the saving grace of passionate sincerity of purpose. The best were written by Robert Bage, Thomas Holcroft, William Godwin, and Elizabeth Inchbald. But only two—*Caleb Williams* and *Nature and Art*—are really impressive, and their power is not derived from their professed object.

In natural gifts Bage was at least the equal of his three rivals. He is sometimes amusing, and his minor characters are alive. But the principal actors who personify his political views are too much absorbed in exhibiting their staring cockades to be natural or even human. A radical rather than a revolutionary, his *Hermsprong : or, Man as he is not* (1796) expresses loyalty to the King and repudiates equality of property. The book, which is the last of his six novels, is typical of his methods. The scene is laid in a Cornish village, where the humble and virtuous inhabitants are " victims of society," tyrannised over by the arrogant landowner, Lord Grondale, his cringing sycophant, Dr. Blick, the sinecurist rector of the parish, and the unscrupulous lawyer who does the peer's dirty work.

On this scene enters Hermsprong, the " natural man," who has been educated—without nurse, priest, or tutor— in the primitive virtues of the Red Indians in the backwoods of America. By a prodigy of courage and strength he saves the life of Lord Grondale's only child, Caroline Campinet. He outrages Lord Grondale by ridiculing distinctions of birth, rank, or wealth, confounds Dr. Blick in theological discussion, defeats the lawyer's attempt to ruin a neighbour, disperses by his arguments a mob of miners who have defied the Riot Act, and wins the heart of Caroline. The magnates of the village plot his removal. A charge is laid against him before the local Bench. It breaks down. But Hermsprong is known to have been educated in North America, to have read *The Rights of Man*, and to have found some good in the French Constitution. He would have fared badly had he not proved himself to be the son of Lord Grondale's elder brother, and rightful owner of his estates.

Frank Henley, in Holcroft's *Anna St. Ives* (1792), is again the natural man. Considering Holcroft's experiences and talents, the novel is surprisingly dull. Stable-boy, cobbler, usher, strolling player, before he settled down to earn his living as a writer and translator, he told his early life in his first novel, the anonymous *Alwyn: or, the Gentleman Comedian* (1780). It is a lively narrative, in which Holcroft, under the name of Hilkirk, relates, in the vein of Smollett's early work, many of his own experiences.

The arid wastes of *Anna St. Ives* illustrate the devastating effect of a political creed. Almost its only interest lies in the picture of the perfect State with which it concludes. Holcroft was one of the chief "oral preceptors" of William Godwin. He had impressed his strong character and convictions on the feebler philosopher, and the prophetic vision of *Anna St. Ives* anticipated the optimistic outlook of *Political Justice* (1793). In the novel, the inhabitants of the perfected world, guided only by reason and free to follow its dictates, live together in equality and brotherly love. Property has ceased to exist. Marriage lasts only as long as mutual inclination continues. Vices and their corresponding virtues have disappeared with the laws and institutions that gave them birth ; both are merged in universal benevolence. Recovering the patriarchal span of life, relieved from excessive labour by simplicity of needs, perfected men and women pass their days in rational enjoyments.

The optimism of *Political Justice* was eagerly welcomed. Thousands of ardent spirits had believed, like Coleridge and Wordsworth, that in 1789 they were standing between two worlds, with one foot lingering among the ruins of the older age, the other touching the threshold of the new. Their dreams of a regenerated humanity were shattered by the horrors of the Reign of Terror. To them, chilled by the shock, Godwin offered an Earthly Paradise, attained, not by force, but by peaceful argument. This sinless Eden was no airy fabric of the imagination ; it rested on a foundation of deductive logic, so firmly compacted that, granting its premises, no flaw could be detected in its solidity. Godwin denied to man any freedom of will. If his reason were convinced, he had no choice but to obey. His actions followed irresistibly from his convictions. Changes of conduct necessarily resulted from changes of opinion. On this view of human nature—in defiance of probabilities, and without regard to experience—Godwin worked out his central idea of perfectibility with a logical pertinacity and precision which, aided by an admirable style, make *Political Justice* an impressive book.

The same uncompromising cogency of reasoning gave his novel *Caleb Williams: or, Things as They Are* (1794) much of its influence. Its defects are also similar to those of *Political Justice*. In both books there is the same disregard of the actual conditions of life. The closet philosopher appears throughout the novel as well as in the political treatise. His friends believed that the book would prove the grave of his literary reputation. They were mistaken. The story is a tale of sombre, dreary power, which stamped its harsh, severe features on more than one generation in the New World as well as the Old. So long as the anonymity of the Waverley Novels was preserved, it was to the author of *Caleb Williams* and *St. Leon* that they were often attributed ; on Bulwer Lytton his influence was marked ; the first novelist of the United States who gained any reputation in this country, Charles Brockden Brown, acknowledged Godwin as his master, and found in his work " transcendent merit."

The book is the first detective novel. A story of crime, it does not transcribe pages from the Newgate Calendar, or seek attraction in ghastly details ; it rather relies for its interest on close analysis of the workings of the human mind, and on the almost morbid skill with which Godwin applies what he calls his " metaphysical dissecting knife." Like *Eugene Aram*, for which Godwin supplied materials to Bulwer Lytton, it states a moral problem. As a proselytising novel, it is a denunciation of social tyranny, a review of some of the " modes of unrecorded despotism " by which, under the existing constitution of society, " man becomes the destroyer of man." Impelled by the perverted sense of honour which society applauded, Falkland murders Tyrell and allows two innocent men to be hanged for the crime. Tortured by his consciousness of guilt, he yet guards his secret. When it is discovered by the fatal curiosity of Caleb Williams, he employs all the resources which the law lavishes on men of wealth and position to dog the footsteps of the too-curious secretary, deprive him of credit and character, and retain him in his power.

In his third Preface to the novel (1832) Godwin explains its composition, and incidentally his own mental processes. He first invented the third volume, and then, working backwards, the second, and finally the first. Having arrived at his conclusion, he reasoned back with singular patience of detail and remorseless logic to the necessary premises. It is to the unremitting tenacity with which the central purpose is grasped that the book mainly owes its impressiveness. Fate itself, and no human persecutor, seems to pursue the helpless Caleb.

Godwin also wrote *St. Leon* (1799), *Fleetwood* (1805), *Mandeville* (1817), and, when he was considerably over seventy years of age, *Cloudesley* (1830) and *Deloraine* (1833). As novels they cannot be compared in effect with *Caleb Williams* ; but the first three show more humanity. Godwin's mind veered towards romance. *St. Leon* is " a Tale of the Sixteenth Century," and *Fleetwood* " a Tale of the Seventeenth Century," and both are crowded with those anachronisms and incongruities which characterise the historical fiction of the period. Like more than one of the revolutionary theorists, he was fascinated by the occult, and *St. Leon* dabbles in the supernatural. The theme and the originality of the story secured it some contemporary success. It undoubtedly inspired Shelley's Rosicrucian tale of *St. Irvyne* (1811), and probably suggested to Bulwer Lytton his *Strange Story*. But Godwin fails to create the atmosphere of mystery. His lack of humour is fatal, and the book never recovers from the shock of the introduction of the stranger who possesses the secret of wealth and immortality. Like *Fleetwood, Mandeville* owes its chief interest to touches of autobiography. Henrietta in *Mandeville*, as well as Marguerite in *St. Leon*, are said to be studies of Mary Wollstonecraft. Her pleadings with Mandeville on virtue and benevolence struck the youthful Shelley, then married to Mary Godwin, as " the most perfect and beautiful piece of writing of modern times."

In the circle of friends from whom—before he was married by Mrs. Clairmont—Godwin proposed to select his second wife, was Elizabeth Inchbald (1753–1821), actress, dramatist, and novelist. The daughter of a Suffolk farmer, named Simpson, she married in 1772 Joseph Inchbald, the actor, went on the stage, and appeared in many characters before and after her husband's death in 1779. Partly owing to a slight impediment in her speech, she never reached high rank as an actress. In literature she succeeded better. When her first novel was published in 1791 she had already written ten comedies, which had been produced at Covent Garden or the Haymarket, and had gained her a considerable reputation as a playwright.

For many years Mrs. Inchbald was, in her own section

of society, one of the most attractive women of the day. " It was vain," said Mrs. Shelley, " for any other woman to attempt to gain attention." Her praise of *The Giaour* delighted Byron more than any other criticism ; Miss Edgeworth wished to see her first among living celebrities ; her charm fascinated Sheridan, and overcame the prejudice of Lamb ; Leigh Hunt was at her feet ; Peter Pindar wrote verses in praise of " Eliza." From the age of eighteen she was wooed on and off the stage, but no breath of scandal ever tarnished her name. Had John Kemble been free to propose himself, she might have married him. Educated for the priesthood, he is said to be in some points the hero of her first novel.

Mrs. Butler records that her Uncle John once asked the actress, when matrimony was the subject of green-room conversation, " Well, Mrs. Inchbald, would you have had me ? " " Dear heart," replied the stammering beauty, turning her sunny face up to him, " I'd have j-j-j-jumped at you." With some irregular lapses into scepticism, she lived and died a zealous Roman Catholic.

Mrs. Inchbald's two novels—*A Simple Story* (1791) and *Nature and Art* (1796)—place her high among the novelists of the period. *A Simple Story* illustrates, by contrast between the character and fortunes of a mother and daughter, the " pernicious effects of an *improper education* " and the benefits of a training in the " school of prudence " and "adversity." The purpose is so little obtruded in the conduct of the story that it scarcely appears, except in the last two paragraphs. It does, however, mar the construction of the novel by demanding an interval of seventeen years between the two parts, and the exchange of the attractive Miss Milner for her insipid daughter, Lady Matilda, as the heroine. Except that the Christian name of Miss Milner is never mentioned, even by her husband, the story has a modern air. It moves briskly. The conventional length is shortened. The style is easy, the dialogue lively and natural, and in her choice of situations Mrs. Inchbald's dramatic experience was of service.

Pitched in a higher key of feeling than most of its predecessors, the first part of *A Simple Story* deals with strong emotions, appeals less to sentiment than to passion, and, without suggesting any comparison between the gifts of Mrs. Inchbald and the genius of Charlotte Brontë, faintly foreshadows *Jane Eyre*. Mr. Milner dies, leaving his only child, a daughter of eighteen and a great heiress, to the guardianship of his friend Dorriforth, a Roman Catholic priest. Dorriforth accepts the charge and receives the beautiful, high-spirited girl, fresh from her boarding-school, at his home in London. She falls secretly and passionately in love with her guardian. Succeeding by the death of a nephew to great estates and the Earldom of Elmwood, he is dispensed by the Pope from his vow of celibacy. He finds that he has given his heart to his ward. They marry and have a daughter. In the second part the results of Miss Milner's education had unexpectedly culminated in infidelity to her husband. She dies an outcast. Embittered by her misconduct, Lord Elmwood has become an unjust, unfeeling tyrant. The story concludes with the restoration of his better nature through the renewal of his affection for his daughter.

In *A Simple Story* the purpose is episodical; it dominates *Nature and Art*, which was written when Mrs. Inchbald was most under the influence of revolutionary theorists. Typical of proselytising novels, the book is constructed to oppose, as it were in parallel columns, the primitive virtues of Nature to the insincerities and depravities of artificial civilisation. Two young brothers, Henry and William, seek their fortunes in London : Nature makes Henry a musician ; Art makes William a dean. All virtues are on the side of the former. The contrasts are sharpened in their respective children. Henry marries a " public singer," William the daughter of a penniless Scottish earl.

Each has a son of about the same age. The dean, to whose care his brother has committed his boy, makes a home for his nephew. The two cousins have had a different training. The young William, whose tutors have been paid to teach him " how to think," thinks " like a foolish man instead of a wise child as Nature designed him to be." The young Henry, bred without books or education among the savages of Zocotora Island, has no knowledge of civilisation, but in his primitive school he has learned to prize honour, truth, affection, independence. His curiosity, pertinacious enquiries, and shrewd simplicity make him a disconcerting inmate of the dean's household. The full-bottomed wig, worn, as his uncle tells him, to distinguish him from inferiors, suggests to the boy the practice of savages who " hang brass nails, wire, buttons, and entrails of beasts all over them, to give them importance." Told that here the poor are born to serve the rich, and that hereafter all will be equal, he cannot understand why, if the future life is better, distinctions of wealth or rank should be allowed in the present world. When guns fire and bells ring to celebrate another victory, he cannot be made to understand the difference between battles and massacres, and, in the argument that follows the explanation, baffles his antagonists.

In manhood the contrast between the cousins is continued. But the real interest of the story lies elsewhere. William has seduced a beautiful village girl, Agnes Primrose, who bears him a son. In the fate of the deserted Agnes, Mrs. Inchbald forgets her mission and shows herself a true artist. The story, told simply and with great restraint, rises to real tragedy. Sixteen years pass. William, succeeding rapidly at the Bar, has become a judge. Agnes, an unwedded mother, clinging desperately to her son, sinks lower and lower, till she falls into the company of swindlers. Charged with uttering a forged note, she is tried before William, convicted, and by him condemned to death. She had recognised in the judge her former lover, and, while awaiting execution, wrote telling him who she was, imploring mercy for herself, or protection for their son. The letter reached William too late. The boy had not outlived the shock of his mother's death. Bulwer Lytton was, possibly, indebted to *Nature and Art* for the similar trial scene in *Paul Clifford* where Brandon condemns his son.

Novels written to advocate political and social changes in the organisation of society were naturally inspired by French writers. Scarcely less marked was the influence of Rousseau and the *philosophes* on fiction of educational and moral purpose. Designed for the improvement, instruction, and entertainment of young people, stories of this class can scarcely be classed among novels. But the best of them deserve some brief notice. Their hold on many successive generations was strong. They were models of the art of narrative and of a simple, easy style. They added a new character—the real child—to the range of the novelist. They opened up to young people a fiction which was one of the literary features of the period. John Newbery, who is introduced into *The Vicar of Wakefield* as the anonymous traveller who relieves Doctor Primrose in his distress, was the pioneer publisher of children's books, and it was for him, and probably by Goldsmith himself, that *Goody-Two-Shoes* was written.

For three-quarters of a century most English boys were brought up on Thomas Day's *Sandford and Merton* (1783–9). In form and method, though it is intended for children, it resembles *The Fool of Quality*. Both books contrast the child of nature, self-taught and simply bred, with the child of art nurtured in luxury ; both use dialogues and tales to convey instruction or illustrate moral lessons. The mysterious uncle in *The Fool of Quality*, who forms the mind of Henry, and, with fabulous wealth at his command, trains him in the right use of riches, is in *Sandford and Merton* represented by Mr. Barlow, who made more enemies among several generations of young people than any other character in fiction by his inveterate habit of improving every occasion. But it was from Rousseau, or from Richard Edgeworth's interpretation of *Émile*, and not from Henry Brooke, that Day derived his scheme of education.

Equally lasting and better deserved was the influence on English childhood of Mrs. Trimmer's *History of the Robins* (1786), Maria Edgeworth's *Parent's Assistant* (1796–1800), *Early Lessons* (1801), and *Moral Tales* (1801), and Mrs. Sherwood's *Fairchild Family* (1818). The scene at the gallows in the latter book is probably still vivid in the minds of some elderly men and women. French writers again had led the way. Both Rousseau and his disciple, Madame de Genlis, had denounced fairy-stories for children. In England a moral crusade was similarly proclaimed against such tales by educational reformers, many of whom, in other respects, recoiled with horror from the doctrines of Rousseau.

A group of women, several of them born story-tellers, set themselves to supply a substitute for Perrault or Madame d'Aulnoy. While Mrs. Trimmer and Mrs. Sherwood wrote under the inspiration of religious motives, Maria Edgeworth's morality was practical and utilitarian. She was also strongly influenced by French writers. Her father was, educationally, a disciple of Rousseau. Herself a student of Marmontel and of his *Contes Moraux*, she began her long literary career by translating the *Adèle et Théodore* of Madame de Genlis. In her own short stories she showed real genius. Some of her best work was done in the natural, charming tales for young people which are contained in her various collections. The eldest of a family of twenty-one, she knew children intimately, and her moral, though firmly pressed, is, except perhaps in the case of *Rosamund*, sympathetically and tenderly enforced.

As a writer of short stories for young people Miss Edgeworth remained for many years supreme. The moral purpose which was not out of place in *The Parent's Assistant* became obtrusive in her longer works of fiction, and crippled her genius for the humorous presentation of human comedies. In one aspect, her *Tales of Fashionable Life* (1809–12) are handbooks of moral instruction ; in another, they belong to the third and most important product of the period—the domestic and social novel which Fanny Burney had created by the publication of *Evelina : or, The History of a Young Lady's Introduction to the World*. The book, which appeared anonymously in 1778, was new in subject-matter, in treatment, in point of view, and, above all, in the simplicity of its theme. It opened the road for Miss Austen.

Frances or Fanny Burney (1752–1840), the daughter of the historian of music, had lived in London since she was a child of eight. Her joy in telling a story, her sense of almost rollicking fun, her quick eye for peculiarities and absurdities, her dramatic instinct which staged men and women and incidents as they passed before her in effective groups— all these were inborn gifts which impelled her to write. Self-educated, she chose her own teachers, and the masters of prose fiction whom she venerated are those enumerated in the Preface to *Evelina*—" Rousseau, Johnson, Marivaux,

Fielding, Richardson, and Smollett." Her stepmother's discouragement failed to check her literary propensities. Before she was fifteen she had written her first novel. The manuscript of the *History of Caroline Evelyn* was destroyed ; but the plot survived in the story of Evelina's parentage, by which her guardian explains the relationship of his ward to Madame Duval.

The choice of subject for her first published novel was happy. She abandoned the tragedy of a disowned wife and mother for the simple story of a young girl's feelings on her first entry into the world and the poignancy of the humiliations that she suffered from the vulgarities of her relations. *Evelina* took the public by storm. It won for Miss Burney the praise of Burke and Reynolds ; it gained her the friendship of Johnson, who named her his " little character-monger."

Johnson's pet name for Miss Burney praised her beyond her due. It is in caricature and not in character that she excelled. Her observation was quick and superficial, rather than close and penetrating. A Smollett in petticoats, she individualised her actors by a feature instead of by their faces. They are incarnations of some single peculiarity or distinctive trait and, by preference, vulgarity. But she is not satisfied with affixing the label. Whatever the point on which she fastens, she illustrates it by such a variety of incidents, detects it under such specious disguises, presents it from so many angles, that her portraits, caricatures though they are, become, like those of Dickens, amazingly alive. Her delight in her narrative power and in the comic wit of her inventiveness is infectious.

There is no sign of strain or effort in *Evelina*. Ease is its distinctive charm, and even the plot, such as it is, tumbles together naturally. Miss Burney perhaps had no great creative gifts, but she possessed a power of literary mimicry, such as belonged to none of her predecessors, which enabled her to reproduce the tone and manners of ordinary society, and keep interest on the stretch without the stock situations and stage properties of previous novelists. It is this simplicity which makes *Evelina* both a landmark and a new starting-point in prose fiction.

It is difficult to realise that in its day *Evelina* was a daring innovation. Hitherto the ordinary events of everyday social or domestic life had been neglected, or used as the background of sensational situations. Miss Burney treated them as the substantive interest of her story. The nearest approach to a light transcript of contemporary society had been made by Francis Coventry in *The Adventures of Pompey the Little* (1751), written in the peculiar form which was a fashion of the period. Writers of picaresque narratives felt that their heroes were unfitted for tea-tables or as reporters of secrets of private life. They met the difficulty by linking their scenes to some inanimate object like a guinea, or to some inarticulate animal like a lap-dog. The ubiquitous and unnoticed presence of both restrained no intimacies, and changes of ownership supplied the necessary variety. A lap-dog of illustrious parentage, Pompey the Little, was born at Bologna in 1735, and died in England in 1749. His experiences abound in lively touches of social life and satirical portraits of individuals, some of which were probably recognised by contemporaries. But the book is too disconnected to be coherent. It is only a novel of manners in the making. *Evelina* carried the type several stages towards completion. The slender plot gives cohesion to the whole, and the narrative scarcely suffers from its epistolary form because, as was the case in *Pamela*, the letters are written almost entirely by the heroine and describe her personal feelings and experiences.

Without Richardson's tragedy, his moral earnestness, and, above all, his minute study of character, Miss Burney left little of his work except sentiment and clothes. Her story was in danger of insipidity. To some extent the risk forced her into exaggeration and caricature. But she had more legitimate resources. Fashion set strongly towards sentimentalism and moral purpose. Against both she appealed to comedy. Her comic wit offered laughter for tears and amusement for gravity. Her shrewd and caustic satire gave a pungent flavour to the whole. The weapon, as well as its use, were then peculiar to herself. Her satire was not of the coarse political or personal kind which owed its point to the identification of its victims. It was not even social. It was domestic and feminine.

Many novelists before Miss Burney had been women. But Aphra Behn and Mrs. Manley had written for men—of men as they desired or thought themselves to be, and of women as ministers to their pleasure. Miss Burney was not a feminist, and probably regarded marriage as a girl's object in life. But she did not accept men as lords of creation. She regarded them critically with a woman's eye as domestic animals, and makes excellent fun of their coxcombries, affectations, and pretensions. If she is not the first novelist who was by sex a woman, she was the first woman novelist.

In her later novels—*Cecilia* (1782), *Camilla* (1796), and *The Wanderer* (1814)—Miss Burney failed to reproduce the simplicity and spontaneity which were the distinctive charms of *Evelina*. The decline was progressive. In *Cecilia* love triumphs in the end over the family pride and social prejudices of Delville, and from the last chapter of the book—where the three words are more than once repeated in the pomp of large capitals—Miss Austen probably took the title of her *Pride and Prejudice*. Longer, more ambitious, and more finished than *Evelina*, the novel is an amusing caricature of English society on the eve of the Revolution. But tragedy and moral purpose crept into the simple story, and Miss Burney was becoming a mannerist. She copied from herself. The familiar figures reappear in the same attitudes, changed to types, and each painted like the Flamborough family with an orange in the hand.

Between the publication of *Cecilia* and *Camilla* Miss Burney served four years at Court as second keeper of the robes to Queen Charlotte. After her release from her services she married a French officer, Monsieur d'Arblay. Whatever loss literature may have sustained by the comparative failure of her last two novels is more than compensated by her vivacious and sparkling *Diary*.

More than twenty years separated *Evelina* from *Belinda* (1801), and in that interval no novel was published on Miss Burney's simple theme. Fashion in prose fiction departed widely from the lines laid down by the great masters.

Truth of observation and analysis of character were thrown
on the scrap-heap ; realities of ordinary life were despised or
distorted to prove theories.   To novels of sentiment and of
purpose were added wild tales of terror, and historical romances
in which modern men and women asserted their connection
with past ages by the medieval flavour of their oaths.

A few of the romantic leaders broke away from their
predecessors deliberately.   Reflecting the growing excitement which heralded the coming outburst of great literature,
they explored the possible contents and emotional range
of the novel, or endeavoured to push its boundaries beyond
the limits of the present.   Their experiments belong to the
next chapter.   But the rank and file of novelists had no
literary aim or standard.   Freed from facts and probabilities,
and recognising no claim of art for art's sake, they wrote for
no other end than the sale of their wares.   One writer,
however, attempted to combine the new elements with
everyday realities and to weave something of poetic feeling,
imagination, strong emotion, and the love of natural scenery
into a romance of real life.   Though the work of Charlotte
Turner—better known by her married name of Smith—
may have shown promise rather than achievement, she
deserves notice for her attempt.

Born in 1749, Mrs. Smith died in 1806.   An unfortunate
marriage and twelve children compelled her to write for
bread and publish too quickly.   *Emmeline : or, The Orphans
of the Castle* appeared in 1788 ; *Ethelinda : or, The Recluse
of the Lake* in 1789 ; *Celestina* in 1792 ; *Desmond* in 1792 ;
The Old Manor House in 1793 ; and to these books were
added more than thirty other publications—novels, poems,
and translations.   The first two titles suggest the insipid
influence of sentimentalism which taints even her best work.
Yet *Ethelinda* produced something of a sensation.   Scott
calls it " a tale of love and passion, happily conceived, and
told in a most interesting manner."   The scene in which
Sir Edward Newenden pleads his cause with Ethelinda,
and is overheard by her lover Montgomery, who is supposed
to be dead, recalls that in which Henry Morton, in the same
circumstances, hears Lord Evandale urge his suit upon Edith
Bellenden in *Old Mortality*.

But *The Old Manor House* is Mrs. Smith's best work, and it is one of the few novels of the last decade of the eighteenth century which can still be read with any pleasure. The book shows traces of the three popular forms of prose fiction. The love-makings of Orlando and Monimia sometimes suggest the Rosa Matilda school, though Mrs. Smith expresses scorn for the extravagances of sentimentalism. The winding stair, the ruined chapel, the ghost who proves to be a smuggler are properties of Mrs. Radcliffe. The sympathy with the American colonists, the hatred of war, the praise of the French, the attacks on the Church and the Law express the sentiments of Godwin's circle, on the fringe of which stood Mrs. Smith, who, as she herself wrote, valued novels as a means of impressing those who were otherwise impervious. But, though the pocket-handkerchief, the dagger, and the programme are all present, they are subordinated to the interest of the story.

The plot, which turns on a hidden will, is sufficient to hold the narrative together ; the incidents are natural as well as varied ; interesting details of social life abound. Descriptions of natural scenery are excessive, but they are unusually definite and local in their colouring. The minor characters are alive. Mrs. Grace Rayland, the last of the three co-heiresses of Sir Hildebrand Rayland, is admirably drawn. " Old Mrs. Rayland," said Scott, " is without a rival," and the determination of the old lady to show General Tracy what an old English dinner is like, without the aid of kick-shaws and French frippery, is worthy of Lady Margaret Bellenden.

One other novel of the period deserves notice. *The Children of the Abbey*, by Regina Maria Roche, reached a fourth edition in 1800, and retained its popularity for several generations. Dunreath Abbey is the home of Lady Malvina, daughter of the Earl of Dunreath. To escape her step-mother, she marries a penniless husband, and, after months of obscure poverty, dies, leaving two children, Amanda and Oscar. " The loveliest of her sex," Amanda is wooed by many suitors, honourable and dishonourable, but all ends well for the children of the Abbey. Oscar inherits the earldom, and Amanda marries an earl.

One element in the prolonged popularity of the novel was its titled company. The rise of the moneyed middle classes accompanied the growth of snobbery in social life. Challenged in their wealth, the old aristocracy entrenched themselves behind their birth. To enter their exclusive circle became a social ambition which Miss Edgeworth ridiculed, especially in *The Absentee*. *The Children of the Abbey* caught this tide of fashion, and remained for years on the crest of its wave. High life absorbed the interest of British matrons for whom the " Silver Fork " school of fiction subsequently catered :

> Oh, Radcliffe ! thou wert once the charmer
>   Of maids who sate reading all night;
> Thy heroes were warriors in armour,
>   Thy heroines damsels in white ;
> But past are such terrible touches;
>   Our lips in derision we curl,
> Unless we are told how a Duchess
>   Conversed with her cousin the Earl.

Even such a distinguishing feature as this is not to be found in the mass of prose fiction which poured from the press in the decades before and after the dawn of the nineteenth century. The depth of degradation to which the novel sank is some measure of the value of the work of Miss Edgeworth. Tears, terrors, and emotional idealism dribbled feebly yet copiously from the pens of a horde of women writers like Mrs. Bennett, Mrs. Parsons, and a score of others. Revelling in their licence of invention, they painted unreal scenes and unnatural characters against the background of an impossible world of illusions. They peopled it with dukes disguised as day-labourers, and wronged damsels of noble birth as milkmaids. Bandits sprang up like mushrooms. Horrors lurked behind each closed door ; mystery lay concealed in every cupboard ; and adventure ambushed behind the simplest incident.

So vitiated was the public taste that these feeble extravagances commanded enormous sales, while Miss Austen could find no publisher for *Pride and Prejudice*. Not only were stories of this type published and sold in four or six volumes; they also circulated in shorter form as chapbooks. Sarah Wilkinson's tales, like *The Eve of Saint Mark: or, The Mysterious Spectre*, adorned with coarsely coloured frontispieces, appeared in the company of older favourites such as *Dr. Faustus* and *Long Meg of Westminster*. It was by laughter that this literary rubbish was at last destroyed. Ridicule marked the gradual return of sanity, and burlesques alone have preserved the memory of their butts. Beckford's Arabella Bloomville was joined by Miss Angelina Warwick in Miss Edgeworth's *Angelina: or, L'Amie Inconnue*, by Elizabeth Marsham in *Romance Readers and Romance Writers* (1810), and (1812) by Cherubina Willoughby in *The Heroine: or, Adventures of a Fair Romance Reader* of E. S. Barrett.[1] With a lighter touch and greater delicacy, Miss Austen used her satiric humour for the same end. But *Northanger Abbey*, though written in 1798, remained unprinted till after her death, and Catherine Morland, Isabella Thorpe, and that " sweet girl " Miss Andrews lay hidden for years in a publisher's drawer.

Not the least of the many services which Maria Edgeworth (1767-1849) rendered to English literature was that she withdrew the novel from a world of day-dreams and nightmares and restored it to the realities of contemporary life. She had already established her reputation as a writer of short stories. Now, in quick succession, she published *Castle Rackrent* (1800), the first of her Irish novels, and *Belinda* (1801), the first of the long series of fashionable tales which ended with *Helen* in 1834. As a national novelist she not only did her best and most permanent work, but broke fresh ground. She was a discoverer, the founder of national fiction, the precursor of Scott. In her social and domestic novels, with which alone this chapter is concerned, she was less original because more under the influence of the time. Yet her tales of fashionable life never entirely fail to amuse and interest as vivid pictures of a society in which the old order was decaying and the new struggling into existence.

Those who only know Miss Edgeworth by the reputation

---

[1] Republished in 1909 with a Preface by Sir Walter Raleigh.

of her short stories for young people associate her with the buckram dignity of a schoolmistress who, without appealing to higher motives, inculcated selfish prudence and illustrated the utility of virtue.   They think of her as a stiff personification of morality,

> a walking calculation,
> Miss Edgeworth's novels stepping from their covers.

If they read her letters, they will be surprised at her keen sense of fun, her power of light and humorous description, her artless enthusiasms, the width and warmth of her interests.   Or, again, they picture her as buried at Edgeworthstown in the company of her clever, conceited father, paying rare visits to Dublin as the prim chaperon of a younger sister, separated from neighbours by Serbonian bogs, engaged in teaching her numerous brothers and sisters, keeping estate accounts, or copying in a characteristically careful hand her father's letters.   Such occupations form only one side of her active career.   She knew, and won the regard of, most of the people who were worth knowing in England and America ; she travelled more than most of her contemporaries, and had seen the best society in Paris ; she was not only a literary lion in London, but her mingled modesty and brilliance made her a welcome guest in innumerable country houses in the United Kingdom.

Miss Edgeworth wanted neither the opportunity nor the capacity to enjoy, observe, and describe the humours of the fashionable world.   If her social novels fall short of the standard which her genius might be expected to reach, one reason for the comparative failure is obvious.   Through her father's influence the educational and ethical theories of French *philosophes* had deeply impressed her precocious childhood. The spell lasted. Moral teaching was her first object ; the interest of her tale came only second. She was more intent on erecting signposts of conduct for the guidance of future travellers than on accomplishing her own journey with directness and despatch.   The polestar of her teaching was enlightened selfishness.   As her pattern children were always rewarded, so her good heroines were sure to prosper, inherit fortunes, or marry into the peerage. She allowed small space in her system for imagination, passion, or enthusiasm ; their strength might disturb her simple balance of right and wrong and endanger the rule of the understanding over morality.

To this limited conception of the novelist's art, and this partial insight into human nature, are mainly due the minor faults and graver defects of her social novels. They account for her didactic manner, her repetitions, her obtrusion of moral instruction. They explain also why—both in the presentation of character and in the construction of plots— she belongs to the middle of the eighteenth century.

Like Miss Burney, she fastens on one prominent characteristic and brings it into emphatic relief. Miss Burney caricatures in order to amuse ; Miss Edgeworth exaggerates in order to instruct. If her principal heroes and heroines are good, they are so complacently prudent and well intentioned that they are tiresome ; if there is one flaw in their compositions, it is certain from the outset that the defect will lead to their ruin, or, if corrected, will secure their happiness. The framework of her stories is similarly distorted to heighten the moral lesson. Though the incidents are not impossible or even improbable, they are too providential to be natural. A string of fortunate coincidences or a series of unlucky catastrophes is made to spring from some predominant virtue or vice in the principal actors.

In spite of the faults into which Miss Edgeworth was betrayed by her conscientious discharge of her duties as a teacher, her novels have many of the excellences of the best prose fiction. Written in a pleasant, easy style, full of shrewd observation, abounding, if not in humour, at least in fun, they are lively sketches of social life. The by-play is generally brisk and full of movement ; the conversations are often animated, natural, lit up by smart, pungent sayings ; the secondary characters, who are remote from the didactic purpose, are sometimes spirited portraits. Her first novel of social life is also her best. *Bolinda*, admired by Miss Austen, comes near to being a great book. It has more of the merits and less of the defects of Miss Edgeworth's other works.

Belinda Portman, a more composed and collected Evelina, passes through her first season with discretion. Though the shadow of her mission to reconcile Lady Delacour with her husband and her daughter falls early on her path, she is a natural girl, and finds in Clarence Hervey a not inadequate hero. They are becomingly rewarded. By three remarkable interpositions of Providence, Clarence is released from Virginia Hartley and freed to become Belinda's accepted lover. At the same time, the bad or defective characters are appropriately punished. The flaw in Vincent, the creole millionaire, is revealed in time ; his passion for gambling loses him Belinda and brings him to the verge of ruin. By the discovery of Mrs. Luttridge's fraud at the E.O. table, she is exposed as a sharper. Harriet Freke, the mature hoyden of " rantipole " manners, who dresses like a man, talks like a man, and drives a unicorn, is caught in a spring-trap, which so mars the beauty of her legs that she can never again wear male attire.

There is the inevitable contrast between the abode of folly and extravagance and the well-regulated home. But the lively, entertaining sketches of society under Lady Delacour's roof make the companion picture of the sententious Mr. Percival, the estimable Lady Anne, and their well-behaved children tame and insipid. Although Lady Delacour is reformed as well as rewarded, her portrait makes *Belinda* memorable. In the sympathetic study of the lady of fashion Miss Edgeworth seems to forget her pedantry and let herself go.

Miss Edgeworth helped to restore prose fiction to sanity. For higher achievements in the novel of social life she was disqualified by her misconception of her art. Her insistence on moral instruction, like the missionary zeal of political or social reformers, falsified human nature. So in other writers the indulgence in sentimentalism or in the extravagances of romantic imagination distorted, almost beyond recognition, their pictures of life.

Such preoccupations or excesses disappeared from the work of Jane Austen (1775–1817). Her social comedies are so vividly contrasted with contemporary fiction that they mark the beginning of a new era. During her lifetime she

18

paid the penalty. Her own generation scarcely knew her, and the Annual Register did not record her death. But if her fame was mainly posthumous, it has lasted and grown continuously. Among the Immortals, yet never placed on the shelf, she is more modern than any of her predecessors and than most of her successors. Men are still disputing which of her novels is the best, arguing whether Elizabeth Bennett was impertinent, or wondering whether the grace and pathos of the renunciation and rebirth of love in Anne Elliot lifts a corner of the veil of her shrouded personality ; and still the stream of pilgrims flows to her resting-place in Winchester Cathedral from the New World as well as the Old.

Of her six completed novels, three—*Pride and Prejudice, Sense and Sensibility,* and *Northanger Abbey*—were the work of a girl not yet four-and-twenty, written, in the order named, between 1796 and 1798. The second group, written between 1811 and 1816, includes *Mansfield Park, Emma,* and *Persuasion.* None of the six deals with characters, incidents, or situations outside ordinary experience. So careful is she to introduce nothing that might not have come within her own observation that no conversations carried on by men alone among themselves are recorded. Her stories challenge and satisfy the severest of tests. All the world can judge of their truth to real daily life. Between the work of Miss Austen's youth and that of her maturity there are no essential differences. If in *Persuasion* the morning brilliance of *Pride and Prejudice* is mellowed into a sunset glow, it is natural ; she was dying when the book left her hands. Otherwise, the distinctive qualities are the same in the first novel as in the last—the creative power, the dramatic faculty, the patient observation, the variety of the characters, the truthful preservation of their individuality, the quiet irony, the pervasive satire, the limpid style, so easy and natural in its flow that it conceals the careful polish and nice discrimination in the choice of words.

The order of publication differed from that in which the novels were composed. *Sense and Sensibility* appeared in 1811, *Pride and Prejudice* in 1813, *Mansfield Park* in

1814, *Emma* in 1816, *Northanger Abbey* and *Persuasion* in 1818, the year after Jane Austen's death. She had brought the novel of character and domestic life to a perfection which, within its limits, is almost flawless. Her work is of the finest quality, wrought with infinite art to an exquisite finish, and, in her own narrow range, her creative power is unsurpassed. No detailed criticism will be attempted. The roads by which the goals were reached, rather than the goals themselves, are the subject of the present volume.

The influence of her favourite authors may be traced in Jane Austen's work. There is in her novels something of Richardson's minute analysis, of Johnson's honesty and contempt for the cant of sentiment, of Miss Burney's satiric comedy, of Cowper's elaboration of detail, of Crabbe's intense realism. But the breach with contemporary prose fiction is absolute. Except as materials for burlesque or parody, none of the distinctive features of novels of the period or of the movements that they represented is to be found in her work. She has no didactic purpose, revolutionary, moral, or educational; she has no mission to form opinions or reform characters. She simply aims at sharing with her readers the amusement that she herself derives from the observation of human nature. Godwin's disciples were to her mind " raffish." She enjoyed life too much and was too content with the existing social order to desire a return to the State of Nature. Sense and self-command were her divinities, and not the Goddess of Reason. Except that she once flares up in defence of governesses, she stood aloof from the Revolt of Women.

Impersonal as Shakespeare, she speaks in character, and rarely reveals her own opinions; but, for the education of women, she seems to have preferred the " old-fashioned boarding-school," where girls have plenty of food and fresh air and " scramble into a little education without any danger of coming back prodigies." With a similar caution, she seems to have thought that, when no choice of profession was offered to women, their happiness lay in marriage and maternity on a sufficiency of money. Sentimentalism she despised, and showed no mercy to its affectation. Impulsive, enthusiastic sensibility might be lovable, if it was genuine ; even then it deserved a husband who was nearing forty, had loved before, and wore a flannel waistcoat.

Tragedy and romance were as absent from her pages as they were from the empty lives of her neighbours which she records. She might have found them, as Crabbe found them, among the cottagers ; but she knew, with the self-knowledge of an artist, the limitations of her powers, and she had no such opportunity for the minute study of the lives of the poor as she had in her daily intercourse with the rural squirearchy and the country clergy.

Almost fastidious in her refinement, she shrank from " guilt and misery " as " odious subjects." The most tragic events in her novels are that Lydia Bennett runs away with Wickham and Maria Rushworth with Harry Crawford, and that Willoughby had seduced a girl in whom Colonel Brandon was interested. But seduction is never treated sensationally. The fact and its consequences are mentioned and relegated to the background. The beauties of nature appealed to her strongly, especially the sea, though she makes the odd blunder of assembling a party to pick strawberries when apple-trees are in blossom. But she was repelled by the fashionable jargon of the picturesque, and preferred a neat cottage to one in ruins, and well-grown trees to those that were crooked and blasted. To worship of rank she never pandered, and ridiculed impartially both aristocratic pride and social sycophancy.

Miss Austen's detachment from the literary interests, preoccupations, and fashions of the day to some extent explains her neglect by the public. In her novels she stood equally aside from the great movements and events in which the nation was absorbed. Her aloofness was partly dramatic truth in the presentation of her own little world—the rural squirearchy, the country clergy, their wives and daughters, a sprinkling of officers from the nearest barracks, and the professional classes of a country town like Basingstoke. After Trafalgar no fear of invasion disturbed the even tenor of their lives ; they knew of no problems ; no breeze from the tempest of the French Revolution ruffled their quiet backwater. But in her intimate letters allusions to contemporary events occur almost as rarely as in her novels. The silence seems to show that the limitations of her own nature corresponded with those of dramatic truth, and that her outlook was similar to that of her neighbours. To them she was a good-looking, normal young woman, loving balls and theatricals, interested in her clothes, not averse from a flirtation, enjoying the life of which she was an amused, ironical, but never cynical observer. Beyond the family circle her literary gift was unknown. She concealed her satiric humour as she did her manuscripts. The self-control which she admired in Elinor Dashwood, Fanny Price, and Anne Elliot was what she herself practised in her novels by the rigorous exclusion of her personality and the measured expression of feeling. But here and there in her unimpassioned pages a passage breaks the surface of self-repression, discloses depths of emotion and tenderness, and creates the doubt whether we know, or ever shall know, the real Jane Austen.

Of the pleasures and rewards of fame she experienced little. Her silence between the two groups of her novels may have been partly due to discouragement. If so, she kept her secret. One compliment she received from an unexpected quarter. It should be remembered to the credit of George IV that he admired her writings and intimated his willingness to accept the dedication of one of her novels. In *Emma* his wish was gratified. But Miss Austen, had she lived to receive it, would have been prouder of Walter Scott's generous tribute. In a well-known passage in his Diary, he says : " Read again, for the third time at least, Miss Austen's very finely written novel of *Pride and Prejudice*. That young lady has a talent for describing the involvements of feelings and characters of ordinary life which is to me the most wonderful I have ever met with. The big bow-wow strain I can do myself, like any one now going ; but the exquisite touch which renders ordinary commonplace things and characters interesting, from the truth of the description and the sentiment, is denied to me."

CHAPTER XVI

In the hands of Miss Austen the novel of real life, character and contemporary manners triumphantly vindicated its independence of the drama as a separate branch of representative art. Another literary trend, which in the latter half of the eighteenth century was moving in a different direction, has been described as the romantic revival, the Gothic reaction, the Renascence of wonder, the revival of imagination. Such phrases carry us back to the twilight of the past, when the art of minstrelsy first took shape in prose as well as verse. They imply the recapture of some lost possession, the reunion of some severed link, the reclamation of ranges of feeling which had fallen out of cultivation. They suggest, not merely the challenge to drama, but the reconquest of some of the provinces of poetry.

Medievalism may be the most comprehensive description that can be given of the movement in the shape which it eventually assumed. The Middle Ages became a rallying point of the revolt against the authority of pagan antiquity. But in this country the aims of writers of prose fiction were less conscious and definite than they subsequently became on the Continent.

Romantic temperaments found their outlet in qualities, tendencies, methods of treatment, rather than in special periods of literature. The attempt to reproduce the life of Christian and feudal Europe was only one of their varying forms of expression. They were represented in the medieval architecture and the appeal to the supernatural of *The Castle of Otranto*. They were represented also in the spirit of adventure and curiosity which stirs in *The Life and Adventure of Peter Wilkins*; in the gorgeous colouring of the Oriental tale of *Vathek*; in the quiver of suspense and the fascination of wild and savage scenery in *The Mysteries of*

Udolpho ; in the graveyard and charnel-house of *The Monk*. They found emotional thrills in the present as well as in the past. Thus many of the novels dealt with in the previous chapter, though their scenes are laid in the England of George III, might reasonably be classified among their products. *The Man of Feeling* is romantic, for the luxury of sensation is indulged by melancholy and pathos as well as by terror. In their discontent with existing conditions and their desire for a better world, propagandist novels of revolutionary purpose strike definite notes of romance. *The Fool of Quality* is romantic, both in its enthusiasms for reform and in its leanings towards mysticism.

In prose fiction the permanent product of the romantic movement was the historical novel. For its advent the eighteenth century was, in two essential points, a preparation. In spite of its comparatively recent origin, the novel of contemporary life was, in a sense, its parent. The relationship is natural. Until truth to human life and nature was recognised as the aim of prose fiction, and represented in the present with some success, the external and internal realities of the past could not be attempted without inevitable failure. The methods of Richardson and Fielding were now ready for use in other fields. But if romantic art is picturesque, while its classical rival is statuesque, the materials on which it could work were not yet available.

Men sought for something in literature that they could not find in transcripts of contemporary conditions. Yet history, as it was then understood, gave them little help in imagining the past or in realising its differences from the present. It chronicled events and exploits ; it ignored the environment which, varying with climate, race, nationality and stage of civilisation, profoundly influenced human life and character. A hero of antiquity could only be represented as man in the abstract, moving among thin and pale generalities of description ; or as a man of the writer's own generation, surrounded by the social conditions with which he was himself familiar.

In the latter half of the eighteenth century a truer view began to be taken of history. From a multitude of sources were gathered facts and details which enabled imagination to paint pictures and portraits of bygone ages, which were approximately accurate and glowed with the local colour dear to romantics. Out of the new material, applying to the past the methods by which Richardson and Fielding had represented the present, and blending realism with idealism, the genius of Scott created the historical novel.

Where historical records were available, even if they were only statistics, Defoe had proved their value in giving substance to an historical picture. In 1722 appeared his *Journal of the Plague Year*. Bred in a Puritan home, he was six years old when the Plague broke out. His childish recollections and upbringing enabled him to recapture the superstitious dread which the visitation inspired. To multitudes it was no ordinary sickness; it was rather the manifestation of the wrath of Jehovah against his sinful people. The awe which hung over the land broods heavily on the pages of the fictitious journal. For another feature in the book he was indebted, not to his own memories, but to the command of historical documents. With extraordinary skill he uses the statistics of the Weekly Bills to make his readers actual spectators of the progress of the Plague. The dry bones of figures live again in his hands. Through them he creates a vivid impression of irresistible movement, now creeping from house to house, now leaping from parish to parish, and always advancing.

The *Journal of the Plague Year* dealt with events within Defoe's own recollection. It does, however, illustrate the value of the concrete facts and definite details that are supplied by documentary records in giving life, colour and atmosphere to pictures of the past. The French writers of heroic fiction, whose works were still the staple reading of English lovers of romance, enjoyed no such advantages. If a Cyrus discussed the metaphysics of love as though he frequented the Hôtel de Rambouillet, they could honestly plead in defence the meagreness of their material. In the main facts of the careers of their heroes, so far as they were known, they claimed to be accurate.

Calprenède, who is perhaps the best of the heroic writers, quotes an imposing list of his authorities, and distinguishes between romances like the *Amadis* cycle, which have no truth, probability, charters or chronology, and his own *Cassandre* or *Cléopâtre*, which contains only history, embellished by invention and decorated by fancy. Fighting for existence against the great tragedians, he and his fellows imitated their rivals in choosing for their protagonists the heroes of antiquity. By so doing they challenged, not only the supremacy of the drama, but the authority of history. On these prominent actors, whose careers and characters were familiar, the interest was concentrated. If their speeches, actions and fortunes were ridiculously at variance with truth, the absurdity was too conspicuous to be ignored.

Before the historical novel could assert independence or freedom, its plan of construction must be altered and its perspective changed. Romance and human interest must be brought to the foreground, and history relegated to a background made as representative of the period and as vividly faithful as possible. The principal actors who occupied the front of the stage must be creations of the imagination, free to love and hate as they will, and, if historical personages were introduced, it must be as subsidiary figures. On this plan, so far as his choice of characters was concerned, Prévost had constructed his *Cléveland* (1732). On similar lines, whether Leland, Horace Walpole and Clara Reeve had or had not read Prévost's story of the natural son of Cromwell, was developed the first stage of the historical novel. The heroes and heroines of their stories were imaginary persons.

No historical novel appeared till 1762. Before the accession of George III, the matter-of-fact common sense of eighteenth-century England looked with suspicion on imaginative literature, especially on that which dealt with the past. An " understanding age," it stigmatised ignorance and barbarity as " Gothic," and, in popular usage, interpreted the word " romantic " to mean something fantastic, unbalanced, exaggerated. Yet, at the height of the triumph of the prose fiction of character and contemporary life, the spirit of romance flickered up in *The Life and Adventures of Peter Wilkins, a Cornishman* (1751). The book was published without a name. But the author is now identified with Robert Paltock (1697–1767), an attorney practising at Clement's Inn, of whom little more is known.

Peter Wilkins sails from Bristol to seek a fortune. After many escapes and adventures, he alone survives a shipwreck on the ironstone cliffs that guarded an unknown land near the South Pole. Passing through a fissure in the line of rocks, he finds himself in a fertile country, fixes his habitation in a cavern by the side of a lake, and, like Robinson Crusoe, settles down to make himself comfortable. Sometimes human voices seemed to reach his ears ; but of human footsteps he heard no sound. One night, a body crashing through a tree-top fell at his feet. It was a beautiful woman, who " seemed to me to be clothed in a thin hair-coloured silk garment, which, upon trying to raise her, I found to be quite warm, and therefore hoped there was life in the body it contained." She belonged to a race winged with " graundees," or cases of their own skin, which, when expanded, enabled them to fly. He marries Youwarkee, who has none of the elfishness of a wild creature, but has, as wife and mother, the charms of one of the most attractive heroines of the century.

The interest of the continuation of the story shifts from the creations of a delightful fancy to some of the directions in which the thoughts of the world were beginning to move. Peter Wilkins not only saves the winged people in a great war and devises a scheme of aerial tactics which might be useful to the Air Marshal ; he also creates a new form of popular government, breaks down the tyranny of a corrupt priesthood, establishes a rational system of education and abolishes slavery.

Peter Wilkins is one of the few novels of the period that were translated into French and German, and in this country have been reprinted both in the nineteenth and twentieth centuries. It owes its vitality to the creation of the flying people. The story is not, like *Gulliver's Travels*, a fable in which the marvellous is employed to accentuate the points in a satire on humanity. Written without any satiric or moral purpose, it appeals to the sense of wonder and curiosity which characterised the romantic movement. Yet Paltock is too dominated by the mathematical realism of Defoe to

be wholly a pioneer of the new school. Eager to authenticate
the existence of his winged race, he piles up details of their
life and language, forgetting that, though Defoe's methods
might convert plausibilities into certainties, belief in the
supernatural is the child of imagination and not of proof.
His elaborate accumulation of evidence is tiresome and
unconvincing.

Peter Wilkins appeared too soon. In this country its fame
was long in coming. It waited thirty years before it reached
a second edition (1783). More to the taste of a large section
of the English public was a burlesque of heroic romances.
In *The Female Quixote* (1752) Charlotte Lennox ridicules
the readers of Calprenède and Scudéri. From her childhood
the Lady Arabella knew nothing of life except as it was
painted in such romantic folios as *Cassandra, The Grand
Cyrus* or *Clelia*. She regulates her conduct, and interprets
that of others, by precedents from the careers of her beloved
princesses. When she enters the world, she sees in every
well-appointed gentleman a would-be ravisher. As Clelia,
to preserve her chastity, plunges into the Tiber, so Arabella,
at the approach of a cavalcade of horsemen, leaps into the
Thames. At last, reasoned out of her delusions, in one short
chapter, by the " pious and learned doctor ——," she gives
her hand to her cousin who throughout had been her
mystified lover.

The Female Quixote was popular with the wits and the
town, and it installed Charlotte Lennox as first favourite
among Dr. Johnson's ladies. Yet the burlesque would have
had no point unless there had been a public to which the heroic
fiction of France still appealed. The taste was there, and it
persisted. As late as 1796 Bage represents the narrator of
Hermsprong as an ardent student of *Cassandra*. On this
starvation fare, during the first sixty years of the eighteenth
century, the popular demand for imaginative prose fiction
had been kept alive.

Meanwhile, students had been active in exploring the
records of the past, literary as well as historical. The
romantic revival was slow in coming, and, when it had
definitely gathered strength, its progress was halting. It
had no champion who could cope with Johnson. It had no

conscious purpose or concerted action. English romantics were linked together by no bond of union like that which bound the French *Cénacle* or the German *Romantische Schule*. When, in the first decade of George III, a number of books seemed suddenly to break the surface and at once to attest and stimulate the force of the movement, they came from men who were working in different directions and independently of one another. To those ten years belonged Hurd's *Letters on Chivalry and Romance*, Percy's *Reliques of Ancient English Poetry*, Macpherson's *Ossian*, Gray's poems from Icelandic and Celtic sources, instalments of Chatterton's *Rowley Poems*, and the first two historical novels—*Longsword, Earl of Salisbury: An Historical Romance*, and *The Castle of Otranto: A Gothic Story*.

The anonymous author of *Longsword, Earl of Salisbury* (1762) preceded Walpole by two years. In date and material, therefore, the book is the first historical novel. The honour of priority is somewhat barren, for *Longsword* excited little interest and exercised no influence. Nor is it certain to whom the honour belongs. In 1831 the book was reprinted with "By John Leland, D.D." on the title-page. That a learned divine should turn novelist would to-day cause no surprise. But in the early years of the reign of George III it would be highly improbable, and history was not among the known studies of John Leland, whose chief work—*A View of the Principal Deistical Writers*—appeared in 1754–6. Assuming that the title-page gives the correct surname, the authorship has in recent years been attributed to the Rev. Thomas Leland, of Dublin, to whose historical writings the subject of the novel is less foreign.

The novel is rather a revival than a starting-point. In shortened form it is a romance of chivalry, modernised by a tinge of sentimentalism, and a thin veneer of history, the support of which the author claims for " the outlines and some of the incidents and minor circumstances " of his story. The scene is laid in the reign of Henry III, and the hero is William, Earl of Salisbury, called Longsword, said to be the son of Henry II and Fair Rosamund. Escaping in a vessel from France, Longsword is driven ashore on the Cornish coast. He and his companions find shelter

with an old comrade-in-arms. In the style of a Greek
romance, two long-winded narratives introduce the actors.
In one speech, Longsword recounts his adventures during
his long absence from England ; in the other, his Cornish
friend, Sir Randolph, tells the Earl how his wife, their
son, his lands and his castle are in the hands of his enemies.
Subsequent events introduce Henry III, who swears " By
my halidome," and culminate in the Earl's denunciations
of the villainies of Hubert de Burgh, the great Justiciar who
in history defeated the French fleet under Eustace the Monk
and ruled England firmly and wisely during Henry's minority.

Flat in its colouring and vague in its historical background though it is, *Longsword* is not inferior to its successors
before Sir Walter Scott. But it possessed none of the
distinction that was needed to inaugurate a new school of
fiction. In spite of its absurdities, *The Castle of Otranto*
(1764-5) was the real starting-point of the English historical
novel.

As burlesques contained the germ of modern novels of
real life, so the seed of modern historical romance was
sown in a work of serious trifling. It is impossible to think
that Horace Walpole (1717-97) was wholly in earnest when
he wrote *The Castle of Otranto*. In his serious moods he
would not have obtruded the supernatural so grotesquely
as to excite laughter rather than fear. Suspicions of his
earnestness will perhaps be confirmed by his reputation
for whimsical inconsistency, and by recollections of his
gimcrack castle on Strawberry Hill, built on the appropriate
site of the villa of the keeper of a fashionable toy-shop.
On the other hand, Walpole was one of the most suggestive
forces of his time. In more than one direction he initiated
movements which have been rich in results, and not the
least fertile of these was the " Gothic Story," which inaugurated a new species of literature. *The Castle of Otranto*
affected the *Rowley Poems* ; it influenced the Oriental tale
of *Vathek* ; it was the parent of *The Mysteries of Udolpho*
and *The Monk* ; it inspired the numerous historical novels
which preceded Sir Walter Scott ; it was the lineal ancestor
of *Ivanhoe* and its vast army of descendents, foreign as well
as English.

Walpole's own statements on the origin and object of the story were inconsistent. His first Preface represented it as a translation made by " William Marshal, Gent." from a black-letter print of an Italian manuscript belonging to the period of the Crusades, 1095–1243. No one was deceived by the device. The hand of Walpole was recognised. Writing to the Rev. William Cole (March 9, 1765) a few weeks after the publication, he depreciates the work. It originated, he says, in a dream. He thought himself in an ancient castle, and saw " on the uppermost banister of a great staircase " a gigantic hand in armour. The idea engrossed his mind. He began to write " without knowing in the least what I intended to say or relate," and finished the tale within two months.

But in the Preface to the second edition of the book he acknowledged its authorship, asserted a definite purpose and claimed to have consciously created " a new species of romance." The story was " an attempt to blend the two kinds of romance, the ancient and the modern " ; to set free " the great resources of fancy," which " have been dammed up by a strict adherence to common life " ; and yet, unlike the old romancers, to make the actors " think, speak and act, as it might be supposed mere men and women would do in extraordinary positions." " If," he continues, "the new route he has struck shall have paved a road for men of brighter talents, he shall own, with pleasure and modesty, that he was sensible the plan was capable of receiving greater embellishments than his imagination or the conduct of the passions could bestow on it."

In *The Castle of Otranto*, Walpole challenged the methods and the subject-matter of contemporary novelists. It substituted invention for observation, a picture of the past for that of the present, the supernatural and the marvellous for ordinary daily experiences. At the same time he broke away from the ancient romance, and tried, in his own words, to " blend the wonderful of old stories with the natural of modern novels." The conception was original and, in spite of its half-hearted execution, abundantly rich in results. Against the moral lessons, sentiment, domestic familiarities and boisterous rowdyism of middle-class fiction, Walpole was honestly in revolt. For the arts of the Middle Ages his zeal, though it may have outrun his knowledge, was warm. Why then did he give a grotesque turn to a serious design? Probably the whim of the fribble triumphed over the judgment of the literary critic; or the pretended contempt of the man of fashion for letters allowed an affectation of frivolity to overpower the real earnestness of his purpose.

The story itself moves briskly, not by long-winded narratives, but by dialogue and action; it has no digressions; it never drags. The scene is laid in Italy at some vague period during the Crusades. The choice of a feudal castle as the historical framework of the tale was happy. The literature of the Middle Ages was beginning to inspire scholars; illuminated manuscripts, tapestries, painted glass, coins, armour, weapons, were becoming the delight of specialists. But it was medieval architecture which seized the imagination of the general public. Its memorials were everywhere present. Cathedrals and churches, ruined abbeys, baronial strongholds, gave the first popular impulse to the romantic movement. It was the Church of St. Mary Redcliffe at Bristol which possessed the heart and brain of Chatterton. Of this feeling Walpole took advantage with the instinct of genius. He used the Castle of Otranto as Victor Hugo used Notre-Dame. It was more than the setting to his story. It gave a medieval flavour to the whole. Itself a romance in stone, its dim galleries, huge halls, underground vaults, trap-doors, and subterranean passages combined to excite wonder and curiosity, to suggest mysteries and terrors, to attune the mind to the marvellous and the supernatural.

On the stage of the Castle assemble the actors who play their parts in the fulfilment of a mysterious tradition. With eager haste, Manfred, the reigning Prince of Otranto, was pressing on the marriage of his only son Conrad. As the tale developes, the reason of his impatience is disclosed. Many years before, Alfonso, Prince of Otranto, had sailed for the Holy Land to join the Crusade. Detained in Sicily by storms, he had secretly married Victoria, a beautiful Sicilian, purposing on his return to avow his marriage.

After he had resumed his voyage, his wife bore him a daughter. In Palestine the Prince was poisoned by his Chamberlain, Ricardo, who forged a will by which he inherited Otranto. Fearing shipwreck, the poisoner vowed to St. Nicholas a church and two convents if he lived to reach Italy. In a dream the saint promised Ricardo that his " posterity should reign in Otranto until the rightful owner should be grown too large to inhabit the castle, and as long as issue male should remain to enjoy it." Manfred, the grandson of Ricardo, and his only son, Conrad, alone represented the male line.

On the eve of Conrad's wedding, a colossal helmet dropped from the moon, crashed through the pavement of the courtyard, and in its fall crushed the boy to death. Without a male heir, Manfred determines to divorce his wife and himself marry his son's intended bride. Round this design revolves the human action of the story, in which Theodore, an unknown peasant lad, plays an increasingly important part. He is, in truth, the grandson of Alfonso and Victoria, and the only child of their daughter. Supernatural agencies establish his claim to his grandfather's title and estates ; portents and ghosts multiply ; and a tempestuous agitation of the sable plumes on the helmet accompanies each manifestation. A gigantic foot and part of a leg, both in armour, appear in the great chamber ; the tremendous rattling of armour was heard as though some giant was rising from the ground ; a colossal mailed fist grasped the banister of the staircase ; an enormous sword, with difficulty borne into the courtyard by a hundred bearers, leaped from their shoulders to fix itself by the side of the helmet ; the portrait of Ricardo sighed, left its panel, and, with a dejected air, passed down the gallery : three drops of blood fell from the nose of Alfonso's statue in the church ; a cowled figure spoke its warning in a hollow voice, and revealed " the fleshless jaws and empty sockets of a skeleton." The end was approaching. A clap of thunder was followed by " the rattling of more than mortal armour " ; the walls of the castle were rent by a mighty force ; the form of Alfonso, " dilated to an immense magnitude," towered among the ruins, and crying, " Behold in Theodore the true heir of

Alfonso ! " rose to heaven and the bosom of St. Nicholas. Great writers have used the supernatural rarely and with the utmost care. Where it has been employed, they have created the proper atmosphere, prepared a sense of expectancy and foreboding, or filled the minds of the spectators with thoughts of which its appearances become the natural expression. Walpole was not a poet, or even a literary artist. He used the supernatural to an excess which bred contempt for its terrors, and, except for the scene of its occurrences, nothing could be more violent and abrupt than his methods of treatment. Yet his crude manifesto of the novel of the future faintly resembles the confession of poetic faith put forward, forty years later, in *Lyrical Ballads*. The " natural of the modern novel " removed from the eyes the scales of custom, and revealed the unexpected treasures which were neglected because of their familiarity. The " wonderful of old stories," outside the range of daily experience, received the semblance of reality, and awakened the emotions which would be aroused if the supernatural events were true. Transferred to the realm of poetry and generalised into a philosophy, these were the respective spheres of Wordsworth and Coleridge.

Walpole's parade of the supernatural suggests that *The Castle of Otranto* was partly written in jest. Clara Reeve, an industrious, unimaginative woman of letters, at the age of fifty-one, followed him in solemn earnest In *The Old English Baron : A Gothic Story* (1775) she accepted his conception of a new kind of prose fiction, but criticised and corrected his excesses.

Her novel, as the Preface states, attempts to blend the romance with the modern novel by supplying enough " of the marvellous to excite the attention ; enough of the manners of real life to give an air of probability to the work ; and enough of the pathetic to engage the heart in its behalf." It was in the use of the marvellous that she tried to improve upon Walpole by reducing it to a minimum, and keeping her ghost " within the utmost *verge* of probability." Confined to a cupboard, where his groans led to the discovery of his skeleton and his murder, he is as prosaic and utilitarian as a ghost can be, and as dull. Miss Reeve did not, like Coleridge, try to make the supernatural natural ; she rather aimed, in the spirit of the middle of the eighteenth century, at making it credible. She appealed for belief, not to the imagination, but to the very faculties which need to be suspended. Raw and violent though its methods are, *The Castle of Otranto* is truer to romantic art than *The Old English Baron*.

Without the thrill of terror Miss Reeve's story has little that is Gothic. Neither has her picture of the fifteenth century any medieval flavour. *The Champion of Virtue*, which was the original title of the novel, best describes its true character. A disciple of Richardson and a friend of his daughter, to whom the book was dedicated, Miss Reeve transplants Sir Charles Grandison into the Middle Ages, and her morality and sentiment are as edifying as those of her model. Her actors talk the stilted language of contemporary novels of high life. Their manners and habits are those of her own generation. Like Walpole, she professes to write from an ancient manuscript, and constructs her story on lines similar to those of *The Castle of Otranto*. But she reintroduces the features of middle-class fiction from which Walpole had contrived to escape. The champion of virtue triumphs ; injured innocence is righted, and wrongdoing punished. The sentiment and moral lessons, still dear to the public, largely explain the prolonged success of the novel. Her timid compromise between the credible and the marvellous robbed the story of its life, and left it, as Walpole said, so probable as to be less interesting than " any trial for murder at the Old Bailey." Yet, in her use of the supernatural, Mrs. Radcliffe approached more closely to *The Old English Baron* than to *The Castle of Otranto*.

Walpole had made his supernatural unnatural by raising the apparition of Alfonso to gigantic proportions. In this device he may have imitated Eastern tales, in which enormous size not only embodies power, but strikes terror. Various forms of Oriental fiction had, in the first twenty years of the century, become popular in this country. Most of the works reached England from France. Among them was the English translation of Antoine Galland's French version of *The Arabian Nights' Entertainments* (1708–1715). In a few years followed Turkish, Persian, Arabic,

Chinese, Mogul *Tales*, translated from the French of François Pétis de la Croix, Jean Terrasson, Jean Paul Bignon and Simon Gueullette. But, except in the apologues, which were favourite pastimes of essayists, Oriental fiction had little influence on English literature. No native writer used it, like Anthony Count Hamilton or Voltaire, as the vehicle of witty satire on contemporary life. It was not Oriental literature which attracted Johnson to seek in Abyssinia the scene of *Rasselas*, but the growing interest in voyage, travel and discovery. Nor did it inspire Dr. John Hawkesworth, when in 1761 he produced *Almoran and Hamet*. He only followed Johnson, and his treatment of the occult is purely Occidental. But twenty-five years later (1786) appeared *Vathek*, the most famous Oriental tale in the English language. William Beckford (1759–1844) wrote other books ; but it is by *Vathek* that he lives.

In its English form *Vathek* is a surreptitiously published translation by the Rev. Samuel Henley from the incomplete French original. Beckford had revised and approved the version, but, to the translator's knowledge, he was still working on additional episodes for the book, and intended to publish it first in its French form. Past the age of seventy, he told Cyrus Redding, his biographer, that he wrote the book " in one sitting and in French. It cost me three days and two nights of hard labour." But autograph letters show that he had " slaved " at *Vathek* for many months previously. Lovers of literary tradition must either recognise that the old man's memory played him false, or believe that, his brain seething with the subject of his studies, he first committed the whole to paper at a single sitting in the stated time.

Many readers are repelled by the exuberance of Oriental fiction, dissociated as it generally is from any development of character. They will find in *Vathek* the defects of its type. The incidents are extravagant, the descriptions luxuriant. Delineation of character is scarcely attempted ; Vathek himself has none, and the outlines that are traced in Nuronihar are not fully developed. Yet few resist the fascination that the book derives from the personality and circumstances of its author. Young—he was little more than twenty-one—possessed of great intellectual gifts, master of fabulous wealth, temperamentally a voluptuary, he dreams of the unbridled desires and limitless ambitions of his Caliph which earth alone could not satisfy. So much did these fantastic dreams possess him that, as he wrote them down, " I have not," he says, " a nerve in my frame but vibrates like an aspen."

Oriental fiction is less the inspiration of the book than Beckford himself. Nor did he owe much to his French predecessors. Scattered through the book are comic episodes and witty or satiric touches which will, he hopes, make Count Hamilton " smile upon me when we are introduced to one another in Paradise." But the spirit in which he wrote was totally different from that of the brilliant author of *Les Quatre Facardins*. His tone does not ring with the light mockery of Western incredulity ; it rather seems charged with confidence in the realities of his wildest fantasies. It is this note which redeems the extravagances of *Vathek* from grotesqueness, and raises its final scene in the Hall of Eblis above the level of theatrical effects into a region of sombre magnificence which has rarely been reached in our literature.

In the French romantic movement Oriental fiction filled an important place. It was not so with English romantics. They found sensations, not in the wonders of the East, but in one or other of the directions marked out by *The Castle of Otranto*. The historical novel, of which Walpole made little and Clara Reeve less, progressed so feebly before the advent of Scott that it needs only brief notice. The novel of terror, inspired by the supernatural or the marvellous, became the most characteristic literary expression of the orgy of mental and emotional excitement, which, swollen by the romantic movement, the religious revival, the preparation for the French Revolution and its aftermath, and the influence of German literature, reached its height as the eighteenth century closed and its successor dawned.

That writers of prose fiction should seek material in the picturesque past seems a necessary consequence of the romantic revival. But they were attracted to history by no respect for its sanctity ; they rather welcomed it as a refuge from present-day realities and an opportunity for invention. In their search for romance they traversed the centuries from St. Dunstan to Kosciusko. They entered light-heartedly on a difficult task in which success is rare and at its best relative. None of them tried so to steep himself in a period as to make it the atmosphere of his mental life, or to project this imaginary self into his creations that they might live and move as real men and women. Without knowledge or preparation they attempted to ride two horses at once, and lost their seats on both ; they were false to history and untrue to human nature. Only Joseph Strutt had the detailed familiarity with a period which was requisite for the rich local colour of a representative historical background. But he was so deficient in imaginative or dramatic power that his *Queenhoo Hall* (1808) is not a living picture of the times of Henry VI, but as dry a compilation of antiquarian facts as was ever penned by a Dr. Dryasdust.

Conscientious writers might study a period for their purpose. Few took the trouble. Some relied for their medieval or Elizabethan flavour on a sprinkling of obsolete words or descriptions of Wardour Street trappings of dubious authenticity. Others, lured by the ready-made interest of famous characters of the past, indicated their period by attributing their most impudent inventions to great historical personages. Of these offenders Sophia Lee, in *The Recess* (1783–5), is one of the most flagrant.

The story is told by Matilda Howard, the eldest of the twin daughters of Mary Queen of Scots by a secret marriage with the Duke of Norfolk. The two girls are brought up in The Recess, a suite of rooms concealed in a ruined abbey and reached through sliding panels and trap-doors by a subterranean passage from the neighbouring house. There the Earl of Leicester is hidden from assassins by the two girls, and before his return to Court he marries Matilda. Leicester is sufficiently well drawn to suggest comparison with the companion portrait in *Kenilworth*. But the faint interest of the first volume is washed out in its successors by a sentimentalism which Burleigh, Walsingham, Queen Elizabeth, Essex, the Countess of Somerset, James I, Prince

Henry and others cannot save from an overpowering sickliness.

With *The Recess* began a stream of predecessors of Scott. Between its publication and that of *Waverley* (1814) a list might easily be compiled of upwards of seventy historical novels. Among them may be mentioned Isaac D'Israeli's *Despotism : or the Fall of the Jesuits* (1811), because, like the social novels of his famous son, it has a political purpose. It sketches, with a romancer's imaginative licence, the circumstances which led up to the expulsion of the Jesuits from Portugal and Spain and their ultimate suppression, and was probably occasioned by their secret re-establishment by Pius VII.

To Jane Porter (1776–1850) more literary importance has been attached. She wrote two novels of which most people have heard, and she claimed to have shown the way to Walter Scott. Irish by birth, she sympathised with oppressed nationalities. The struggle for independence in Poland or in Scotland is the theme of *Thaddeus of Warsaw* (1803) and *The Scottish Chiefs* (1810). Thaddeus Kosciusko is the real hero in the first, William Wallace in the second.

The war which followed the partition of Poland in 1793 was recent. Its actors were of Miss Porter's own generation, and she herself probably met many Polish refugees. *Thaddeus of Warsaw*, therefore, is not an historical novel. In its tear-drenched pages the hero, who had been the brother-in-arms of Kosciusko, becomes a teacher of languages in London. He is described by Sophia Egerton as " a soldier by his dress, a man of rank by his manners, an Apollo from his person, and a hero from his prowess." The extravagantly sentimental book has one claim to remembrance. The thought of Thaddeus determined Shelley, reaching London after his expulsion from Oxford, to take lodgings in Poland Street.

The Scottish Chiefs, on the other hand, opens in 1296, and ends with Bannockburn. For her difficult task of writing an historical novel Miss Porter carefully prepared herself. She claimed not only that she had read " every writing extant on the period of her narrative," but that she

UA

had seldom mentioned " any spot in Scotland " which she had not herself visited. For this unusual preparation she deserves credit. But the result is a book which is scarcely less rubbishy than the work of her most careless contemporaries. Neither her reading nor her travels produce a trace of local colour. Her historical sense is so weak that her pictures of the past are completely wanting in verisimilitude. Her spiritless fighting is continually interrupted by magnanimous speeches. Her Scottish ladies are the Angelinas of the sentimental fiction of the day. The language is bombastic, and in the conversations absurdly high-flown. It is impossible to admit Miss Porter's claim to be the founder of the historical novel. It is almost incredible that Scott, even in the most punctilious mood of his courtesy in acknowledging literary obligations, should ever have admitted any debt to a book which, with all its excellent intentions, is feebleness itself.

Two attempts at the new type of prose fiction were made by the most successful novelist of the day, if not of the century. With an historical novel Ann Radcliffe, whose maiden name was Ward (1764–1823), began and closed her literary career. The scene of *The Castles of Athlin and Dunbayne* (1789) is laid on the north-east coast of Scotland. Beyond the use of bows and arrows in warfare, there is no indication of the date of the action. But the book derives some interest from the early recognition of the romantic potentialities of the Highlands and from the picture-making power which is shown in the description of the Castle of Dunbayne, perched on a rock whose base is washed by the sea.

In *Gaston de Blondeville* (written in 1802 : published 1826) Mrs. Radcliffe made a more serious effort, for which she had carefully studied the period. Between her first and last historical novel many literary adventurers had sought the vein of romance which lay concealed in history. Mrs. Radcliffe's faith in the existence of the buried treasure was strong enough to induce her to return to her first love, desert her own peculiar field, and change her style. It is a story of the times of Henry III. Though historical personages, like the King, Prince Edward and Simon de

Montfort, appear, the incidents and chief characters are fictitious.

An imaginary manuscript dug up in the ruins of Kenilworth, and a few obsolete words or inverted sentences, are used to give the narrative a Plantagenet origin and flavour. Pictorial truth to the period is sought in trappings or accessories. But the more essential element of dramatic truth to character and sentiment is neglected. The conversations and dialogues adopt the high-flown, stilted style of contemporary fiction, and express the most modern ideas in the most modern phrases. Nor does the conduct of the story show much originality. The peasant heir is identified by a strawberry mark, and a resolute ghost, working by day as well as by night, disposes of the principal villains. Only in this historical novel does Mrs. Radcliffe follow Walpole in leaving the supernatural unexplained.

Gaston de Blondeville failed. Mrs. Radcliffe probably knew it, for the book was never published in her lifetime. History still withheld the secret of the historical novel. When Scott found the clue, he owed little, except by way of warning, to the blind gropings of his predecessors.

It was in the other direction marked out in *The Castle of Otranto* that Mrs. Radcliffe won the triumphs which made her the most influential pioneer of the romantic movement. Appealing to the new-born passion for night and solitude and the craving for something strange and unfamiliar, she worked on the vein of " the supernatural " and " the marvellous " which Walpole and Clara Reeve had suggested. Out of it she created the novel of terror or suspense to which Monk Lewis and Maturin added fresh horrors.

Living a retired life, she knew little of the outer world. Her figures are not built up from experience and observation ; they are created out of herself. As with her actors, so with her scenery. She had never visited the countries in which her plots are laid ; her landscapes are creations of her imagination. Her stories are still further removed from ordinary life by being told of distant countries and of bygone times whose spirit she makes no effort to reproduce. Divorced from realities, they are the poetry of prose romance.

In her distinctive vein she wrote four novels : *The Sicilian Romance* (1790), *The Romance of the Forest* (1791), *The Mysteries of Udolpho* (1794), and *The Italian* (1797). The first is so inferior to the other three that it may be ignored. Of the three later novels, *The Italian* is the most powerful, perhaps because in the Inquisition it contains the solid substance of a formidable reality.

The plots of her three novels are constructed on a uniform plan. A persecuted heroine of mysterious birth is brought into the hands of a crime-stained villain—a needy and desperate noble or a remorseless monk. She is immured in an ancient building—a half-ruined abbey plunged in the depths of the forest, an immense castle among the peaks of the Apennines, or a convent of the Black Penitents. These buildings become important actors in the story ; their huge rooms hung with tapestry, their hidden doors, sliding panels, secret stairways and passages, subterranean dungeons, add nameless terrors to her solitude. Sounds unexplained, sights indistinctly caught, the flutter of the tapestry in the draught, dim shadows endowed with motion by the flicker of the firelight or the tremulous shimmer of the moonbeam suggest superstitious fears. Incidents which often prove to be innocent or trifling arouse unreasoning apprehensions from their indefinite menace of possible designs. Mutilated manuscripts, unearthed from their concealment and stealthily read at midnight by the feeble light of a lamp, lead up to the revelation of some hideous crime, perpetrated on the very spot, only to break off at the moment when their secret was about to be disclosed.

In the heroine's terrors nature plays its part, and its changes are skilfully used to harmonise with her moods. The savage wildness of the Apennines or the depths of the unexplored forest exclude human aid and darken solitude. The wind howls, whistles, or moans ; the clouds lower ; the roll of the thunder is ominous ; the flash of the lightning intensifies the blackness of the night by its momentary glare. Again and again hope seems dead, or is snatched back to life from the very verge of despair. But in all three novels there is a happy ending in which heroine and lover are united.

Mrs. Radcliffe's use of scenery was one of the new resources which she added to the art of the novelist. In this respect she and Charlotte Smith stood almost alone among their predecessors or contemporaries. Yet the difference between their descriptions is marked. Mrs. Smith's landscapes are definite and local. Mrs. Radcliffe, as might be expected from scenes which are not observed but imagined, is typical and general in the impressions which she produces. Even in the famous description of the Castle of Udolpho, as it first comes into sight, there is such vagueness in detail that no two artists would draw it alike. Yet, however much her pictures are creations of the fancy, they show an intense sympathy and intimacy with nature. Her sunrises—and all her heroines are early risers—her sunsets and twilight, are close studies of atmosphere and cloud-effects. If she is immoderate in using scenery to suggest or accompany emotional moods, the excess may be pardoned in the discoverer of a novelty which was of great potential value.

There are no characters in Mrs. Radcliffe's stories. Her heroines are pensive, melancholy, sentimental beings, with a pretty taste for a sonnet or an elegiac ode, who shed floods of tears and seem to pass from swoon to swoon. But, soft though they seem to be, they have in them a harder element. Driven by a fearful curiosity, they meet and even court danger. Powerless in the hands of the villain, they yet face him boldly. Emily confronts Montoni and tells him that the death of her aunt makes it improper for her to remain unchaperoned in his Castle of Udolpho, and demands to be restored to her relatives. All drawn to the same pattern, one girl cannot be distinguished from the other. La Motte, Montoni and Schedoni are equally stock villains. La Motte is the most human, because there is vacillation in his criminal purposes. Byron modelled his scowl on that of Schedoni, and *Lara* and *The Giaour* owed much to the really powerful description of that monastic villain in *The Italian*.

It is difficult for the present generation to recapture Mrs. Radcliffe's thrill. Immune from many of the terrors which tortured her heroines, it cannot realise what the extinction of a lamp meant to the solitary inmate of some vaulted room or gallery so readily as a generation which

knew neither matches nor artificial light. Mrs. Radcliffe
is a mistress of hints, suggestions, associations, silence,
indefiniteness, emptiness. But, though she uses her
machinery with literary craftsmanship, her processes are
ruder than those of her successors. The methods by which
she works cannot compare in delicacy and subtlety with the
means by which the poetic genius of Coleridge produced
the weirdness of " The Ancient Mariner," or the witchery
of the serpent gaze of Geraldine in " Christabel," or by
which, in later times, prose writers like Nathaniel Hawthorne
and Stevenson have created their atmosphere of foreboding.
But she does possess, to a rare degree, the power of suggesting
those doubts whether something inexplicable may not lie
behind material certitudes which, in given circumstances,
readily pass into the thrill of superstitious fear.

Mrs. Radcliffe's use of the supernatural is peculiar to
herself. Walpole left it inexplicable ; Clara Reeve laboured
to make it credible ; Mrs. Radcliffe, while allowing it to
fascinate her imagination, carefully reduces it to an illusion.
Artistically she would have gained if, without affirming
or denying belief, she had left its existence a possibility.
Whether her motive was piety or reason, the simplicity of
her explanations so completely destroys her mysteries that
her books can scarcely be read a second time. In this
respect, her work bears an inverted relation to the poetry
of the future. Instead of seeking supernatural or mystical
meanings in familiar objects, she finds for her idealised
terrors a natural basis.

Matthew Gregory Lewis (1775–1818), nicknamed the
" Monk " from the title of his most famous book, followed
Mrs. Radcliffe. *The Monk* (1795) was published when
Lewis was only twenty. Begun, as he tells his mother,
" in the style of *The Castle of Otranto*," he " was induced to
go on with it by reading *The Mysteries of Udolpho*." A
cheerful, round-faced, foppish little tuft-hunter, he can with
difficulty be taken seriously. " Tell me," he asks his mother,
" whether you see any resemblance between the character
given of Montoni . . . and my own. I confess that it
struck me." But his boyish enthusiasms, which he retained
throughout life, made him hosts of friends, and, both as an

original writer and as a purveyor of German fiction, he
exercised a considerable influence on his literary contemporaries.

Between beginning and completing *The Monk* Lewis had
steeped his mind with *Werther* and with the recent marvels
of German imaginative literature. Like Mrs. Radcliffe, but
by more violent and brutal methods, he appealed to the
sense of fear. He added thrills peculiar to himself. One
was physical repulsion from the horrors of the charnel-house.
Another was sensuality, which, though modified in warmth
of expression under the threat of legal proceedings, remained
an object. Scene after scene in *The Monk* is painted in
crude colours, with imaginative extravagances which may
have been due to boyish immaturity, to German models,
or to the morbidity of a diseased mind. But Lewis's gift
of vivid narrative grips the reader's attention, and even
maintains interest through the absurdities of the catastrophe.
Ambrosio, the monk whose spiritual pride has been turned
to his moral ruin by Matilda, half woman, half fiend, has
strangled his mother and violated his sister. In a dungeon
of the Inquisition he awaits his summons to an *auto-da-fé*.
The steps of the guard approach the cell, when he yields to
the temptation of the Evil One himself, signs the conveyance
of his soul with the conventional iron pen and drops of his
blood, is wafted away to the mountains, and there, dropped
by the demon from a dizzy height on the rocks below,
perishes in the fall.

The *diablerie* of Lewis was primitive and childish compared
with that of Charles Robert Maturin (1782–1824). An
Irish clergyman, dramatist, and romance-writer, he wrote
many novels, the first of which was *The Family of Montorio*
(1807), " misnomed (*sic*) by a bookseller *The Fatal Revenge*,"
and published under the assumed name of Murphy. Appealing for its only interest to what he calls the universal and
irresistible " passion of supernatural fear," the clumsily
constructed book follows the crude methods of *The Monk*.
Corpses and spectres circulate so freely that they are scarcely
to be distinguished from the living.

Still working on the same passion, but by subtler methods,
he produced in 1820 *Melmoth the Wanderer*. He had freed

himself from the influence of Lewis. No longer gross and emphatic, he ceased to aim at creating physical terror by visible objects. He rather sought to communicate the haunting dread of the approach or presence of something supernatural. He used, and with great power, Mrs. Radcliffe's method of suggestion. Melmoth himself may have owed something to the Wandering Jew, to Faust, to Rosicrucian ideas. But the conception remains original and impressive. By what means he has won earthly immortality and the command of supernatural powers is a secret which none can hear without loss of reason. The strange glare of his piercing eyes, and his smile, at once malignant, mocking and pathetic, burn themselves into the memory.

At each final stage of the episodes in the disconnected narrative—whether in the madhouse, the subterranean passage of the convent, or the dungeon of the Inquisition—Melmoth's appearance is awaited with a tingling of the nerves. The victims to whom he offers escape on conditions which are incommunicable are brought to the last stage of despair. With remarkable command of detail are accumulated the external circumstances which gradually close the door of hope. To the pressure from without is added the pressure from within. Maturin possessed a knowledge of human nature which belonged to no other writer of his school. With acute analysis he traces the workings of the mind as it passes from resistance to apathy and on towards the verge of insanity. The climax of agony which preludes the approach of Melmoth is internal as well as external.

Melmoth the Wanderer is the work of an unwholesome genius. In England it appeared too late for the author's reputation. Sobriety was taking the place of mental intoxication. On the Continent the book made something of a sensation, and it fascinated Balzac. Maturin's love of display, extravagances and affectations write, as it were, the epitaph on the extinction of a school of writers which had become decadent and diseased. When he was writing, he fixed a large black wafer on his forehead as an injunction to silence. Often in pecuniary difficulties, he once spent the borrowed money on a reception, hiring a room in which, seated with his wife on a dais surmounted by a crimson canopy, he received his guests. Bewick, who visited him at Dublin in the early part of the last century, has left a graphic description of his interview with the novelist. He found Maturin dressed to receive him :

> " pacing his drawing-room in elegant full dress, a splendidly bound book laid open upon a cambric pocket-handkerchief, laced round the edges and scented with eau-de-Cologne, and held upon both hands ; a stylish new black wig curled over his temples, his shirt collar reaching half-way up his face, and his attenuated cheeks rouged up to the very eyes."

As the century closed, the native stream of novels of terror was swollen by the influx of a German tributary. In Germany a movement similar to that in England, but more conscious of its purpose and led by men of genius, was in progress. In revolt against the supremacy of French classicism, it demanded freedom and a national literature ; it discovered Shakespeare and plunged back into the Middle Ages. In 1773 Bürger published his ballad of *Lenore*, and Goethe his tragedy of *Götz von Berlichingen*, or *Goetz with the Iron Hand*. In 1781 followed Schiller's play of *The Robbers*. Before the close of the century these three books had been translated into English. Walter Scott's first publication was an anonymous version of *Lenore* and *The Wild Huntsman* (1795). Four years later he published a free translation of *Götz von Berlichingen* (1799), with the name of " Wm. Scott " on the title-page. *The Robbers* had already been translated by his friend Frazer Tytler. A horde of inferior invaders followed, with melodramatic ballads, plays and tales. If they were written under the influence of Walpole and Mrs. Radcliffe—and Goethe himself had read *The Castle of Otranto*—the debt was repaid with interest. Bandits, monks, feudal barons, poisonings, dungeons, tortures and shrieking spectres poured into the country. Even Scott seemed for a moment to be swept from his feet. He contributed two translated and three original ballads to the " repast of hobgoblins " offered in the metrical *Tales of Wonder* (1801), in which " wonder-working " Lewis made a churchyard of Parnassus.

The effect of this riot of the imagination, half native, half foreign, may be illustrated by the influence that it exercised on the mind of Shelley, who, as a child, revelled in moon-illumined castles, cadaverous monks, scowling desperadoes and obtrusive spectres.

> While yet a boy I sought for ghosts, and sped
> Thro' many a lonely chamber, cave and ruin,
> And starlight wood, with fearful steps, pursuing
> Hopes of high talk with the departed dead.

He made the garret at Field Place the abode of an alchemist, old, grey and bearded. At Sion House and at Eton he dabbled in chemistry and conjurations of the Devil. La Motte, Montoni and Schedoni were the first fictitious characters by whom he was impressed. The German books which he read in translations fostered his taste for the marvellous and romantic. His own novels, *Zastrozzi* (1810) and *St. Irvyne* (1811), are curiosities of literature of the melodramatic and blue-fire type. As works of art they are worthless imitations, written when his mind, like that of Scythrop, was filled with dreams of " Illuminati and Eleutherarchs," and marked by every fault of juvenile extravagance. Five years later, " the Monk " was one of the famous party who in 1816 gathered in the Villa Diodati at Geneva, and planned the unearthly tales of which Mrs. Shelley's *Frankenstein* (1818) and Dr. Polidori's *Vampyre* (1819) were the outcome.

From the gush of sentimentalism and the surge of imaginative excess Maria Edgeworth, sane and serene, stood aloof. She felt no impulse to strengthen the treatment of romantic themes, historical or emotional, with the best elements of novels of contemporary realities. Yet the national novel which she inaugurated with *Castle Rackrent* (1800) expressed a definite side of the romantic movement. The classic school studied man in the abstract and dwelt upon the typical attributes of humanity. Romantics, on the other hand, fastened on all that was distinctive, characteristic, peculiar—all that made up the different personalities of individuals or the local colour of nations and races. Of the one school the outcome was the universal brotherhood of man ; of the other the passion for nationality. Miss Edgeworth's hand fired the train which had been already laid for the simultaneous development of national novels, not only in Ireland, but in Scotland and Wales.

Hitherto, Smollett alone had tried to distinguish a Scotsman by other characteristics than a national dialect. No other effort had been made to penetrate the individuality of national manners, habits and feelings. That Miss Edgeworth should have been the first to discover this unworked vein is at first sight strange ; at a second glance the strangeness seems partly to disappear. The true Irish novelist, says O'Leary in Lady Morgan's *Florence M'Carthy*, is bound to be " Irish body and soul ; Irish by birth, by blood, and by descent ; Irish every inch of her, heart and hand, life and land." Had Miss Edgeworth fulfilled these conditions, had Irish manners and customs been the familiar surroundings of her childhood, she might possibly have overlooked the material of which she became the first observer. Many of her predecessors and contemporaries among writers of prose fiction came nearer than herself to fulfilling the conditions demanded by Lady Morgan ; yet they were blind to the wealth of material around them. Thus the credit of creating the national novels of Ireland belongs to a woman, who in mind and character was the least national of all the gifted writers who have been Irish by birth. Her books are not racy of the soil ; neither are they emerald-green from cover to cover. But she paved the way for her immediate successors—for the patriotic enthusiasm of Lady Morgan in *The Wild Irish Girl* (1806), for Maturin's *Wild Irish Boy* (1808) and Griffin's *Collegians* (1829), for the gloomy realism of John and Michael Banim in *The Tales of the O'Hara Family* (1825, etc.), for the sunnier yet not less truthful pictures in William Carleton's *Traits and Stories of Irish Peasantry* (1830–3).

Miss Edgeworth never saw Ireland till she was fifteen years old. In 1782 her father, taking his children with him, settled at the family home at Edgeworthstown, near Mullingar. The clever schoolgirl, carefully educated by her father and at school in Derby and in London, instructed during the holidays by the eccentric author of *Sandford and*

Merton, was suddenly plunged into a new country, and introduced to strange surroundings. Everything combined to heighten the vividness of the contrast, for in Ireland she practically became her father's agent, and was brought into daily contact with his tenants. Though not a languishing London beauty, she could scarcely have felt the difference between her old and new circumstances less acutely than did Lady Juliana in Miss Ferrier's *Marriage* (1818) on her first visit to her husband's Highland home and her Scottish relations. It is a contrast on which she often insists, and an experience which she allots to Lord Glenthorn in *Ennui*, and Lord Colambre in *The Absentee*.

The comparisons which were forced upon her as a quick-witted, observant girl were the parents of her Irish novels. They gained her the fame of creating national fiction ; they imposed upon her limitations which she never overcame. She writes of the Irish as an alien rather than as a native. She draws her pictures of Irish life and character with the acute but superficial observation of a foreign resident, and colours them with the amused deliberation of an English-woman. Her *Essay on Irish Bulls* (1802) is now chiefly remembered for the fact that, in the growing enthusiasm for farming improvements, it was ordered by the secretary of an English agricultural society. It contains some excellent stories ; but the person who could sit down to compose it was scarcely the woman to write a national novel of Irish life.

Of Miss Edgeworth's Irish novels *Castle Rackrent* (1800), *The Absentee* (1812), and *Ormond* (1817) are the most successful. In the first, the narrative of Thady O'Quirk, the old steward, who recounts the fortunes of the successive baronets—the drunken Sir Patrick, the litigious Sir Murtagh, the fire-eating Sir Kit, the lie-about Sir Condy—has the easy flow of a country gossip's history. Its brevity saves it from becoming wearisome, and its construction obviates the necessity of a plot, in which Miss Edgeworth never succeeded. But it contains no creation like that of King Corny and no penetrating study like that of Sir Ulick O'Shane in *Ormond*. In all her stories the minor characters are vigorously drawn, and, moral puppets though they often are, they are alive and human. Her gallery of national portraits is varied, and rich in such pictures as Lady Clonbrony, Father Jos, Sir Terence O'Fay or Nicholas Garraghty. But, apart from the tragic figure of Ellinor O'Donoghoe and the warm-hearted fidelity of Larry the postilion and Moriarty Carroll, her humble actors leave the impression of superficial observation rather than that of insight into character.

" Do explain to us," wrote Sir Walter Scott, " why Pat, who gets so well forward in other countries, is so miserable in his own." For such a task Miss Edgeworth knew herself to be unfitted. To a woman of her sensible, practical temperament, with her talent for truth rather than for invention, holding her feeling and her imagination under firm control, and always responding to the appeal of reason, the Irish peasant was a sealed book, beyond the covers of which she scarcely attempted to look. She had little sympathy with his intense nationality, and no knowledge of his native language. She lived in the midst of Thrashers, Whiteboys, Hearts-of-Oak-boys, White-Tooths, Defenders, and other offspring of agrarian, religious and political discontent. With her usual good sense, she refused to allow the disorders around her to disturb her equanimity, and quietly pursued her daily tasks. " I cannot," she says, " be a captain of dragoons, and sitting with my hands before me would not make any of us one degree safer." Not anxious to probe very deeply the causes of the discontent around her, she offers as her one panacea a resident landlord.

Miss Edgeworth herself used to say that she did not know the Irish peasant till she had read William Carleton. Always generous in her appreciation of other writers, she also speaks in high praise of the work of the two Banims. " Have you seen," she asked in 1827, " the *Tales of the O'Hara Family*—second series? They are of unequal value ; one called *The Nowlans* is a work of great genius." With this verdict on John and Michael Banim many people will agree. Of the true character of the Irish people less is learned from Blue books and parliamentary speeches than from these three Irish writers—peasant-born and peasant-bred. Without glozing over the darker passions of their compatriots, they tried to explain to England why Irish peasants considered themselves at war with the law of the land.

Miss Edgeworth brought to Ireland opinions and standards formed in England, and it was mainly through this accident that she discovered her new mine of material. But her title to have created the national novel is firmly established, even if, in some respects, it may be doubted whether she was herself a national novelist. The vein which she was the first to strike has since been worked by many hands and in many countries. To her, more than half a century after the publication of her Irish novels, Turgenieff acknowledged his debt for his pictures of the Russian peasantry. But the greatest tribute to her genius was paid by Scott in the Postscript to *Waverley*. Speaking of his characters he says, " It has been my object to describe these persons . . . so as in some distant degree to emulate the admirable Irish portraits drawn by Miss Edgeworth."

There is no resemblance between Miss Edgeworth's outlook on Ireland and the passionate devotion of Walter Scott (1771–1832) to the country of his birth, to the people, history, scenery and traditions of Scotland. His generous compliment did not imply that she had suggested the matter of national novels. From his childhood—long before the publication of the Irish novels or Jane Porter's *Scottish Chiefs*—he had been gathering the material which he poured forth in his romances, both in verse and in prose. His tribute meant exactly what it said. It expressed the hope of an untried novelist for some success in a field in which the older writer had won fame.

Lame and weak in childhood, Scott shaped his own mind before it was forced into the framework of mechanical education. His grandmother and aunt stored his childish brain with Border songs and tales as he lay crumpled up in the window-seat at Sandy Knowe. At the age of six he was determined to be a " virtuoso, one, that is, who wishes to, and will, know everything." Under the plane-tree at Kelso he devoured Percy's *Reliques*, and at twelve years old had begun his own collection of ballads, as well as of weapons and antiquities. Through Edinburgh High School

and University he continued his omnivorous self-education.
During his long illness in 1784 he absorbed masses of *The
Faerie Queene*, Tasso, and the latest works on chivalry,
and ravaged the shelves of the circulating library, which
groaned under ponderous tomes of *Cyrus* and *Cassandra*.

From school and University he carried away little philosophy or science, some Latin and no Greek. But he had
accumulated treasures of romantic lore, wide knowledge
of history, and stores of antiquarian learning. An indefatigable student, he never became a recluse. Habits of
early rising and methodical industry, learned in his apprenticeship as a writer to the signet, freed him during many
hours of the day, in spite of his colossal literary labours,
for social life, rides, rambles and outdoor sports. When
he changed to the other branch of the legal profession,
and became an advocate (1792), his first professional
appointment opened to him fresh scenes for the study of
human nature. As Sheriff depute for Selkirkshire, like
Cervantes in his tax-gathering circuits, he was brought
into touch with all sorts and conditions of men. His
military enthusiasm as a Volunteer added to his experiences,
and it was to the gallop of his charger on the Portobello
Sands that he set the rhythm of his battle stanzas in
Marmion.

As a child he had been the companion of the milkmaid
and the " cow-baillie." As a man he possessed the same
powers of gaining the confidence of those he met. Even
the " Blenheim cocker," which barked at the " acrid
quack," fawned at his feet. Kith and kin with everyone,
he made and kept hosts of friends of all degrees. As he
sat by the side of Old Mortality on the gravestones, or
walked the rounds with Edie Ochiltree, or supped at the
bountiful board of some Liddesdale Dandie Dinmont, or
caught from the lips of Elspeths the songs which they
crooned to the humming of their wheels, he stored in his
tenacious memory those singularities of look, speech, habits
or movements which gave life and individuality to his
varied actors.

In the atmosphere of his reading and experience his mind
was steeped. He used to the full his varied opportunities

of snatching back from the verge of oblivion legends, anecdotes, scraps of old songs and ballads, local customs, usages and prejudices. Convention had not yet smoothed to uniformity the strongly marked characters which he preserved of Edinburgh lawyers, Glasgow citizens, or inhabitants of rural districts and quiet country towns. To his sympathetic ears were narrated many picturesque incidents of recent history, told with the vivid detail of eye-witnesses or with the freshness of oral tradition. The meetings of the Jacobites were events of yesterday. Men still lived whose fathers had been hunted down by Claverhouse and Dalzell, or who, like Hogg's uncle, could not bring themselves to repeat old ballads for thinking of " covenants broken, burned and buried." In the Lowlands the stern zeal of the Cameronians still survived. The Highlands remained an unknown region, in which glowed the flame of fidelity of clans to their chiefs and of picturesque loyalty to the House of Stewart.

Throughout the preparatory period of his literary career Scott was an adventurous student of history, ballads and romantic literature, and the direction in which his solid work would be done could not be predicted. He was not born, like Keats, a poet, or, like Jane Austen, a novelist. Neither was it by the path of literary experiments that he reached his rhyming romances and historical novels. Chance seemed to determine his methods of shaping his sentiments, knowledge, memories and experiences. When the form of expression came to him, he used it without apprenticeship and with the natural ease of a master. But he was forty-three when he published *Waverley*.

Bürger's *Lenore* encouraged Scott to rhyme. Goethe's bold picture of the robber barons of the Rhine in *Goetz with the Iron Hand* recalled to him the life of Border chiefs, their moss-troopers, and their forays, and from it he drew at least one suggestion for *Marmion*. His own labours in collecting and editing Border minstrelsy, his studies of the metrical romance of *Sir Tristrem*, the suggestion by Coleridge's " Christabel " of a modern rhythm suitable to a long story, are links in the chain. *The Lay of the Last Minstrel* (1805) was his first original work of any length,

and won him his first great success. He followed it with
Marmion (1808) and *The Lady of the Lake* (1810). His
later poems were less successful. He abandoned story-
telling in verse, partly because the method had lost its
freshness, partly because, as he said himself, he was beaten
by Byron, but mainly because in prose he found greater
freedom in the use of his materials, and an opportunity for
dialogue that was denied him in rhyme.

Scott's masculine sense rescued him, not unscathed, from
the English and German plague of ghosts and goblins. So
his literary instinct freed his poems, even in descriptive
passages, from excess of luxuriance. Restrained in tone
yet essentially romantic, they illustrate the bent of Scott's
sympathies, the depth of his imaginative feeling, the direction of his reading. They express the fascination which the
past and its idealised feudalism exercised on his mind, the
spell laid on him by the Middle Ages—their picturesqueness
and glow of colour, their fervent faith, their chivalrous and
warlike spirit. The poems breathe also the ardour of his
patriotism—a Scotsman's proud yet mournful memories
of Flodden Field, and his enthusiasm for the scenery of the
Highlands, now wild, now tender in its beauty, and rich
in associations with the history of the people. But the
poems are romantic rather than human in their interest.
They necessarily make little use of Scott's stores of experiences. He needed some literary form in which he could
combine the two elements hitherto separated and blend his
romantic feelings and imagination with the vivid details of
life and character which his keen observation had harvested.
His prose novels met his need.

In the early summer of 1814, rummaging in a drawer for
fishing-tackle, Scott found the unfinished manuscript of
Waverley. He had begun it, as the sub-title suggests—
" 'Tis Sixty Years Since "—in 1805. Now he worked again
upon the story, added two-thirds and published it on July 7.
1814. By the end of 1820 twelve novels had appeared,
and among them were : *Guy Mannering, The Antiquary,
Old Mortality, Rob Roy, The Heart of Midlothian, A Legend
of Montrose, The Bride of Lammermoor,* and *Ivanhoe.* Other
notable novels followed in the course of the next eight years.

Wᴀ

Throughout Europe, Scott was recognised as the chief of the romantics. In the capitals of the world the book-markets competed for his stories, even for those which were most racy of the soil of his native country. The novel, but yesterday struggling for independence, now challenged the supremacy of poetry and the drama in representative art.

In Scott's work the second goal is reached, and no detailed criticism will be attempted. But the stage which he represented has none of the finality to which Jane Austen attained. By her artistic conscience, and the ruth-less truth of her presentation of the whole of the life of her narrow circle, she survived the changes which since 1875 have gradually transformed English prose fiction. Scott's influence was less permanent. It extended throughout the great mid-Victorian outburst, because he combined the chief elements and summed up the progress of the eighteenth-century novels on which that group of novelists worked with the same zest of creation, the same absence of self-consciousness, the same disregard of any canons of their art. There Scott's influence may be said to end. The position to which he raised the novel had far-reaching consequences : his historical and national novels had im-portant successors. But otherwise, and so far as the prose fiction of to-day is concerned, he rather closed a period than inaugurated a new era in its history.

Waverley and its successors were the first historical novels. They created a new type of prose fiction, and, for years to come, established the conventional formula for its construction. Pictorially true to the conditions of the period that is represented, they were dramatically true to its characters and feelings. In intention, at any rate, Scott always subordinated the shifting interest of his decorative background to the unchanging interest of human nature. Trappings and tournaments rarely diverted him from the novelist's mission of interpreting life. In foreign countries and to some extent in England, it was probably by *Ivanhoe* (1820) and *Quentin Durward* (1823) that his universal fame was finally established. Their broad effects and splendid audacity made a cosmopolitan appeal. But they lost much by their divorce from Scotland and its people. So long as Scott stood on his native soil, he could use to the best advantage his detailed observation of types of Scottish character which were true to all time. In England or in France he was less sure of his ground.

Many of the Waverley novels are historical only in date ; in essence they are national. In these idiomatic, native, home-grown studies he employed his stores of experience as the material for his vivid, humorous transcripts of the habits of thought, life and character of the Scottish people. On this national side he was a pioneer of many workers in the same fertile soil—in the immediate future, of Susan Ferrier, John Galt and David Moir ; at a later period, if a happily descriptive title may be used, not in depreciation, but in admiration, of the recent " Kailyard " school.

Scarcely less important to its immediate development was the expansion which Scott gave to the novel proper. In him met and were united the opposing forces of the preceding century. His assimilating genius enabled him to absorb elements which had been hitherto divorced, and to infuse into novels of contemporary life and character something of the deeper range of feeling of imaginative romance. Fielding was a dramatist before he became a novelist, and he asserted the novel's independence of the drama. Scott came to the novel through poetry, and from it he reclaimed for prose more than one lost province. He took the " prose epic " of contemporary life, with its accurate observation, insight into human nature, comedy, humour, and catholicity, and transferred it to romantic scenes of history, near or remote, striking the tragic notes of passion, terror and pity, and adding the delight in natural scenery. Both types of fiction profited. The imaginative re-creation of the life of the past gained solidity from the best elements of the novel of contemporary realities ; the realistic presentation of life and character was enlarged in range by the addition of the poetry, imagination and strong emotion which underlie the placid surface of ordinary society and create the tragedies of real life.

The stress that has been laid on Scott's preparatory years is justified by their importance to his work. When Scott

sat down to write his best novels, he was neither obliged
to read for his purpose nor tempted to leave the scaffolding
up when the building was completed. His imagination
transformed his own experiences and recollections into a
vivid story. His memories of men whose characters had
been moulded by the political and religious struggles of the
past brought him into living contact with the soul of
Jacobites or of clansmen, of Covenanters, Cameronians, and
military adventurers like those who served with Gustavus
Adolphus. The material which he thus employed gave to
his novels a reality that none of his romantic predecessors
attempted, and that filled a larger and more public stage
than that on which Fielding had worked.

Scott frankly abandoned himself to the delight of telling
a story. He never regarded his novels as works of art or
gave himself time for correction and polish. He produced
them rapidly, almost shamefacedly, and it was not till
1827 that he publicly acknowledged their authorship. His
mind was too full of external impressions and recollections
of other ages and other individuals to spare a thought for
himself. This self-suppression is not only one of his charms ;
it was also a corrective to the subjective excesses of the
romantic movement. It stood out in striking contrast to
the self-concentration of the great poet who was his only
contemporary rival in universal popularity.

Not unnaturally, Scott had no message to deliver. On
that charge Carlyle denied him greatness. It is true, and
it was undoubtedly one of the causes which contributed to
the disparagement of his writings. Scott had no faith in
the benefits that were promised in the wake of locomotives,
factories and democracy. On the contrary, he believed
that they would destroy the Scotland that he loved. In an
age of millennial hope, his illiberal attitude towards modern
ideas of progress damaged his literary reputation. Men
were predisposed to assume that his methods were as obsolete
as his political opinions were reactionary.

To-day, judgments formed on political hostility or
sympathy go for little. The neglect into which Scott has
fallen is due to literary faults that have been accentuated
by new conceptions of novel-writing as an art. Living

novelists have made an advance in technique that renders
his openings tedious and his methods clumsy ; their artistic
consciences revolt from his careless style ; their higher
standard of truth throws his historical errors into strong
relief. To these and other points of literary criticism no
adequate answer can be made. Once embarked upon his
story, he tells it with a power which few have rivalled ; his
narrative gains in swiftness of movement from his refusal
to search for the *mot précis* ; he knew as well as his critics
the difficulty of reconciling the legitimate claims of history
with the creation of a living interest in the minds of his
audience. These are not defences, and Scott can afford to
plead guilty to the charges. His genius can only be
measured by the amazing mass of his achievement as
a whole, and by the varied world, with its multitude of living
characters, which he created with so joyous a freedom
from self-consciousness.

For living novelists he is almost as antiquated as Heliodorus. They certainly stand farther from him than they
do from *Tom Jones, Tristram Shandy*, and *Pride and
Prejudice*. Yet the spell that he laid on his own contemporaries and on succeeding generations was once irresistibly strong. In 1827 Mary Ann Evans was a child of eight,
living at her father's home at Griff, and playing in its old-
fashioned garden and among the barns and cowsheds. A
copy of *Waverley*, lent to her elder sister, was returned
before she herself had finished the book. To keep what
she had read in her memory, she wrote out, in her childish
hand and " In lines that thwart like portly spiders ran . . .
the tale of Tully Veolan." With that recollection in her
mind, George Eliot could never have felt or written dis-
passionately about Scott. Thirty years later the spell
still held those who were growing to boyhood, and they, too,
remembering what they owed him, find it hard to be critical.
The generations of those who in their youth fell under the
influence of Scott, while it was still strong, have passed,
or are passing. Yet in one part of the British Isles his
glamour lasts. Scotsmen, said Johnson, are not a fair
people ; they " love Scotland better than truth." Whether
in these sayings the doctor was right or wrong, it will be

an evil day for Scotland when Scotsmen think impartially of Sir Walter Scott.

From the Milesian Tales to the Waverley Novels is a period of two thousand years. Throughout those twenty centuries one thread seems to run, sometimes broken, sometimes indistinct, always persistent. It is the gradual perception that life must be presented truly, though not as yet in its whole truth. But, even when the journey over the long track is pursued by chronological stages, and contemporary groups of obscure writers are explored by the way, no law of progress emerges in the processes by which the novel took literary shape as a means of telling a story and creating characters. Something was achieved by the compromises that followed on the alternations of excess and reaction. More was accomplished through the creative energy of individuals, or of groups of individuals, appearing simultaneously. From time to time a genius came, did his work of creation, and passed away, leaving the novel in some way different from what it was. The mystery of the coming of genius can no longer be compared to that of the wind which " bloweth where it listeth." Science has penetrated the wind's secret, and predicts its force and direction. But the movements of genius defy analysis. Sometimes, as with Jane Austen, it appears without warning. Sometimes, as with Scott, its approach is heralded by the atmosphere of expectation which is created by the widespread independent search for expression of a new interest. In either case the mystery is unsolved.

More novels that are worth reading have been written by living writers than were produced in the twenty centuries which preceded 1832. Why, then, stop at the death of Scott ? Why not include the mid-Victorian outburst of creative genius ? Why not carry forward the history to the last quarter of the nineteenth century, when the novel of the present day first began to take shape ?

It might be a sufficient answer to plead the title of this book. Novels produced in our own lifetime or in that of our fathers and grandfathers do not, in ordinary language, form " The Light Reading of Our Ancestors." Nor would the inclusion of the mid-Victorians really carry the story beyond the stage which it had reached in the Waverley Novels. Compared with novelists of to-day, they are as old-fashioned as Scott. Between him and them there is no breach of continuity ; they initiated no new departure, introduced no essential novelties, either in theory or in practice. Dickens, Thackeray, Trollope, Bulwer Lytton, the Brontës, the Kingsleys, Charles Reade, Wilkie Collins, Mrs. Gaskell and George Eliot followed the same English traditions. Like Scott, they scarcely conceived of the novel as a work of art, or concerned themselves with their manner as well as their matter. Mainly for this reason, they shared his freedom from self-consciousness and his ecstasy of creation. Like him also, they enjoyed, except in one fatal respect, the liberties of a literary Alsatia. Critics did not ask whether a novel satisfied the canons of art ; they only demanded—and they did so with increasing insistency— that it should conform to the moral conventions required by society.

Working in the past, Scott scarcely felt the restraint imposed by the social morality of his time. Yet in *St. Ronan's Well* (1824), his one novel of contemporary society, he ruined his plot by deference to its authority. A quarter of a century later the conventional code had become despotic. Uncompromising in its rigidity, it held the mid-Victorians in bondage. Right and wrong were strongly and grimly divided. No room was allowed for graduated shades of feeling, for complexities and difficulties of choice, for balanced problems of conduct. Men and women were sharply distinguished as sheep and goats, and the goats were to be driven into the wilderness. Unless a writer was wholly on the side of the angels, he was anathema.

Mid-Victorian novelists were not only shackled in their liberty of creation ; they were also driven into insincerities and prevented from setting their shoulders squarely to face facts. Their reticences concealed the meaning of life. Their complacency was hollow. In the light of the whole truth their half-truths were falsehoods. Most of them chafed against their fetters ; few attempted freedom. Even the rebellious spirit of Charlotte Brontë was broken, and she expiated her offence in creating Rochester by loading him with punishments. The one direction in which there was no restraint was that of sentimentality, and novelists were sentimental to excess. Thus a literature which, for its glorious gift of creation, should have been an everlasting possession already shows symptoms of decay, because it is preserved neither by the imperishable touch of art, nor by the salt of sincerity to life.

It was in reaction against these conditions that the modern novel came into existence. France had owed much to Richardson, Sterne and Scott ; now she repaid the debt. Her masters were the models of the new English novel. Their worship of art, their skill in technique, their unsparing truthfulness to the whole of life, were grafted on to the native stock, and the work was partly done by two men not of English birth—Henry James and Joseph Conrad. The fruit has been rich in quality and abundant in quantity, and without the infusion of the new elements the tree might well have become barren.

Novelists to-day, in the doubts, tumult and fluctuations of present-day existence, may sometimes envy their more fortunate predecessors and, above all, their freedom from self-consciousness. Yet they have given not a few proofs that the creative zest still survives the exacting anxieties of the artistic conscience. Whatever changes may be in store for the form and substance of the novel, living writers have created a brilliant literature, in which they have expressed, as nothing else has done, the varied aspects of modern life. Among all the uncertainties of the future, their art at least is stable, and it is incredible that poetry and drama should ever again reduce prose fiction to its former dependence.

Index of Authors and of Titles of Books